This book is to be returned on
or before the date stamped below

UNIVERSITY OF PLYMOUTH

PLYMOUTH LIBRARY
Tel: (0752) 232323
This book is subject to recall if required by another reader
Books may be renewed by phone
CHARGES WILL BE MADE FOR OVERDUE BOOKS

The Technical Fix

Education, Computers and Industry

Kevin Robins and **Frank Webster**

M
MACMILLAN

First published 1989

Published by
MACMILLAN EDUCATION LTD
Houndmills, Basingstoke, Hampshire RG21 2XS
and London
Companies and representatives
throughout the world

Printed in Hong Kong

British Library Cataloguing in Publication Data
Robins, Kevin
The technical fix: education, computers
and industry
1. Great Britain. Schools. Curriculum
subjects: Computer systems
I. Title   II. Webster, Frank   III. Series
004'.07'1041
ISBN 0–333–42900–1 (hardcover)
ISBN 0–333–42901–X (paperback)

For Danny and Joe, Frankie and Isabelle

'I turn my eyes to the Schools and Universities of Europe
And there behold the Loom of Locke, whose woof rages
    dire,
Wash'd by the Water-wheels of Newton: black the cloth
In heavy wreathes folds over every Nation: cruel Works
Of many Wheels I view, wheel without wheel, with cogs
    tyrannic
Moving by compulsion each other, not as those in Eden,
    which,
Wheel within Wheel, in freedom revolve in harmony &
    peace.'

William Blake, *Jerusalem* (1804–20)

Contents

List of Tables

Acknowledgements

An important initial stimulus for the development of this work came from Les Levidow, and I would like to thank him for his continuing support. The background to this book has been very much shaped by the project of *Radical Science Journal* and its successor *Science as Culture*, and it is the ideas developed by Les Levidow and Bob Young in these journals that have given me an intellectual framework for many years now. *Science as Culture*, along with other publications from Free Association Books, is recommended as a journal to follow up many of the issues developed in this book.

Newcastle   KEVIN ROBINS

Writing a book of this sort is unavoidably an isolating affair. At a time of acute economic anxiety, when education is called upon to do its duty by helping industry escape recession by training the young in appropriately technical (and other) skills, undermining 'computer literacy' initiatives is not likely to make one popular. We did not expect approval and anticipated the Luddite labels. In such circumstances it is important to have colleagues, near and far, who may deflect criticism, absorb pressure, and from whom one may draw strength.

I am fortunate to work at an institution that is both supportive and academically stimulating. From the commencement of this book early in 1986, I have had nothing but encouragement, even if sometimes quizzical, from colleagues at Oxford Polytechnic. Harry Hendrick deserves a special mention since it was at his invitation that I fired a first salvo at 'computer literacy' programmes during a History Society seminar in February 1985. The responses to that paper encouraged me to develop the arguments. In particular I must mention the assistance of Keith Lambe, Martin Joseph, John Astley, Tony Harding, Rob Pope, Peter Madgwick, Alan Jenkins, David Pepper and David Watson. Several of these friends were present at Harry's seminar, and their interest in the 'anti-I.T.' book has helped mine.

Thanks too to the members of the Sociology Subject Committee at the polytechnic, particularly the regular attenders of the Thursday Evening Seminar at the 'Black Boy'. They have been important in bolstering my belief in the validity of education which is more than instrumental.

Many of the themes were rehearsed on students from the Computing and Sociology Fields who enrolled on my courses 'The Information Society?' and 'Issues in Computer Communications Policy'. Their responses helped immeasurably in clarifying my ideas. I thank them.

Acknowledgement too should be made of the Modular Course at Oxford Polytechnic. Its openness to ideas and organisational flexibility allowed me to introduce into several Fields courses which incorporate themes touched on in this book. This refusal of colleagues to reduce education to training has been a source of encouragement to me in my years at Oxford.

Further afield, I have drawn heavily on the community of scholars concerned with information and education. In particular, David and Douglas Noble, Len Masterman, Michael Young and Peter Abbs have been constant stimulants to my thought and writing.

Special mention must be made of Herb and Anita Schiller. They have been intellectual mentors as well as fine friends and hosts to me for several years now. More than anyone else they have asked and tried to answer the central questions of the 'information age'. I salute them and their joint endeavour.

Bill Melody happened to be living in Oxford while much of this book was being written. His keen intellect and enthusiastic manner helped it along, as did his friendship on and off the terraces of Oxford United. The Woolgar family gave similar support and diversion.

As ever, I offer special thanks to Liz, Frankie and Isabelle who put up with me writing this book, though I swore the previous one would be the last.

Oxford   FRANK WEBSTER

Introduction

'Suppose the question is misconceived. What if we reject the premise behind this whole discussion, that industrialism fosters political and economic progress?' (Christopher Lasch, 1985, p. 41)

According to a recent White paper from the Department of Trade and Industry (DTI), 'the competitiveness of industry and commerce depends on our ability to harness the energy, develop the intelligence and promote the enterprise of our people, especially amongst the young'. 'Bridging the historical divide between business and education', it continues, 'is vital to encourage the enterprise culture, to encourage young people to work in industry and commerce, to bring greater relevance to their education, and to prepare them better for working life' (Department of Trade and Industry, 1988, p. 19). We must 'bring business into education and encourage education to consider the needs of business', and to do this we must 'combat the past anti-enterprise bias of British culture' (ibid, p. 3). As part of this project, the DTI also wishes 'to ensure that young people become aware of the value of information technology (I.T.), and that I.T. is used across the curriculum... Where young people are regularly using technology to enter, use and manipulate information at school, they will be better placed to help industry and commerce to compete effectively' (ibid, p. 20).

This has become the great educational orthodoxy of our times, only repeating the commonsense wisdom of report after report. It is the consensual verdict on both Left and

1

Right of the political spectrum that economic growth and productivity have been thwarted by the elitism and 'anti-business snobbery' of what has become known as the 'English disease'. What is now called for is a new realism: a new spirit of enterprise; a new vocationalism; the encouragement of 'technological literacy'; rapid and enthusiastic adaptation to computers and communications. And this is what we are getting, with a vengeance. Schools are increasingly being manoeuvred into the arms of business. The Manpower Services Commission (MSC) (now called the Training Commission) has shaped non-advanced further education according to the 'needs of industry'. Universities and polytechnics are spawning technology and enterprise parks to promote high-tech industries.

Our own view is that a dismal consensus has arisen around this issue. To be sure, there are debates about the appropriateness of aspects of strategy. For example, the TC's Youth Training Scheme (YTS) has been criticised for its censorship of political education and for the poverty of its philosophy of training. Within this framework, debate tends to focus around the relative significance of vocational education on the one hand, and liberal education on the other. We understand this focus, and taking a side, we would emphasise that, in a world in which education is becoming increasingly functional and instrumental, reminders of the importance of independence of mind are crucial. We should heed Peter Abbs' reminder of what education should be:

> Education is quite simply the expression and development of a primary impulse for truth, a deep epistemic instinct which we inherit as part of our biological nature. A civilisation which cannot recognise the intrinsic value and beauty of education has, perhaps, already condemned itself either to permanent ethical and cultural stagnation, or, worse, extinction. (Abbs, 1987)

However, we should also be aware of the increasing difficulty of maintaining such a position. It now seems 'soft', unrealistic, idealistic, anachronistic, indefensible in the Britain of the 1980s. Mary Warnock's observation on the philosophy of university education identifies the predicament for all levels of education. 'No one', she writes, 'appears to believe in their higher purposes except themselves. Are the high purposes therefore imaginary?' (Warnock, 1988, p. 24).

But it is not just that vocationalism has come to outweigh liberal education. What we would argue is that the liberal versus vocational opposition has now become an inadequate framework for formulating the educational choices that are open to us. Our own argument probes the modern condition further to argue, in fact, that the issues are far more complex and difficult than the antinomy suggests.

One part of our thesis in this book is that advanced capitalist societies are now undergoing fundamental transformations, ones that have been described as marking a transition from what has been called a Fordist system to one characterised as neo-Fordist. This transition is associated with new flexible and decentralised forms of production, with new class segmentations and with new forms of social control. In this process it has become necessary to subordinate the education system to the changing needs of business and industry. Schools and colleges are directed to produce the skills, expertise and orientations appropriate to the new forms of production. They must also produce new forms of control and consensus to ensure the stability and durability of the emerging neo-Fordist system.

The upshot of this has been the emergence of a new pedagogy which has sought to regulate and redirect young pupils and trainees. A recent survey, reported in the DTI's public relations magazine for education/industry liaison, outlines what are now considered to be the desirable qualities of young workers. The study differentiates those trainees who improved and did well compared to those who did not:

Improver	*Non-improver*
Versatile	Doesn't follow instructions
Takes initiative	Bad timekeeper
Has good personal	Dislikes supervision
relations	Careless about quality
Listens to instructions	Can't concentrate

Has a wide viewpoint	Chats and gazes around
Seeks work when slack	Has personal problems
Quality conscious	Has bad personal relations
A good timekeeper	Over-confident for his or her ability
Asks questions	Doesn't pull weight
Methodical and neat	Doesn't like change
Reports faults	Doesn't report faults
Remedies the problems	No loyalty to company

(Turner, 1987, p. 16)

The new pedagogy replaces didactic and explicitly disciplinary methods with a new student-oriented focus which emphasises competence, capability and responsibility. To a large extent, what we have is the appropriation and incorporation of what have been referred to as progressive educational strategies by those eager to make education functional for changing socio-economic needs. Moreover, this new pedagogy, which we call instrumental progressivism, aims to develop the qualities listed above not just in work situations, but also as guiding principles for the student's wider life. In this respect it effectively undermines the liberal/vocational dichotomy by subordinating the trainee's whole identity and personality to the new productive order. What is now demanded are the right attitudes and dispositions, and these must guide work and non-work time alike. This leaves little if any space for liberal beliefs in education either as ends in themselves or as a means of enriching the life of a citizen. Instrumental progressivism's claim is that it includes principles of liberal education within its response to what the changing economy demands, thereby usurping liberal education's role.

If one fundamental objective of this book is to situate our understanding of current developments in education in the socio-historical context of the shift from Fordism to neo-Fordism, then a second is to explore the increasingly close relationship between education and technology. In recent years, education has come to be seen as central to technological development and 'progress' more generally. And within this world view, technology is considered to be a neutral force – one that may occasionally be misused, but one that for the most part is directed towards the benefit of society. Our view, however, as we shall reveal, is that technology is a much more problematic force.

Because this book argues that the real issues confronting education policy cannot be addressed without an understanding of the wider processes of social, economic and technological development to which it has become subordinated, its contents might seem, at first sight, to stray from the relevant focus. For this reason it is useful to provide a map of the terrain ahead.

The book is divided into three parts. Part I sets out to examine the premises of the 'I.T. revolution' and of I.T. initiatives in education. Our argument is that we do live in a society in which information is more central to affairs than before, but that this is due to social, economic and political factors that have been unfolding over decades and which have accelerated, rather than through breath-taking technological breakthroughs. In our first chapter we take issue with the view that it is innovations in technology that are leading to social changes to which education must respond. Against this, we outline the genesis of the 'information society' in Chapter 2 and plot its major contemporary contours in Chapter 3, in opposition to the plethora of futurists who claim that we are on the threshold of a break with the past.

Our depiction of the social roots of the 'information society' allows us to contest the technological determinism that underpins so much current education policy. Further, we think that the acknowledgement that new technologies can be better comprehended as integral parts of developments taking place within society as a whole enables us to see that I.T. is not some supra-social phenomenon to which everyone must adjust as best they can, but rather an expression of values and priorities. By extension, when educational institutions are instructed to change in the name of adaptation to technological progress we may properly ask, what are the values that lie behind this technological imperative?

Part II focuses more centrally on education policy and practice with regard to I.T., endeavouring to cut through the rhetoric associated with the 'computer revolution' to expose the reality of developments in education and the reasons for them. Chapters 4 and 5 set current issues in a wide and comprehensible context. We delineate the new orthodoxy that an 'English disease' has incapacitated the education system and, in turn, the economy, arguing that this nostrum has played a key role in legitimising the imposition of changes on education. Contending that Britain is under-going important transformations, and that education is being called upon to oil the wheels of change, we argue that these entail far more than adjustment to new technologies and overcoming a distaste for contact with industry. Our view is that the neo-Fordist epoch which we are entering requires above all 'flexibility': of production, of marketing and of course of employment. This lays a series of demands at the door of education which lead to an emphasis on it being market-oriented, entrepreneurial and, most important, sensitive to changes required by industry in those whom they seek to recruit. In a word, this requires the manufacture of employees who are 'flexible': that is, adaptable, imbued with an 'enterprise culture' and willing and able to train and retrain to meet the challenges of rapidly changing technolo-gies.

Chapter 6 observes that a key element of education's reform is that it should come to terms with I.T. Computer communications are a crucial element of the restructuring of industry, so if education is to rid itself of its anti-industrial ethos, then it must incorporate new technology in the curriculum and produce the kind of graduates required by employers. This chapter scrutinises the rationale behind 'computer literacy' programmes and contends that its assumptions are mistaken and its vocational promises illus-ory. Chapter 7 takes up what we believe is the real goal of 'computer literacy' – the production of a more malleable workforce – in order to reflect more closely on the socialising role of education. We describe and speculate on the dis-ciplinary requirements of neo-Fordism and the role to be played by education in providing future generations with the

skills and mentality to adapt to the emerging situation. Here
we discuss the significance of policies aimed at 'education for
capability', of shifting conceptions of what constitutes knowledge, and of changes in learning from didactic models
towards a more self-regulated approach.

Part III returns to issues raised in our opening chapters.
The gravamen of our case is that I.T. should not be viewed
as a neutral and inherently progressive phenomenon. We
need to disabuse ourselves of the conventional wisdom that
technology holds a rational and liberatory centre which may
advance the human condition provided enlightened policies
are put into practice. Our argument, which develops out of
earlier work on the politics of computer communications
technologies (Webster and Robins, 1986), is that technological innovation, and the rationality of which it is expressive,
is deeply and indissociably imbued with power relations.
Technology – its origination, development and application –
cannot be extracted from relations of power and the social
values (priorities, goals, beliefs) these entail. It is folly to
believe that technology can be segregated from the ruck of
social, economic and political processes in such a way as to
rescue an untainted level of 'progress'. Technology is always
shaped by, even constitutive of, prevailing values and power
distribution. Instead of persistently accounting for the development of particular technologies as but the misapplication of scientific discovery, we should do better to concede
that substantive technologies are what we have and it is the
rationality they represent with which we must come to
terms. It is our view that the technocratic assumption – the
conviction that change stems from the cold compulsion of
technical reason that is aloof from values and power – which
underlies 'computer literacy' (and educational change) scenarios must be thoroughly examined. For us, the most
fundamental premises of enthusiasts for I.T. are that technology has come to be seen as containing progress within
itself, and that the search for control – over nature and
fellow human beings – is the unquestioned motor of technological innovation.

Chapters 8 and 9 develop this line of thought by focusing
on the most distilled expression of the technocratic outlook:

the development of military technologies which deeply implicate education and I.T. We contend that command and control networks are not some unfortunate misapplication of technological knowledge, but that, with their compulsion towards surveillance, secrecy and spying, they are expressive of the real – and value-laden – history of technological development which, under the guise of a neutral and beneficent progress, has extended control throughout society and advanced the prospect of cybernetic order and automated war. I.T. in the industrial sphere has exhibited a similar, if less spectacular, history. We suggest that the new technologies extend and intensify processes of technocratic control that have a long, and under-examined, history. Identifying the values which have guided technological innovation and application, we argue that the fundamental issue today is not the 'English disease' of which education must be cured so the nation might reclaim its former glory, but whether the 'progress' represented by instrumental reason is either inevitable or desirable. Unless we confront this reality of technology, and until we see through the hidden values of technocratic thought, we shall be unable to come to terms with the 'information revolution'. Sadly, we find among the political parties a depressingly uniform capitulation to the technocratic ethos.

Part I
The Myth of the Machine

1

Technological Futures and the Technical Fix

'Taken as a whole, benefits of this kind constitute what I would call mythinformation: the almost religious conviction that a widespread adoption of computers and communications systems along with easy access to electronic information will automatically produce a better world for human living.'
  (Langdon Winner, 1986, p. 105)

Introduction

It is surely beyond question that Britain today faces formidable difficulties. At the forefront of public concern is the unprecedented level of unemployment, which is particularly acute among young people. Compounding this are regional imbalances that manifest the problem of worklessness, but which also extend far beyond this as 'deindustrialisation' takes its toll. Coal, steel, shipbuilding and manufacture continue their remorseless decline and with these industries goes a whole way of life. Underlying these trends is a deep-seated international recession which is having the effect of tightening competitive pressures, to which Britain does not seem able to adequately respond. The upshot is an apparently inexorable economic collapse, still further unemployment and bleak prospects for the future. On top of this, such is the internationalisation and integration of economic affairs mediated by gigantic transnational corporations and inter-state agencies, that people commonly sense their destinies – and that of their own nation – as being beyond their control.

As if this were not enough, in the inner cities are trapped what is increasingly solidifying as an underclass, composed disproportionately of racial minorities and the transient young. This class is burdened by a cumulation of disadvantages in housing, jobs and education. This class' expressions of discontent are evidenced in high crime rates, broken families, vandalism and, more frightening and prophetic, intermittent rioting and looting. Shrouding even this, and indeed all else, is the new Cold War and the widespread apprehension that a nuclear holocaust may terminate human existence. On a lesser scale, post Chernobyl and Three Mile Island, most people realise that nuclear power entails huge risks for the environment.

The chronicle could be extended, but this description is sufficient to highlight the fact that we learn from opinion surveys that the public is distinctly glum about the future (Heald and Wybrow, 1986, p. 251).

Since empirical analysis reveals that control is moving further away from the individual citizen as well as from once sovereign nations, and that crises are intensifying and cumulating, we should not find the public mood remarkable. What we do find astonishing, however, is that in the present period one regularly encounters a strain of opinion, loud and persistent, which adopts an almost messianic faith in the future. Far from being anxious about what is looming on the horizon, there are those who envisage the year 2000 as a time of super abundance, contentment and social harmony. They look forward to the future with enthusiasm and unalloyed utopianism. One of them, Professor Tom Stonier, peers from the windows of the local university and sees far beyond the ruins of Bradford's textile mills to an era in which 'everyone [is] an aristocrat, everyone a philosopher', where 'authoritarianism, war and strife' will have been eliminated, and where

> For the first time in history, the rate at which we solve problems will exceed the rate at which they appear. This will leave us to get on with the real business of the next century. To take care of each other. To fathom what it means to be human. To explore intelligence. To move out into space. (Stonier, 1983, p. 214)

Professional diviners like Stonier screw up their eyes and, possessing a vision denied the majority, discern universal improvement: 'better education, better news media, better forms of human communication, better entertainment, better medical resources, less pollution, less human drudgery, less use of petroleum, more efficient industry, and a better informed society' (Martin, 1978, p. 15). Public apprehensions are soothed by a large dose of optimism.

This panglossian outlook is not at all insensitive to the difficulties many must face in the here and now. On the contrary, it makes a great deal of its 'realism' and 'determination' to come to grips with the present. Alvin Toffler, for example, is 'under no Pollyanaish illusions' about the world today. He taps baldly on to his word processor:

> As I write this, the front pages report hysteria and hostages in Iran, assassinations in South Korea, runaway speculation in gold, friction between Blacks and Jews in the U.S., big increases in West German military spending, cross burnings on Long Island, a giant oil spill in the Gulf of Mexico. . . Waves of religious revivalism crash through Libya, Syria, and the U.S.; neo-fascist fanatics claim 'credit' for a political assassination in Paris. (Toffler, 1980, pp. 3, 17–18)

These futurists appear to regard the magnitude of present-day problems as indicative of the immanence of their nirvana. The very depths of today's crises announce to these optimists the scale and wonder of the forthcoming revival. Recession, terrorism, unemployment, crime and industrial collapse are perceived in terms similar to Christian's progress: each obstacle and torment a test of faith and fortitude, endurance of which ensures safe arrival at the Celestial City (cf. Kahn, 1983).

Technology as saviour

What pulls the future enthusiasts through the present Slough of Despond is technology, and especially the range of computer communications technologies that go by the neologism Information Technology (I.T.). 'The computer is the most important single invention in recorded history' testify Tom Stonier and Cathy Conlin (1985, p. 7). It announces an 'electronic renaissance' trumpets another visionary (Williams, 1982, p. 234). We are living through, and have been for nigh on a decade, a 'microelectronics revolution' which has resulted in the dispersal of computer technologies far and wide: in washing machines, in motor cars, photocopiers, watches, televisions, machine tools, typewriters, finance houses, printing ... In almost every conceivable place the 'mighty micro' is finding a role. Symbioticly, telecommunications has been extensively computerised and updated to string together many of these disparate applications and pave the way towards an 'electronic grid' through which will course information in the emerging 'wired society' (Dordick, 1986). These technologies herald the development of a network of electronic highways linking houses, shops, businesses and schools which will allow instant access to and communication of information to everyone.

I.T. will undeniably be pervasive in reach and profound in effect. Of course, a good many are already aware of its potential and fear loss in employment, deskilling and the further encroachment of surveillance agencies. From this perspective I.T. is regarded as part and parcel of the malaise we described a few sentences ago and which is depressing for so many. But the optimists will have none of this downheartedness. On the contrary, their view is that I.T. will solve all the problems presently imposing themselves as it sweeps everything before it. Those who refuse to believe this prognosis, who persist in carping and quibbling about I.T.'s possible negative features, are scorned in the manner of heretics. They are castigated as 'future haters' who suffer from the dementia 'technophobia'. Technology being presented as the panacea for any and every malady, the message from the converted is unequivocal:

Rather than lashing out, Luddite-fashion, against the machine, those who genuinely wish to break the prison hold of the past and present could do well to hasten the ... arrival of tomorrow's technologies [because] it is precisely the super-industrial society, the most advanced technological society ever, that extends the range of freedom. (Toffler, 1980, pp. 282–3)

The combination of range of application, depth of effect and speed of arrival of new technology is obviously disruptive and understandably disturbing. Nonetheless, the I.T. zealots are emphatic that if in the future we hope to survive let alone to prosper, then we must in no way resist its arrival. To do so would be unwise for it would hold back the cornucopia that I.T. will release. Moreover, it would be futile since I.T. will arrive willy-nilly.

Alvin Toffler's wave metaphor which thematises his best-selling book *The Third Wave* (1980) is especially revealing of this widespread sentiment. The first wave was the agrarian revolution: it was irresistible and unsettling, but everyone gained immeasurably from vast increases in food; the second wave was the industrial revolution: it hurt the weavers and stockingers, but it could not be stopped by frenzied protest, and just look at its benefits in the material advantages we enjoy today; the third wave is crashing about our heads right now: the Jeremiahs are moaning, but this tidal wave will envelop us all irrespective of our predilection. The sane and sensible will not despair, but will rather catch the wave as it rises, go with the flow and surf effortlessly on to the beach where they will find the 'electronic cottage' of the 21st century. It is not insignificant that British Telecom was using precisely this symbolism in its corporate advertising campaigns on British television during 1986 and 1987.

Post-industrial society

Those who yearn for the future do not conjure up this wonderland to which we will all be spirited on an electronic flying carpet simply from the void of their excitable imaginations. They also draw on the work of a distinguished sociological thinker, Daniel Bell of Harvard University, in support of their vision. It was Bell who originated the term 'post-industrial' society a generation ago and it is this concept which has become emblematic to much futurism

(Robins and Webster, 1987). Few I.T. enthusiasts appear to have read Professor Bell closely, but his major book, *The Coming of Post-Industrial Society* (1973), is ritually cited as an authoritative description of the order towards which we are moving, courtesy of new technology. Furthermore, over the years, with Bell as with his followers, the concept 'information society' has come to be used synonymously with that of 'post-industrialism'. As we shall see, this is for reasons that are intimately connected with developments in I.T. and which give Bell's speculations still greater resonance.

Andrew Neil is representative of futurism's style of argument in so far as a 'post-industrial information society' is presented as the destination to which I.T. is directing us:

> Britain is on the brink of a post-industrial revolution every bit as big as the move from an agricultural to an industrial society 200 years ago. The modern information technology of telecommunications-allied-to-the-computer has already nurtured the blossoming of a new 'information society'. (Neil, 1983, p. 3)

To those enamoured of the future, the discovery of I.T. and Daniel Bell's depiction of a heightened role for information combine to suggest a new and brighter dawn.

There are two features of Daniel Bell's argument that concern the role of information and I.T. The first of these is more qualitative and it contends that the 'axial principle' of 'post-industrial' society is the 'centrality of theoretical knowledge' (Bell, 1980, p. 501). Bell claims that in the nineteenth century innovation was achieved by 'inspired and talented tinkerers who were indifferent to science' (Bell, 1973, p. 20), but that nowadays change is initiated from and guided by known theoretical principles with the detail of experimentation and the gathering of data to effect the change a matter of 'codification': Stephenson invented the railway without benefit of scientific knowledge because of pressing practical problems of transporting coal; the development this century of electronics has been steered by theoretical understanding of energy and matter well before the microprocessor was created. For Bell, this shift signifies the replacement of a 'labour theory of value' with a 'knowledge theory of value' and a new stage of human history.

In our view Bell's identification of the primacy of theoretical knowledge as a distinguishing feature of 'post-industrialism' is interesting and provocative (cf. Giddens, 1981, pp. 261–4), but this is not the feature of his writing that most appeals to I.T. enthusiasts. While this 'strategic resource' does require computers to bridge formal theory and stores of empirical data, it does not explain the ubiquity of I.T. It is the more quantitative aspect of Bell's forecast, that which highlights trends which have increased the amount of information in society, which speaks most directly to those concerned with I.T. To grasp this element we need to review Bell's descriptions of the evolution of 'post-industrial' society.

Bell's argument is that over the centuries society has evolved through a number of stages because increases in productivity in one sector of the economy have allowed the transfer of people into others without loss of wealth. Since each stage of development can be characterised by the preponderance of employment in any one sector, Bell argues that we have passed through a pre-industrial society where people chiefly worked in agriculture; to an industrial society where employment was primarily in factories with workers located there because the agrarian revolution provided sufficient food to support them, though it required fewer farmers than previous to produce it so that most could transfer their labour to industry; to a post-industrial society where work is chiefly in services, with employees there paid out of the wealth that has emanated from industrial automation, with people employed in services because industry, even with increased productivity, needs fewer personnel than ever to operate.

For Daniel Bell, services in general mark the development of 'post-industrial' society, but it is the especially rapid growth within them of the 'professional and technical class' (Bell, 1973, p. 17) which is most important because its expansion supports his claim that 'post-industrialism' is not only a 'white-collar society', but that it is also one in which the professional is predominant. The category of services

which is decisive for 'post-industrial' society is health, education, research and government because 'this is the category
that represents the expansion of a new intelligensia' (Bell,
1973, p. 15). The primacy of such professions allows Bell to
declare 'post-industrialism' a 'knowledge society' (p. 242),
for such occupations chiefly involve utilising and generating
this resource. Therefore a 'post-industrial' society is an
'information society' – one in which 'the weight of society
. . . is increasingly in the knowledge field' (p. 212). Professor
Bell's epigones are at pains to underline this heightened
importance of information: 'We have become an information society in which the knowledge industry is the major
growth area and in which the bulk of the labour force has
become information operatives' (Stonier, 1981).

The growth of services – and hence information work – is
not merely a matter of changes in occupation. It also has
profound consequences for class structure, attitudes and the
organisation and operation of the wider society. Stratification undergoes significant change as the manual occupations
that once dominated industrialism are displaced by information professionals who do not share the proletariat's oppositional class outlook. Further, 'post-industrial' society has a
more graduated system of inequality where people are
allocated a place in the hierarchy by qualifications that have
been gained in an increasingly meritocratic education system
(Bell, 1973, p. 409). Conflict continues, attests Bell, but it
shifts from class against class towards tension between
'situses' such as universities and government, social services
and military departments. Moreover, because service employment is a matter of interaction between people rather
than working with objects, as with manufacture, it is more
fulfilling and caring than its predecessors. This interpersonal
and service oriented ethos extends throughout the society to
stamp 'post-industrialism' with a 'new consciousness' that
promotes the 'community rather than the individual' (Bell,
1973, p. 128). Therefore, the rise of professions encourages
'more conscious decision-making' in society and thereby
more effective planning of socially desirable and socially
agreed goals.

Even a thumb-nail sketch like this suggests the appeal of

the 'post-industrial information society': more professional, more knowledgeable, more caring, more in control of itself, more meritocratic and healthily competitive yet without the malice and destructiveness of the class conflict so much in evidence in Thatcher's Britain. Not surprisingly, sanguine futurists who put their trust in I.T. have been keen to draw on the impressive sociological speculation of Professor Bell (cf. Stonier, 1983, pp. 21–32). His theory has been especially appealing since it connects with, and Bell himself explicitly makes links to, developments in I.T.

We have already noted how commentators like Andrew Neil latch on to the 'information society' concept to claim that I.T. is bringing it into being. Daniel Bell's earlier sociological account does not offer much direct reference to I.T., but his devotees do not do him disservice in stressing the role of I.T. since in Bell's *oeuvre* it is crucial to the evolution of 'post-industrial' society in several ways. First, because 'post-industrialism's' major resource is information there has to be a technology capable of handling it and computer communications are the means to manage 'organized complexity' (Bell, 1973, p. 28). Second, technological innovation hastens the arrival of the 'information society' by continuing the automation of agriculture and industry and thus freeing workers to fill vacancies made available in services. Third, and most important, advanced technology is the means by which the service society is funded. This is the case because services consume wealth rather than create it and agriculture and industry are called upon to provide the wherewithal to fund service expansion.

If we are to expand services then we must encourage the adoption of I.T. in the wealth-creating sectors to boost output. Further, introduction of I.T. is more urgent because services, since they are matters of qualitative relations rather than of quantities of output, are performed by people rather than by machines. Therefore there are unavoidable limits imposed on the productivity of service workers since one cannot readily mechanise a 'relation between persons' (Bell, 1973, p. 155). On the one hand this is a fine thing for employment since opportunities in services are constantly created. On the other hand services are very expensive since costs cannot be reduced by machinery. The upshot is that further pressure is placed on the wealth-creating sectors to increase their productivity by constant automation in order that more services jobs may be funded.

A leisure society?

While Bell's forecast of a 'post-industrial' society has driven almost all writers favourably disposed towards I.T. to appropriate the term, the fact that his work makes no reference to unemployment makes it rather hard to take the theory aboard wholesale. An 'information society' ushered in by I.T. is attractive, but there are few people living in Britain who can accept that there will be service jobs aplenty given present levels of unemployment, slow economic growth and the likelihood that I.T. will reduce rather than increase job opportunities. To be sure, the Thatcher administrations have always insisted that services will mop up the pool of workless (cf. Lawson, 1983). Thus Kenneth Baker's faith is representative and orthodoxically Bellian:

> In the early 1950s in Britain around 40% of the workforce was in manufacturing, by 1970 it had fallen to 37% and by 1981 to 28%. This trend will continue as American experience has shown, but I do not believe this will lead to massive unemployment since more and more people will be needed to provide the service activities which the new technologies are already stimulating. (Baker, 1983, p. 3)

In spite of the Education Minister's conviction few people – indeed even few Conservatives – believe that services will solve the problems of the unemployed (Heald and Wybrow, 1986, p. 96). The evidence suggests that it is doubtful that services will continue to expand in real terms and that even its increase relative to manufacture will be constrained by I.T. (Levitt, 1976). Already the service sector is stagnating and with public expenditure, which accounted for the majority of services growth in the 1970s (Robertson *et al*, 1982, pp. 50–51) being reduced, the likelihood is that things will worsen. Confronting such obstinate realities, most writers about I.T. find endorsement of the service society scenario untenable.

But the notion of 'post-industrialism' doggedly remains and enthusiasm for I.T. refuses to dwindle. They resurface in the prospect for a leisure oriented 'information age'. Although there are several variations on the theme – job-sharing, early retirement, shorter working week, regular sabbaticals, extended education and so on – all share the idea that the 'work ethic' must be changed, either to make acceptable permanently high levels of unemployment or to redistribute present work in a more equitable manner (see, *inter alia*, Robertson, 1985; Jones, 1982; Jenkins and Sherman, 1979; 1981).

The goal of more leisure as part of a desirable and achievable future is pursued by the broadest range of political opinion. On the Marxist Left, for instance, we have André Gorz, who urges socialists to abandon their call for a right to work. In his view the 'post-industrial proletariat' (Gorz, 1982, p. 69) should abandon the 'obsolete religion of work' (Gorz, 1983, p. 216) because jobs currently performed by the working class are dead-end and, more, they 'will be largely eliminated by automation' in the near future (Gorz, 1982, p. 69). Traditional socialist calls for 'workers' control' and 'jobs for everyone' are empty slogans in face of 'the micro-electronic revolution [which] heralds the abolition of work' (Gorz, 1982, p. 69). Yet this does not dismay Gorz, although he is well aware of and sympathetic towards the miseries of the unemployed. Refusing to be downcast he sees hope in a policy of redirecting the Left towards 'winning the power no longer to function as a worker' (Gorz, 1982, p. 67). That is, he advocates an extension of leisure for people who are to be granted a generous 'social wage' paid for by 'taxing automated production' (Gorz, 1985, p. 44). The price of technological redundancy is a large subsidy to those who are displaced. From an analysis that evokes the gloom and despondency of mass unemployment, Gorz manages to project a future composed of 'liberated time' (Gorz, 1983, p. 213) from stultifying labour thanks to the bounty of advanced technologies. A frightening image of millions cast out of work while the remainder are trapped in meaningless jobs is reportrayed as the newly discovered freedom from labour, with ample leisure and means with which to develop one's true self.

From a radically different political persuasion, Conservative Sir Francis Pym arrives at a remarkably similar conclusion. He considers that 'the continuing pace of new technology will prevent conventional policies from reducing unemployment to an acceptable extent' (Pym, 1985, p. 12). The prospect of permanent worklessness for up to 20 per cent of the population is an extremely bleak prognostication, but Pym has a solution that may turn sorrow into joy. His belief is that 'we can assimilate the lower demand [for labour] by reducing the number of hours worked by each individual in a working life' (p. 179) and by massively boosting leisure. Dark clouds are blown away and the future is radiant because what was a 'problem of huge proportions' is now converted into 'an opportunity of huge proportions' (p. 177), as long as policies are devised and accepted that rearrange present patterns of work and leisure. At the core of this proposal is I.T. which, while under *laissez-faire* policies worsens unemployment and further divides the nation, will facilitate a dramatic reduction in working hours 'without harming productivity or competitiveness' if its introduction is undertaken speedily by a caring government.

Technological determinism

Whether the future will be a 'post-industrial' society run by service professionals ministering to our needs, or one in which voluntary idleness is the norm, it is certain that advanced technology is its essential requisite. Without I.T. extensive services employment will not be sustainable and generous leisure will not be affordable. This is a fact agreed upon by all commentators.

Daniel Bell, for instance, regards 'productivity' as the 'transforming fact' (Bell, 1983, p. 191) of economic life and, in turn, 'technology . . . is the basis of increased productivity' (p. 155). For the theorist of 'post-industrialism' it has been the ethos of 'more for less', of rationalisation, that has led to technological innovation and concomitant leaps in production. With this appliance of science comes the where-withal to pay for services and hence to allow the evolution into an 'information age'. It follows that with more I.T. will come more productivity to support still more services.

André Gorz shares this perception, although he frames it in socialist language. Adopting Marx's distinction between the 'sphere of necessity' and the 'sphere of freedom', Gorz argues that we live in a 'dual society', with one side supplying goods to satisfy our 'primary needs' (Gorz, 1982, p. 97), and the other – to date limited – in which we may enjoy the fruits of our labour that traditionally has been given over to producing the necessities of life. Gorz contends that, until now, work in the 'sphere of necessity' has been onerous and unwelcome, but a requirement of survival imposed by the 'technical imperatives' of material production (p. 92). In the current period he perceives work becoming no longer so important in securing material plenty due to advanced automation. Thanks to technology we can secure sufficiency with many fewer workers than before. His advocacy proceeds logically: since people do not much like the work that has hitherto been imposed on them, and since technology means that workers are no longer required in the numbers they once were, then more leisure – expansion of the 'sphere of autonomous activity' – is the obvious and desirable strategy. Leisure being equated with the 'sphere of freedom', it follows that with more I.T. will come more production from still fewer workers to support still more leisure and thereby ensure still more freedom.

Sir Francis Pym shares the same outlook, although he puts it in the idiom of one-nation Conservatism. He grieves for the unemployed and refuses to leave them out in the cold. But he also recognises that they are surplus to the economy's needs because I.T. has had, and will continue to have, a profound effect on production. His resolution is obvious: we must change 'the entire way we think about our working lives' (Pym, 1983). What we must do is reduce working hours, redistribute remaining labour as best we can, and change our attitudes towards the unemployed. This can only be achieved, of course, if technological innovation proceeds apace, since humane employment policies are not feasible without 'sustained economic growth'. It follows that with more I.T. adroitly applied will come further opportunities to reduce working life – and thus increased leisure – without blunting the competitive edge or threatening output levels.

We would emphasise that these approaches to social change share a deep-seated technological determinism. There are two interconnected aspects of this which require special attention. First, technology is regarded as the determinant factor of social life. It is taken as a given, a requisite of all else, the bedrock, the base, the premise of social existence and the ultimate determinant of our future existence. Second, technology is isolated from society, and is granted an autonomous existence beyond the arena of morality and human decision-making. To be sure, there are choices regarding how to distribute the bounty that technology pours forth and we are called upon to act to facilitate the introduction of technology, but there is no place for values and politics, for human intervention, in the development of technology itself.

In this manner technology is invariably regarded as socially determining because it is seen as an exogenous phenomenon that appears from outside to act on society. It is in this way discerned as somehow supra-social, as an intervention from without society which is to have the most tumultuous effects. It appears to be a bolt from the blue, an immense force which possesses its own volition, a phenomenon set on its own trajectory of 'progress'. If it has a history it is one that is merely immanent: from integrated circuits to microprocessors, from one technical discovery to another, devoid of influence from social forces yet devastating in its social consequences.

This perception – technology comes from without society although it then determines social arrangements – is evident in much of the comment. Thus Francis Pym: 'Over recent years, new technology has come out of the science-fiction books into our lives' (Pym, 1985, p. 172); similarly Christopher Evans: 'This book is about the future . . . It is a future which will involve a transformation of world society at all kinds of levels . . . It's a future which is largely moulded by a single, startling development in technology whose impact is just beginning to be felt. The piece of technology I'm talking about is, of course, the computer' (Evans, 1979, p. 9).

Now invasions such as this can be highly disturbing, and not everyone will respond positively to a mysterious thing invented in 'Silicon Valley' which is set to change their way of life. In response to such apprehension those who place their faith in I.T. are quick to assure the public that it is benign. It is not merely from afar, but it is a genuine *gift* from the gods. Margaret Thatcher spoke illuminatingly when she wooed her audience with the following analogy: 'Information Technology is friendly: it offers a helping hand; it should be embraced. We should think of it more like *ET* than I.T.' (Thatcher, 1982, p. 29).

Technology might be a beneficial imposition, but we are also instructed that it is a neutral force. This could scarcely be otherwise given that technology is thought to be asocial, but it does give rise to a quite extraordinary rhetoric of choice among futurists. Perhaps the most distinguishing feature of writing on I.T. has been commitment to the nostrum that we are free to choose how it is used (Webster and Robins, 1986, pp. 75–81). Big Brother or Power to the People, education or entertainment, centralisation or decentralisation . . . choices present themselves everywhere when it comes to I.T. From the premise that 'just like any other technology, I.T. is intrinsically neither good nor bad' (Marsh, 1982, p. 638), it follows that people may do what they will with it. Ironically, choices do not extend to acceptance or rejection of I.T. itself, since accedence is essential to realise the options. But who could possibly want to refuse a technology which is inherently beneficient and, moreover, entirely malleable? Bow to the technology, goes the refrain, since this is inevitable; accept it and adjust without protest and it will shower society with countless opportunities to create any sort of society one may wish for.

Legitimacy from technology

Because technology is presented unproblematically as the

driving force of change, it is a powerful legitimator of social, political and economic policies. No matter how partisan they may be, the public is assured that particular policies must be accepted because technology has changed circumstances irrevocably. Debates about policies, about who benefits, who loses, whose interests are dominant, about the need to adapt are subordinated to the new agenda of adjustment to inevitable technological change.

In the present period this is especially noticeable. At once we come across commentators who insist that the massive difficulties we must come to terms with in the here and now will be resolved by a technical fix that will usher in a 'post-industrial' society. At the same time, although the message is unambiguous that I.T. itself will ensure a brighter future, we are advised that we must adapt to the new technology *post haste*. No matter that it is disruptive and unsettling. It is here now and we must make the best of the situation and not be bloody-minded Luddites. Nothing can be made to bar the path of 'progress': 'Technological change will not be halted' (Williams, 1985, p. 52) so there is no point in carping about potential downside effects.

Thus recalcitrant and obstructive groups are swept aside in the name of technological imperatives. If printworkers resist changes in employment practices, if coal miners object to redundancies and new work patterns, or if telecommunications engineers hesitate to endorse the introduction of computerised exchanges, then they are lampooned as Canutes bent on resisting the inevitable tide. No-one can, no-one must, be allowed to hinder the onward march of technological progress. New technology is conceived as having a momentum akin to planetary orbit: 'sunset' industries will inexorably disappear, steelworks and shipyards scarcely need the sweat and skill of working people now that technology can do the bulk of it and other countries produce at lower prices; meanwhile we the people must await the coming of the 'sunrise' businesses, equipped with video display terminals and managed by the 'computer literate'. Since technology of itself is asocial, favouring neither capital or labour, Left or Right, how can it be objected to when all it gives is self-evident improvement, palpably more for less?.

'To stand in the way of technology is, almost by definition, to be labelled reactionary . . . [It] is equated with modernization, with progress, with a better and healthier life for all' (Dickson, 1974, p. 42). This perception of technology as an innocent, as an immaculate conception which will tell heavily on social arrangements, takes responsibility for historical development out of the hands of human beings who make choices, pursue interests, exercise power and leave their mark on artifacts, and presents it as 'progress', as an objective, self- (and selfless) driven process which is unstoppable.

Technological innovation and social values

These are the premises on which all policies, from Left and from Right, are based. From the assumption that I.T. will surge through society in the manner of a tidal wave comes the lesson that we must make haste to prepare for its unavoidable consequences by changing industrial practices, introducing computers into the school curriculum and rapidly becoming 'I.T. literate' so that we may sail into the 'information age'. From the premise that I.T. is an instance of the awesome powers of the demigods of Bell Laboratories follows the widespread acceptance of new technology, with enthusiasm from those on whom the deity shines, with fatalism when its victims experience deskilling or redundancy. With I.T. perceived as socially neutral all may welcome it, convinced that appropriate policies – more service employment or more leisure – can best take advantage of the additional resources it will hand over to society for distribution as politicians so decide.

We would challenge these assumptions. The gravamen of our case is that perspectives which conceive of technology as separate from society, even while it exercises a formidable influence once it sweeps into the social domain, are mistaken. Similarly, analyses which imagine society is amenable to division into separate levels – Gorz with his 'spheres' of necessity and freedom, Bell with his distinctions between industrial and service sectors – fall into the same trap of claiming that one element is in some way desocialised (it is usually technology, but it may also be portrayed as production, science, industry, or even as the wealth-producing sector of society: there is an odd conflation of these terms in writing about social change), and hence beyond the reach of values and policies, while another is conceived as the locale of policy, though it is dependent on, and shaped by, the desocialised sector which provides the materials to be consumed in leisure or used to subsidise services.

Our argument is that technology is an integral part of the social process and that, far from being autonomous, it is expressive of social relations. In much the same way, it is our case that society is much more integrated than those who see distinct realms imagine. Take for instance Bell's theory of 'post-industrialism'. The germ of it is that one part of society makes available resources that may be spent on service employment. It does this by virtue of productivity increases which give more wealth to spend on service needs. Note the principles of the model: one sector is driven by the search for more for less and this the axis – and ultimate determinant – of all else. The productive sphere of society is beyond the reach of politics, driven rather by the self-directed logic of rationalisation/efficiency – which is, of course, expressed primarily in the development of technologies that enhance productivity growth. Without automation the services which announce the coming of an 'information society' are unsustainable.

The problem with this model is that services cannot be detached from production in the way Bell presumes. The work of Jonathan Gershuny and Ian Miles (1983) has demonstrated, for example, that the expansion of the service sector has owed much to a desire to improve production (cf. Cohen and Zysman, 1987). Banking, finance, advertising, even a great deal of education have expanded not because productivity in the industrial sector has provided sufficient excess wealth. They have increased because they make more effective production and because, quite simply, they are sensible matters of the division of labour (Gershuny, 1978, p. 92). It will not surprise any teacher to read that manufacturing employers send their apprentices along to college because they find this a convenient and cost-effective way of training them to be better workers, not because they feel obliged to dissipate the wealth they have generated on a bit of education.

Further, social change has not come about because industry has produced such surplus that people have turned to services as a means of ridding themselves of excess. Far from wealth-production coming first and thereafter people looking to services to spend their income on, widespread desire for services has shaped production itself. It has been market demand for service products like washing machines, televisions and automobiles which has guided production, rather than, as Bell contends, services expanding because some undefined 'productivity' has supplied us with abundance which we must then spend. An alternative version is that Bell's sphere of production is not aloof from social values, is not a mere repository of wealth, but is actually intimately shaped by social priorities. That is, technological innovation itself is influenced by, and even incorporates, social values.

André Gorz's theorisation shares the same shortcomings as Bell's. Gorz suggests that the 'sphere of necessity' imposes work which carries 'technical imperatives' that must be conformed to if society is to meet its basic needs. This has long been the major constraint on human beings, but at last this tyrany of unwanted and unsatisfying labour may be broken because I.T. reduces it to a minimum. Gorz's assumption is that work is imposed by the demands of production and that now both work and production can be profoundly affected – and relieved – by technology. But this is to presume that work is beyond society, something natural which 'just has to be done' in generally unpleasant circumstances. However, a moment's reflection must lead one to question Gorz's premises. Work is in truth greatly influenced by social relations, from the very definition of a given activity as 'work' (chopping a log can be work or leisure depending on context), through the creation of particular places of work in particular forms (factories, offices, workshops), shift work schedules, supervisory roles, specialised tasks, time-sheets and assembly lines. Work as we know it – paid employment – is most definitely not a legacy of the *condition humaine*; it is a social creation, indicating the values and priorities, the very architecture, of society (cf. Rose, 1985).

Insistence that work is a social construct also provides an insight into technology. Leisure society theorists presume this is merely a neutral force that provides the means of decreasing working hours. But if we regard technology as part of society rather than as an exogenous factor we may recognise that, notably in this century, technologies have been designed and applied specifically as a means of getting more out of employees. Nowhere have engineers or investors seriously considered creating machinery that might ennoble work, but because they have not done so does not mean that they have left behind social values when it comes to technological innovation. On the contrary, what have been predominant have been the values of minimum cost and minimal concern for the workers' quality of life. As we shall see (in Chapters 2 and 3), I.T. is being developed with similar priorities to the fore. Since this is the case we find it dubious in the extreme that people should perceive I.T. as a fortuitous instance of scientific 'progress' that will grant liberation from the servitude of work. If the issue is approached from our perspective it is far more relevant to ask: why have technologies and work been designed so as to appear anathema to so many people and how and why is I.T. being designed in the here and now?

Conclusion

We cannot but be struck by the accumulation of problems Britain must face as we approach the year 2000. Energy blight, urban disorder, economic crisis, declining competitiveness and increased vulnerability to international movements of capital are just some of them. Yet we are also amazed by the assurance of so many seers. Seizing the assumed promise of the 'microelectronics revolution' we are proferred a technological paradise against which our apprehensions and fears seem absurd. No matter how entrenched and worrisome, I.T., adroitly managed and rapidly accepted, is the solution, the technical fix.

This resurrection of McLuhan's faith in technology is perhaps not altogether surprising and we are tempted to draw on the historian's concept of the 'chiliasm of despair' to explore the inner motives of the 'post-industrial' converts. But we are neither historians nor psychoanalysts and our concern is with the present and technology's place there. Here we must say that this way of thinking represents a failure to come to terms with existing realities, that it is an escape from the substantiality of this world and a refusal to squarely face the genuine difficulties the country now endures. This is especially ironic given the fact that the imminence of I.T. is emphasised as a means of implementing policies – industrial restructuring, market-orientation, vocational education, youth training – that are indicative of identifiable values and priorities about which debate is ignored, repressed and pushed aside in the name of necessary adjustment to the 'I.T. revolution'.

In this chapter we have suggested that technological change can only be adequately understood if we stop seeing it as aloof from society. Those writers who separate I.T. from society, only to erect an entire future on its largesse, misconstrue the meaning of technological – and social – change. Against these approaches we want to insist that technology – and any future – will emerge as part of established social relations. For this reason we are sceptical of claims that we are on the edge of a 'new age'. Certainly we are aware of change all around, but we do not believe this is a transcendence of the society in which we find ourselves. Indeed our argument throughout this book is that past and present circumstances are important pressures bearing on the origination, design, development and application of information technology and that an understanding of these is a requisite of comprehending the social construction and adoption of I.T. We want to bring examination of I.T. back into society, out of the hidden world of the laboratory and away from the mystifying language of 'progress'. Axial to this exercise is scrutiny of the origins of the 'information society', not in terms of an analysis of the

32   *The Myth of the Machine*

immanent history of technological invention, but from a point of view which includes technological innovation as an integral and indivisible part of social change. It is to this that we turn in the following chapter.

2

The Origins of the Information Society

'The *bien-pensants* of the information explosion seem almost
obtuse in their good intentions to add to knowledge, almost
disarming in their innocent enthusiasm for a 'complete record'
which could be exceeded only by the mind of God in the
amount of information it contains.' (Edward Shils, 1967, p. 343)

Introduction

We share with I.T. enthusiasts the view that information –
its collection, storage, analysis and transmission – plays an
increasingly key role in society. However, we disagree
profoundly with the idea that this is a consequence of an
Information Technology 'revolution' that came about in the
late 1970s courtesy of the 'mighty micro' and is destined to
change everything with which it comes into contact.

The aim of this chapter is to challenge this now conventional wisdom which has it that the arrival of advanced
technologies heralds an Information Society in response to
which education must introduce *tout de suite* courses in
'computer literacy' so that the younger generation can fit
easily into the new era. Against this, we shall argue that the
roots of the Information Society, and indeed the cluster of
technologies identified by the term I.T., can and should be
examined from a historical perspective. Doing this, we can
at once better understand the character and import of
information technologies in our society and at the same time
resist the technological imperative that propels 'I.T. awareness' initiatives.

33

Our argument in outline is simple, in detail it is complex. It is that social, economic and political relationships have been characterised by their being increasingly *organised* over this last century and more, and that this *systematisation* of life has been orchestrated by state and corporate groups in ways expressive of relations of power. We contend that the most significant feature of the development of advanced capitalism and the nation state has been their endeavour to integrate diverse areas of life into domains over which they have control. Drawing in and extending into once exempted activities, corporate capitalism and state agencies typically have achieved a greater management of social relationships, have increasingly 'scripted' roles and encounters, at the same time as they have advanced their criteria as those most appropriate for conducting affairs. This process should be seen as the rationalisation of control in pursuit of particular interests.

The imperative to move towards greater regulation of affairs, in our view, has engendered a special emphasis on information, since information gathering, scrutiny and dissemination are requisites of effective and systematic control. Without reliable information on sales, consumer preferences, labour processes or currency exchanges, modern corporations could not conduct their business; without accurate information on income distribution, health or even demographic trends, the efficacy of the state in social security, welfare or conduct of elections would be severely curtailed. In pursuit of our thesis that the original 'information revolution' should be traced through time, and long before the invention of the microchip, as the history of growing corporate and state interest in extending their influence, let us sketch what we consider to be landmarks in the development of an 'information society'.

Corporate requirements

One of the most striking features of life in the late twentieth century is that, wherever one looks for goods or services, one encounters extremely large and relatively few corporations supplying them. The advanced economies are characteristically dominated by concentrated and oligopolistic enterprises that command hundred million and even multibillion pound revenues. Banking? Barclays, National Westminster, Lloyds and the Midland. Retailing? Sainsbury, Asda, Co-op, Tesco. Cars? British Leyland, General Motors, Ford, Toyota. Petrol? Shell, B.P., Texaco, Esso. And so on.

The bulk of these companies have their origins in the nineteenth century, from whence we can trace the emergence of the corporate capitalism of today with its distinctive features of:

• concentration into fewer and fewer dominant participants that is accompanied by the increased relative and absolute wealth of corporations;
• extension deeper into the fabric of society by the establishment of networks of outlets (garages, supermarkets, branches, etc.) and involvement in education and politics, commitment to sponsorship and cognate activity;
•spatial growth, first nationally and, especially since 1945, internationally, such that typically the leading corporate participants in the domestic economy have transnational subsidiaries for production, sales or distribution or a combination of all three.

In addition, corporations have undergone, and continue to undergo, processes of vertical and horizontal integration, the first trend leading towards the placement of manufacturing and retail facilities under one organisational umbrella, the second towards focusing on a distinct product range and market area. An important consequence of these moves towards integration has been that we have witnessed at once a decline in the influence of the market on much corporate activity as 'managerial capitalism' (Chandler, 1977) has evolved to increasingly plan and regulate business affairs, at the same time as market principles have been promoted in areas with which the corporation has come into contact. In other words, as corporations have enlarged and developed, they have been able to limit in significant spheres the operations of the free market (for example, in taking over supplies of parts and producers of complementary goods they have reduced their dependence on the market as a source), while what might be called the incorporation of society (Trachtenberg, 1982) has extended market principles and market relations into wider domains. Thus managerial capitalism has facilitated the intrusion of market principles into social relations, thereby paving the way for the spread of consumerism. This is particularly visible in urban areas, where they are most effectively founded, at the expense of self and local reliance, so that shop and store, rather than family and neighbours, became the source of everyday needs, and the ability to pay became the arbiter of their fulfilment.

Combined and individually these evolving features of corporate capitalism place a heightened emphasis on information collection, analysis and communication. Standardisation and organisation of relations were essentials of a secure corporate order which in turn demanded reliable information processing and transmission if they were to be co-ordinated and implemented effectively. As the corporation grew and spatially extended, so there came about a need to link disparate sites and cohere larger and larger units; as the corporation integrated its activities so there came about an imperative to thoroughly plan and monitor its operations; as the corporation burrowed deeper into the society so there came about a requirement for systematic appraisal and observation of its outlets.

In response to these trends were introduced and/or expanded occupational groups, managerial and clerical categories such as merchandisers, marketers, and sales personnel, all of whom had the fact they were members of a burgeoning sector in common: information work. With these personnel came the introduction of information technologies – electronic calculating machinery, communications facilities, the telephone and telex system – that were essential to manage the increasingly important material of information.

Scientific management

At the turn of the century one of the most pressing problems facing corporate capitalism was how to control its increasingly large (and increasingly unionised) workforce. A few years previous, at the height of *laissez-faire* capitalism, this problem had not pressed itself as an everyday issue. To be sure, there had been explosive and violent confrontations between owners and workers intermittently throughout the nineteenth century, but in the main and for most organisations, everyday discipline had been maintained by employers being able to exercise personal supervision of their employees in the workshop.

Although the image of the Industrial Revolution is one of vast and impersonal cotton mills where multitudinous 'hands' were ruthlessly exploited by distant capitalists, the reality was that most work – arduous though it undeniably was – took place in small units of perhaps a dozen or so employees overseen by a master (Samuel, 1977). Size only became a widespread issue in the later years of the century when cartels and the logic of competition brought into being corporate giants, most of which have dominated the industrial landscape ever since. By then production was organised on too grand a scale for employers to personally supervise and, besides, a good many of the grandchildren of the industrial entrepreneurs who had made the Industrial Revolution with their own hands wished to escape the factory and cultivate the lifestyle of the 'gentleman' (Landes, 1969, p. 336; Thompson, 1963, p. 132). In response to this situation, an appropriate means of engineering people had to be achieved to complement the undeniable advances that had been made in the scale and significance of the engineering of things. The owner/entrepreneur was no longer on the shop floor on a day-to-day basis and the workforce was too big to get to know personally. How could business continue?

The corporate resolution was to initiate the concept of management; that is, to create a new role for the employer or, more correctly, his trusted lieutenants the expanding professional managers, which would be dedicated in large part at least to discovering ways of how best to control the workforce. A crucial factor influencing management effectiveness is that management should know, as fully as is possible, the requirements of the work which is its task to oversee and organise. This is essential if the workforce is to be adequately disciplined to maximise production since, if management is ignorant of constituents of a work process, then it is likely to the same degree to be beholden to its employees who do possess that knowledge. This may be satisfactory as long as the employer maintains the hearts and minds of the workforce, but such commitment is especially hard to induce in large organisations. In such circumstances, as any manager realises, ignorance easily leads to ineffectiveness and over-reliance on the whim and willingness of employees – in short, to indiscipline.

In the opening decades of the twentieth century it is possible to discern the emergence, especially in the bigger corporate concerns, of modern management and its commitment to maximum knowledge of labour processes as the *sine qua non* of effectively fulfilling its functions. Indeed, this creed was articulated by one F. W. Taylor, the man who coined the term 'Scientific Management' and the creator of what we know today as Taylorism.

It is a peculiarity of many contemporary management theorists that they refer to Taylorism as a particular practice (usually 'time and motion') that is outdated, having been superseded by more socially and psychologically sensitive managerial methods. Peculiar, because Taylorism is not reducible to particular strategies, but is better regarded as *the* unifying and underlying philosophy of *all* modern management in so far as its essence is an emphasis on the necessity for management to monitor, analyse and thoroughly plan the activities that are the concern of the corporation.

Various strategic options follow from Taylor's perception that 'brain-work' should be the monopoly of the management which would plan how best to conduct production on the basis of meticulous pre-conceptualisation of the required work. Prominent among these is the possibility of arranging the labour process in such a way as to give least possible initiative to the employee by, for example, designing an assembly line which requires many individual inputs from many workers none of whom do anything calling for more than rudimentary skill. It seems undeniable that this has been a feature of Taylorism and that deskilling has been chosen as a means of effecting managerial control. But we would stress that this follows from the core tenet of Scientific Management, that *knowledge/information* is the crucial ingredient for successful discipline of the labour force: 'Surveillance in the capitalist enterprise is the key to management' (Giddens, 1987, p. 175). With sound information on how work is to be conducted management has the initiative over workers who are compelled to respond to any particular strategy their employers may choose to implement. It is this advantage that falls to management that illuminates the nature of Taylorism: it is an emphasis on surveillance and planning that identifies its particularity. In this sense Scientific Management represents the original information revolution.

What we are arguing is that Scientific Management represented a decline in interpersonal modes of control at work and a shift towards more rational and calculative procedures which crucially involved management collecting, processing and acting upon information about the work process, all the better to control it. Herein lies Taylor's contribution to the Information Society of today. The advocacy of Scientific Management necessarily puts a heightened emphasis on information, stimulating the generation of greater quantities and qualities of data (on output levels, on work organisation, on employee functions) and encouraging additional employment of information workers (wherever it was applied, Scientific Management led to an increase in numbers of supervisors, clerks and general managers). As it undertook these tasks. so did Taylorism contribute to more systematisation and regularisation of the world of work.

Fordism

Henry Ford, pioneering his automobile plant in Detroit,

complemented Taylor by placing knowledge of production in the machinery of his assembly lines. Mechanisation, the characteristic feature of modern industrial production, should be viewed as the fruition of planning operations which have observed and even anticipated the labour process, considered the skills necessary to effect production, and incorporated these wherever possible into technology. Fordism expresses 'technical control' (Edwards, 1979) of the labour process (the assembly line determines the pace of work, the machinery calls for minimal skill from the worker) and may be regarded as an enhancement of Taylor's advocacy in so far as management acts upon knowledge of work still more systematically than previous arrangements that had been limited to organisational innovations. In our view Fordism not only draws attention to the heightened significance of information and knowledge for corporate activities, but it also indicates a further stage in the rationalisation of control, the consequences of which for employees are well documented. (See, for example, Beynon, 1984.)

Taylorist and Fordist principles have continued to be applied remorselessly in efforts to better manage – and thereby induce more productivity from – employees. Computer numerical control, advanced automation, robotics and associated techniques fit easily into this tradition (Shaiken, 1984; Wilkinson, 1983; Noble, 1984). Moreover, in recent years Fordism has penetrated the office, spearheaded by a range of information technologies that promise to extract more for less from an increasingly expensive section of the labour force. After a number of less than wholly successful attempts to revamp the office organisationally (Mills, 1963), advanced technologies are set to radically change that environment. Computer systems, online terminals, electronic filing, 'smart' copiers, dedicated micros, word processors and so forth are technologies being introduced into the primary sector of white collar work (which as a whole now accounts for almost half of the entire labour force) as a conscious effort to contain and restrain the burgeoning cost of information storage and processing.

Ironically, groups that benefited from the Scientific Management of others (notably manual workers) and the overall promotion of information garnering and analysis that resulted from the expansion of corporations throughout society, are now having the techniques of Taylor and Ford applied to their work. New technologies are now finding applications, in conjunction with extensive work reorganisation, to 'solve the problem of office productivity' that has vexed managements forced to watch office costs rise far ahead of inflation to account nowadays for something like 50 per cent of corporate costs while productivity increases here have been minimal over the past decade (Webster and Robins, 1986, pp. 116–20). Today, thanks to reductions in the cost of computer communications technologies and the targeted development of these technologies stimulated by the prodigious potential savings in staff costs, the office sector is undergoing rapid automation. Managements have carefully conceptualised the information routines of their non-manual workers and are now endeavouring to supply and introduce machinery that will speed and even reduce the 'information flow' at a 'cost effective' rate. Already results are manifest in such 'factory offices' as insurance companies, banks and the large word processing centres.

Sloanism

If Henry Ford pioneered modern management in manufacture, his counterpart at General Motors, Alfred P. Sloan, played an equally important role in innovating the management of consumption. As Scientific Management was introduced into factories, and while companies founded special management teams to integrate manufacture and distribution, the impulse to control beyond the work force and corporation through to the customer became more pressing. It seems inevitable, with hindsight, that Taylorist principles of calculation would extend to the crucial area of selling. Thus Herbert Casson, an early devotee, could argue that 'What has worked so well in the acquisition of knowledge and in the production of commodities may work just as well in the distribution of those commodities' (Casson, 1911, p. 7).

There was the additional factor that mass production could not be assured if consumption was left entirely to customer whim, something not lost on a contributor to *Advertising and Selling*:

> Stripped naked of rhetoric, the situation becomes fairly simple: In the past dozen years our factories have grown ten times as fast as our population. We have had, therefore, either to create new buying power or slow down . . . Coming prosperity . . . rests on a vastly increasing base of mass buying. (Goode, 1926)

As elsewhere, corporate capitalism moved to minimise the uncertainties the free market presented for its operations by attempting to regularise relations with customers. Thus by the second decade of the century in the United States (Britain was some years behind the most energetic capitalist nation), procedures were being developed to manage selling. The steady movement of clothing, cigarettes, household furnishings, processed foods, soaps and the like required the creation of ways of reaching customers, taking heed of their needs, wants and dispositions, and responding by persuasion and even redesign of products to make them more or newly attractive (Pope, 1983).

Sloanism exemplified aspects of this extension of control beyond the plant into the customer's home. It was Sloan who in the 1920s introduced into the automobile industry instalment selling, used-car trade-ins, annual model changes, and emphasised styling and brand image (Sloan, 1965, Chapter 9) which had two, connected, features. One was that production was better integrated with consumption than it had been previously, in so far as outlets for goods became better regulated; the other was that this necessarily entailed making sure that the consumer was known about and thereby subject to persuasion.

In a word, modern *marketing* began to be established – a concept that nominates and embraces the three activities of production, distribution and sales. Axiomatic to this principle was the systematic processing and dissemination of information wherever corporate imperatives so determined, in order that maximum influence could be made. The need to gather, aggregate and accumulate information about the consumer led to the rise of market research (for demographic details, class distribution and socio-economic characteristics etc) and the accumulation of detailed sales records and analyses (who buys what, where, when and at what price?).

The embryonic company, International Business Machines, benefited from these trends as its technologies admirably suited record-conscious corporations. Henry C. Link, a contemporary advocate of scientific marketing, described the impulse early forms of I.T. received from the informational needs of business:

> The most highly developed technique for measuring buying behavior is that made possible by the electric sorting and tabulating machines. These ingenious devices have made it feasible to record and classify the behavior of the buying public as well as the behavior of those who serve that public, on a scale heretofore impracticable. Whereas by ordinary methods hundreds of transactions may be recorded, by this method thousands may be recorded with greater ease. Not only have comprehensive records been made possible but, what is much more important, the deduction from these records of important summaries and significant facts have been made relatively easy. The technique developed by various merchants, with the use of these devices . . . is the quantitative study and analysis of human behavior in the nth degree. (Link, 1932, p. 248)

It was also vital, of course, to convey information to the consumer (and already this term was displacing the word customer) and this gave rise most obviously and preeminently to advertising, though it was also evident in packaging and the branding of goods, their display, trade-in deals and various other means of persuading the public to spend.

We are by no means claiming that these attempts at organising and orchestrating the consumer have been entirely successful – people can be fickle and recalcitrant at the point of sale furthest away from corporate pressure (Schudson, 1984) – but these activities have been, we would argue, fundamental constraints on twentieth-century social and cultural life. At the heart of this extension of Taylorism from factory throughout society, a process we would designate Social Taylorism, is that crucial insight of Scientific Management that information control is the life-blood of the modern corporation (and society).

It does not take only radicals to recognise this development. David Potter, author of *People of Plenty*, a hymnal to American productivism this century, makes no bones about it. Given the 'abundance' pouring out of increasingly automated factories, Potter wonders how it is to be put to use by an inadequately educated population. His answer is that thankfully 'advertising [is] an institution of social control – an instrument comparable to the school and the church in the extent of its influence upon society'. Indeed, he continues, advertising is 'the only institution which we have for instilling new needs, for training people to act as consumers, for altering men's values, and thus for hastening their adjustment to potential abundance . . .' (Potter, 1954, pp. 168, 175). We would not so unhesitatingly argue that advertising is successful and neither would we extract advertising from other methods of persuading people to buy, but what we would endorse is the view that Potter's words are simple common sense to the 'Ad men [who] searched for a means of translating Frederick W. Taylor's ideal of scientific management into the selling and distribution processes' (Schultze, 1978, p. 116).

It should be stressed that these indices of a shift towards a more rationalised and organised way of life are considerably more than a matter of collecting, considering and distributing forms of information, important though these undoubtedly are. They were also expressed in structural transformations through which corporate capitalism stimulated the spread of market criteria throughout social life. Thus, as corporate capitalism advanced it transformed the texture of everyday life as it insinuated itself into social relations, with mail order purchase, department and chain stores, instalment payments and the plethora of novel and stylishly packaged goods stimulating and consolidating our distinctively modern way of life: *buying a living* (Lynd and Hanson, 1933). Of fundamental importance was the replacement of self and/or collective provision by market exchange and commodity relations. The overriding principle is one of access and availability to pay for goods and services. With the increased rationalisation of social life, there developed, then, consumer capitalism.

Professionalisation

Amid all of these developments what is evident is a common concern for surveillance and planning within the plant, between sites, and throughout the wider society. During the second and third decades of the century it is clear that a series of movements were coming together, headed towards a more systematic monitoring of life so that corporate enterprise could be reliably conducted. A necessary adjunct of this concern was a heightened emphasis on exactitude, on measurement and quantification of most reliable data, on 'professional' and 'scientific' approaches to the management task. Thus in advertising concepts from psychological research were enthusiastically introduced and campaigns more thoroughly prepared by pre-testing and careful analysis of advertising copy and presentation, while the vulgar hype of P. T. Barnum was superseded by more sophisticated imagery (Marchand, 1985); market research flourished and increasingly drew upon survey literature, census data and social scientific techniques, feeding back its findings into commercial strategies; broadcast ratings were promoted and refined to distinguish types of audience, their patterns of behaviour and their preferences (Hurwitz, 1983); public relations emerged and rapidly enlarged in response to the growing domain of business activity (Tedlow, 1979) and soon took on board up-to-date techniques to manipulate and even create news and affairs that might affect the corporation (Lipsky, 1925; Bernays, 1952). Underpinning these trends, all of which expressed a corporate search for better control, was the faith in business circles that changes were motivated not by vulgar self-interest, but by the search for 'efficiency', and that in this search the 'expert' and the 'scientist', whether engaged in the fabrication of goods or the fabrication of consumers, had a key role to play (Akin, 1977).

  Supporting this too was the establishment of a system of social and economic analysis, institutionalised in journals, publishing ventures and academic posts, centred in a burgeoning university sector that commonly attracted funds from the business world and which was, perhaps most notably in Chicago, consciously shaped by a concern to accurately analyse behavioural patterns in the urban environment. On the basis of the information gathered, the dislocated and alienated could be integrated into a fast changing society (Carey, 1975). To be sure, academe had its autonomy, but what is striking is the congruence of corporate and university concerns: monitoring of behaviour, amassment of relevant data and adjustment of social action to facilitate new ways of living. Not surprisingly, there were many instances of academics and business people working closely together (Noble, 1977).

  Better information collection and dissemination to better control a public suffering the effects of 'modernity' is an overriding theme of the second and third decades of American history, and developments in the UK shared marked similarities. Here, as in the USA, an acute depression was disproportionately hitting the regions and the heavy industries located there with manifest social and political consequences. However, less obvious but highly significant was that between the wars corporations in Britain very rapidly concentrated and that with this trend 'the new mass production economy really triumphed' (Hobsbawm, 1968, p. 185). At the forefront of this development was the discovery that the mass consumption of the working class held sales opportunities, to which is owed the rapid growth of retailing between the wars. As in the United States, this brought with it chain stores and instalment purchase and, of course, advertising (Stevenson, 1984, ch. 4). A number of social trends – the shift to the cities, social and geographical mobility, expansion of manufacturing output, new goods and services, increased real wages – together recommended corporate capitalism, with its need for market growth to sustain itself, to urge the creation of adequate means of regulating the public.

The core means for achieving this was *information*, accurately collected and appropriately disseminated, imperatives which underpinned the rising clamour for professional conduct on the part of information operators. The responsibility was enthusiastically undertaken and approved by John Watson, the founder of behaviourist psychology and vice-president of the J. Walter Thompson agency, who drew attention to the fact that 'Business men are realizing as never before that the sale of their products depends on the accuracy with which they have gauged the requirements of the buying public' (Watson, 1932, p. vii). This exactitude of analysis prior to selling was complemented by expression of its purpose by Walter Dill Scott, a pioneer of 'scientific advertising' and, like Watson, an academic turned 'applied psychologist', who urged that 'it was the job of advertising to move a heterogeneous and distant population to harmonious action' (Schultze, 1978, p. 96). Advertisers like Scott willingly conceived of themselves as 'consumption engineers' (Marchand, 1985, p. 25) and willingly committed their skills in search of shaping public consciousness in ways beneficial to their corporate clients.

Corporate change: adaptation and intensification

We have sketched what we consider to be some of the roots of the 'information society'. The imperative to organise its spheres of activity – which have increasingly enlarged and deepened in scope – has induced corporate capitalism to continue and to consolidate its informational requirements. In order to update our argument, and to underline our thesis of the social origins of the Information Age, let us, in telegrammatic form, point to some more recent developments.

(i) *Corporate consolidation*

This century, and especially over the last 40 years, the world has become much more integrated economically, an integration overseen by the extension of transnational corporations. This much is news to no-one with any idea of the major corporate units in Britain who has travelled abroad and come across the same products and same corporate giants in Europe, Africa, the Far East and even in the United States.

However, what can be overlooked are the enormous consequences this has had for information. The establishment of a system of transnational corporations has placed an inordinate importance on having sophisticated and reliable computer communications networks meshing together operations. The co-ordination involved, for example, in the assembly of a product in several countries from parts drawn from numerous others and materials from still more, is formidable. Add to this the operation of transnationals in what are now regarded as global markets. Consider then the complexities of establishing price and processing revenue (adding to the complexity that significant elements of pricing are intra-corporate). Now one can begin to appreciate the informational requirements of the concerns.

The *Business Roundtable* is clear about what this means:

> The dependence of multinational corporations . . . upon international information transfer is increasing. A 1983 survey, with 380 companies, from 85 countries participating, indicates that 94% of the corporations now use, or are planning to use, international computer-to-computer communications systems. (*Business Roundtable*, 1985)

Westinghouse Corporation reasoned aloud why it has recently put in place an 'integrated worldwide strategic planning process': it would 'provide timely and detailed information for every part of the world. This centralization of planning and intelligence will give Westinghouse a competitive edge in the worldwide deployment of its resources' (Westinghouse, 1982a).

The quantities and qualities of information and data stored in computers around the globe and traversing national borders hour after hour can scarcely begin to be estimated, but it is certain that financial transactions, corporate directives, sales returns, commodity exchanges and the like constitute the essential infrastructure of the corporate network (D. Schiller, 1982).

Increasingly, and as if to underline the pertinence of this information flow, transnationals are opting to develop private data networks such as offered by Citicorp and the General Motors subsidiary Electronic Data Services that can by-pass obstacles encountered on public communications systems. Moreover, some idea of the pertinence of information to transnationals can be estimated by the rise and rise of 'information factories' such as Reuters and TRW. These supply services of economic and strategic significance to the dispersed corporation, offering information from vast data banks at short notice on foreign exchanges and money matters, securities, bonds, energy prices, commodities, shipping, precious metals, historical materials and news of value to investors. So attractive are these rapidly growing information suppliers that they are quickly being absorbed by still larger information corporations which are themselves increasing their presence in this lucrative field (for example, IBM and Merrill Lynch recently began to offer a financial information and brokerage service).

(ii) *Productive decentralisation*

A recent trend observed among transnationals is to decentralise their activities, such that there has been discerned a break-up of the mass production factory located close by corporate headquarters (Ford's plant at Detroit is the classic instance), and the distribution of activities far and wide. Some have greeted this development as a radical transformation that gives power and responsibility back to the people who may in future work meaningfully in communities and small groups.

Against this, we would emphasise that decentralisation is in no way weakening the command of the transnational parent. Rather, it is an instance of the way in which developments in information handling can enable a centralised organisation to decentralise without losing control. In our view, the establishment of, for example, production facilities in Taiwan, Glasgow and Dublin, design in Berkshire and New York, and marketing in London and Los Angeles, is illustrative of the 'new international division of labour' characteristic of what we call 'neo-Fordism' (see Chapter 4), which is enabled by facilities that allow constant monitoring and feedback from units in dispersed locales without loss of control. This is, again, illustrative of the heightened significance of information in the advanced capitalist societies, the demand modern corporations place upon computer communications technologies, the reality that information and knowledge set the limits to decentralization and that these limits are being extended by breakthroughs in I.T. (Webster and Robins, 1986, Part 3).

(iii) *Global marketing*

While most transnationals have very important markets in their host country, they traverse the globe in search of outlets for their produce. This poses an immediate need to know much about local particulars (exchange rates, income levels, demographic details, national cultures) and an ability to mount campaigns capable of merging people in an individual nation into international consumers of their brands. World marketing, exemplified by firms such as Coca Cola, IBM, Shell and Procter & Gamble, demands worldwide market research and advertising, a capacity to scrutinise populations and, on the basis of analysis, to persuade them of the desirability of a product and supplier. The agencies which undertake these activities – information operatives *par excellence* – are themselves transnational enterprises that are increasingly integrated across the information business. Thus Saatchi & Saatchi, the world's number one agency following its takeover of the Ted Bates group, has during its meteoric and acquisition-led rise established skills in public relations, market research, management consultancy and sales promotion as well as in its mainline advertising.

The strategy of Saatchi & Saatchi is visibly to direct its informational expertise towards the biggest market – the 'multinational advertisers [that are moving] towards greater co-ordination in their international marketing activities' (Gill, 1983) and which account for 80 per cent of America's top spenders on advertising. The rationale is obvious. Having applied Scientific Management to some effect at the level of the plant and office, the next stage for corporate capital is the customer wherever he or she might be. As financial journalist Stella Shamoon put it:

> It is a small step from the rationalisation of product lines, and the centralisation of production, distribution and marketing by continent, to world brands. (Shamoon, 1984)

World marketing involves not just the search for images with universal appeal. It demands simultaneously a capacity to scrutinise the particularities of a given country or region, to relate these patterns to those found elsewhere, and to connect all to appropriate advertising campaigns (Janus, 1984). It requires, in the words of Saatchi & Saatchi, 'analysis of all demographic, cultural and media trends', so that marketers 'can survey the world battlefield for their brands, observe the deployment of their forces, and plan their international advertising and marketing in a coherent and logical way'. In the present age, this involves at once having a capability to know precise conditions on the ground (to be able to detail how 'there are probably more social differences between Manhattan and the Bronx ... than between midtown Manhattan and the 7th Arondissement of Paris'), an ability to fabricate an advertisement 'so deep in its appeal that it can transcend national borders previously thought inviolate', and a capacity to deliver where appropriate specialist messages to specified audiences: 'the rifle rather than the shot-gun approach to planning advertising campaigns' (Saatchi & Saatchi, 1984).

The spread of global marketing not only represents the emergence of a particular kind of information. It also has profound effects on I.T., especially in the media. The press, radio and television, major information providers to the general public, have long been shaped, often in decisive ways, by the pressures of advertising (Barnouw, 1978). The predominance of escapist entertainment on the screens and in much of what passes for journalism owes much to advertising's need for maximum audiences. It is likely that, for the most part, the new communications technologies of cable, satellite and video will be harnessed to the established role of selling (Robins and Webster, 1986). Certainly, these novelties may be used for more discriminating advertising than previous: sponsors for particular types of programming – for example classical drama – may be interested in specific audience segments, video may be produced with distinct socio-economic groups in mind. However, this will not break with the hold of marketing, but rather it will consolidate it (Saatchi's 'rifle rather than the shot-gun approach'). Cable in particular, with its capacity for two-way communication, promises to provide new means of monitoring watching habits and a possibility thereby to more precisely target images at specified audiences. If we can be sure of nothing else, it is that the new communications technologies for the home will be dedicated to purveying and harvesting information that aids the selling process.

Already on a modest scale, but ultimately society-wide, these will enable 'teleshopping'. But a cognate innovation, propelled by the same corporate desire of attaining maximum information as a means of maximising market share, is the rapid growth of credit cards supplied by banks, garages and department stores, and credit worthiness data bases. What credit cards facilitate is the monitoring of purchases and thus the economic and social standing of large sections of the public. They give access to what people buy, at what price, how regularly, where, and how readily they foot the bill. This is the sort of information for which corporations yearn, and a sharp reminder of the motive and meaning of the approach of an 'information society'. Already there are enormous data banks holding information on the public concerning their credit worthiness. *Infolink*, for example, boasts data on the entire electoral register of 42 million voters, which it processes at a rate of 48 000 transactions an hour (*Financial Times*, 24 March 1986).

The state

The state, which we take to be a given territory over which sovereignty is held, has always, and necessarily, had a major stake in information and communications. Surveillance is a requisite of any state since at a minimum it must know its subjects sufficiently well so that they can be granted rights of nationality such as passports, and that they can be obliged to serve the nation in times of emergency. Moreover, governments have an acute interest in monitoring the economic affairs of their peoples, not least so that monies can be raised through effective taxation (Domesday was an early attempt to gather information for this purpose).

Despite these historical precedents, the role of the state generally, and its informational concerns particularly, has changed enormously during the twentieth century. The state in all advanced societies is now a pervasive phenomenon which reaches deep into many areas of social, economic and political life. As it has intruded deep and extensively into the texture of everyday life, so has the state widened and enhanced its informational needs and functions. Our view is that, with the growth of the 'programmed' market economy which we have described above, the political process has undergone a similar shift towards the combination of planning and control on a systematic and regularised basis.

Anthony Giddens (1985) has reminded us that the state has always been propelled into the business of surveillance and information gathering. Information and communications capabilities have been fundamental to the state for a number of reasons. First, they have been indispensable pre-requisites for administering and co-ordinating – maintaining the cohesion and integrity of – complex social structures. Second, they have played an important part in policing deviant members of the internal population and in the surveillance of external populations. Third, they have been central to the democratic process of political debate in the public sphere. In the following discussion we want to highlight the shape and force that some of these information functions have assumed in political life during the present century.

As a preliminary, however, it may be helpful to sketch conceptually and developmentally some of the major transformations in the state's use of information and communications. Most important, we believe that the ideal of an open 'conversation' in the 'public sphere' of a modern democracy has increasingly given way to the instrumental and 'efficient' Scientific Management of political life. In his classic account of the emergence of the public sphere, Habermas (1962) underlines the centrality of communications and information to its success. The public sphere is the forum, open equally to all citizens, in which matters of general and political interest are debated and ideas exchanged. It remains distinct from the state and, indeed, in so far as it is the locus of critical reasoning, it operates as a curb on state power. Its fundamental principles are that 'opinions on matters of concern to the nation and publicly expressed by men outside the government ... should influence or determine the actions, personnel, or structure of their government', and that 'the government will reveal and explain its decisions in order to enable people outside the government to think and talk about those decisions' (Speier, 1950, p. 376). Such democratic discussion within the frontiers of the state depends necessarily upon an infrastructure of communication and information availability. Indeed, it is only on this basis that the very idea of a public can have meaning.

But if this is the democratic aspiration, then historical trends have led to a shortfall in practice. Most telling has been the process by which political debate has come to be regulated by corporate bodies and by powerful segments of the state apparatus (Habermas calls this 'refeudalisation'). In this way the public has been 'superseded, managed and manipulated by large organizations which arrange things among themselves on the basis of technical information and their relative power positions'. What results is 'the dominance of corporative forms within which discussion is not public but is increasingly limited to technicians and bureacrats', with the public now becoming 'a condition of organizational action, to be instrumentally managed – i.e., manipulated' (Gouldner, 1976, pp. 139–40). What is being described here is the technocratic and administrative rationalisation of political life, the increasingly Scientific Management of the public sphere and of public information.

What we would emphasise here is the shift from what might be called a principle of public rationality to one of administrative rationalisation. With the latter political debate, exchange and disagreement in the public sphere can come to seem 'inefficient', an inhibiting and frictive obstacle to the 'efficient' management of society. Due to this, rational and informed discourse in the public sphere gives way to the rational, scientific management of society by technicians and bureaucrats.

This technocratic tendency is reflected, of course, in the positivist philosophy of Saint-Simon and Comte, but it is with a later form of practical sociology, that associated with the extension of the principles of Scientific Management to the wider society, that it assumed its most sustained form and the systematic exploitation of information resources was taken up in earnest. A figure of key theoretical and political importance here was Walter Lippmann.

In his book on Scientific Management, Samuel Haber considers Lippmann's 'desire to bring order out of the disorder of capitalism'. What is required, according to Lippmann, was scientific method, professionalism and expertise. Essentially, the problems of society 'had shifted from moral to technical issues', and they required in consequence the engineering techniques of Scientific Management. The close relationship with Taylorism is brought out in Lippmann's stress on administration and rationalisation (the logic of the planning department and its generalised laws). In Haber's words, acceptance of the age of mass participation in politics was balanced by

> an attachment to the expert and his guiding role in active government. Scientific Management, especially when placed within the conditions of industrial democracy, embodied in the factory regime what these progressive thinkers (like Lippmann) envisioned within society at large. (Haber, 1964, pp. 90, 93, 97–8)

Lippmann points to two dilemmas of the modern mass

society. The first refers to the political competence of citizens in democratic society

> The ideal of the omnicompetent, sovereign citizen is, in my opinion, such a false ideal. It is unattainable. The pursuit of it is misleading. The failure to produce it has produced the current disenchantment. (Lippmann, 1925, p. 39)

The second dilemma is that society has attained 'a complexity now so great as to be humanly unmanageable' (Lippmann, 1922, p. 394). The implication is that central government has been compelled to assume responsibility for the control and co-ordination of this increasingly diffuse social structure. This entails 'the need for interposing some form of expertness between the private citizen and the vast environment in which he is entangled' (ibid, p. 378). As in the Taylorist factory, this depends on 'systematic intelligence and information control'; the gathering of social knowledge, Lippmann argues, must necessarily become 'the normal accompaniment of action' (ibid, p. 408). If social control is to be effective, then control of information and communication channels is imperative. With the scientific management of social and political life through the centralisation of communications and intelligence functions, 'persuasion . . . become[s] a self-conscious art and a regular organ of popular government' and the 'manufacture of consent improve[s] enormously in technic, because it is now based on analysis rather than rule of thumb' (ibid, p. 248).

This concern with the management of information is reflected in the massive literature on public opinion theory in American political and social science theory during the first half of this century (the work of Harold Lasswell is especially noteworthy). What is most important here, we believe, is the association of public opinion theory with the study of propaganda in contemporary political discourse. Propaganda has commonly been perceived as inimical to rational political debate and regarded as a force that obstructs public reasoning. In the context of the social complexity and citizen 'incompetence' observed by Lippmann, however, propaganda assumed the guise of a more positive social force in the eyes of many social and political thinkers in the early decades of the century. An increasingly pragmatic and 'realistic' appraisal of the political process suggested that 'in a world of competing political doctrines, the partisans of democratic government cannot depend solely upon appeal to reason and abstract liberalism' (Albig, 1939, p. 301). It became clear that 'propaganda, as the advocacy of ideas and doctrines, has a legitimate and desirable part to play in our democratic system' (Childs, 1965, p. 282). The very complexity of the modern state appears to be such that a free market of ideas and debate must be superseded by the management and orchestration of public opinion. Lasswell makes the point well:

> The modern conception of social management is profoundly affected by the propagandist outlook. Concerted action for public ends depends upon a certain concentration of motives . . . Propaganda is surely here to stay; the modern world is peculiarly dependent upon it for the co-ordination of atomized components in times of crisis and for the conduct of large scale 'normal' operations. (Lasswell, 1977, pp. 235, 234)

Propaganda here should be understood in terms of the regulation and control of channels of communication and information in democratic societies. At one level, this is a matter of disseminating and broadcasting certain categories of information. Edward Bernays (1923) refers to this as 'special pleading'; and Lasswell writes of 'the function of advocacy', suggesting that 'as an advocate the propagandist can think of himself as having much in common with the lawyer' (Lasswell, 1941, pp. 75–6). At another level, it is a matter of restricting access to specific categories of information. As Lippmann makes clear, 'without some form of censorship, propaganda in the strict sense of the word is impossible. In order to conduct a propaganda there must be some barrier between the public and the event' (Lippmann, 1922, p. 43). For Lippmann, propaganda and censorship are complementary as forms of persuasion and public opinion management. In his outlook is evidenced a shift from the idea of an informed and reasoning public, to an acceptance of the massage and manipulation of public opinion by the technicians of public relations. According to Lasswell, society 'cannot act intelligently' without its 'specialists on truth', 'specialists on clarity', 'specialists on interest': 'unless these specialists are properly trained and articulated with one another and the public, we cannot reasonably hope for public interest' (Lasswell, 1941, p. 63).

In our view public opinion has become a condition of organisational action, to be instrumentally managed. Propaganda, scientifically manufactured by experts and professionals, becomes a legitimate – and indispensable – mechanism for achieving the efficient and rational regulation of society. The very complexity and intricacy of the modern state must be reduced to a more predictable and manageable pattern. Propaganda and public opinion theory extend the principles of Taylorism from factory to the state and wider society. The modern state 'cannot follow public opinion', writes Jaques Ellul, 'but it cannot escape it either. Since the government cannot follow opinion, opinion must follow the government', and the masses must be made to 'demand of the government what the government has already decided to do' (Ellul, 1965, pp. 126, 132). Public opinion remains a hallowed principle, but in practice, and in the cause of 'efficient' government, it must be moulded and managed. A more recent writer on propaganda puts the problem thus: 'As a democracy we must renounce propaganda; but as a state, we must make use of it' (Choukas, 1965, p. 281). We would put it somewhat differently. It seems to us that the state function has increasingly come to subsume and regulate the democratic principle; and this to the point that it now seems indissociable from that principle. We would agree with Francis Rourke that 'public opinion [has] become the servant rather than the master of government, reversing the relationship which democratic theory assumes and narrowing the gap between democratic and totalitarian societies' (Rourke, 1961, p. xi).

We have spent some time outlining the development of political management and information control because we feel, again, that this is an important historical context for the development of new information and communication technologies. Through the impetus of Scientific Management, and the development of propaganda and public opinion research, it became clear that social planning and control depended heavily upon the exploitation of information resources and technologies. This was the moment of the information revolution. The most recent technological innovations – space and satellite technologies, data communications, telecommunications – extend what was in reality a fundamentally political 'revolution' in information management. It was this historical conjuncture that spawned the 'modern' industries and bureaucracies of public relations, propaganda, public (and private) opinion polling, news management, image production and advocacy, political advertising, censorship and official secrecy, think tanks and so on. As in the corporate sector, so it was in the realm of the state: continuing trends promoted the importance of information and shaped its form and content in directions that reflected the concerns of powerful groups eager to manage the new age. Let us now illuminate key features of these developments by focusing on four major facets of the state that have important consequences for information, in that they have stimulated its generation and analysis while subordinating it to the priorities of its architects.

(i) *The state and citizenship*

A crucial feature of the modern state is that it monitors the citizenry much more closely, routinely and systematically than any of its predecessors. Educational records, medical files, vehicle registration, employment histories, tax liabilities, housing conditions, criminal records and so on are but some of the ways in which people are scrutinised by local and national authorities in contemporary Britain. Collectively these data bases amount to hundreds of millions of items of information on individuals and there are no signs of slowing down their growth.

Undoubtedly it is the case that the operation of the welfare state is unthinkable without these results of surveillance, since without detailed information the state cannot administer social security, elections, school provision or housing benefits. So we are not necessarily condemning this situation. Indeed, we are willing to concede that the surveillance machinery of the state plays a pivotal role in conferring what T. H. Marshall termed 'citizenship rights'. In fact, it is our view that the emergence of the surveillance state has roots in the Fabian tradition of social reform which placed stress on information amassed and analysed by experts in social and economic research as a requisite of amelioration of the lot of the lower orders (cf. Shils, 1967). One can readily depict a tradition of thought and key individuals – the Webbs, Marshall, Titmuss – who played a central role in the emergence of social research and practical welfare policy. This is not to underestimate the perils to civil liberties that are posed by the creation of data banks, which nowadays and in the near future are to be routinely accessed, networked and maintained electronically, which increasingly may be interconnected and drawn upon by reactionary and publically unaccountable forces (Campbell and Connor, 1986). It is simply to observe that the surveillance state owes its architecture as much to advocates of reform as it does to conservatives (cf. Abercrombie *et al.*, 1986, Chapter 5).

Our point here is simply to draw attention to the prodigious informational role of the state. As it has expanded its reach and range, so has it refined procedures to best harvest, store and scrutinise the results of this surveillance. To appreciate this one only need consider the army of information workers within government, in police stations and headquarters, in welfare agencies, census departments, the central statistical services and a variety of ministerial departments. In view of this it is not surprising to learn that the state is far and away the biggest provider of information on social and economic relations in Britain, far in excess of academic or media researchers. Nor is it unexpected to see that the state is the largest single customer of the I.T. industry, testament to which are the acres of computers in Whitehall and connected branches and the ambitious plans to automate many facets of state information such as police records, social security and Inland Revenue data.

(ii) *The state and economic planning*

There is a current nostrum which has it that the state must be extricated from economic affairs so that we might return to the days of *laissez-faire* and former glory. The record indicates, however, that the state has become – and will remain – deeply implicated in the economic life of the nation chiefly to bolster and facilitate the interests of market enterprise which without state support would be disadvantaged. There has been an inexorable increase in the state's participation in economic issues from and throughout the later decades of the nineteenth century. This for multiple reasons, including the need to harmonise training provision and industrial requirements; managing utilities such as rail, coal and electricity; stimulating and directing economic demand by judicious fiscal measures and public purchases; appropriate policies aimed at assisting in the co-ordination of indigenous corporations faced by foreign competitors that frequently have material support from their governments; supporting research and development initiatives that might benefit large numbers of strategically placed enterprises; attending to currency prices on the international market and trying to ensure that these benefit domestic concerns. Examples could be multiplied easily, but these must suffice to give the lie to the idea that non-intervention is feasible in the late twentieth century.

The state also intervenes in industry in less directly economic, but nonetheless economically weighty, ways, such as in policies towards trade unions (whether to weaken or support, legislation and state practice regarding trade unions have consequences for corporate operation), educational institutions (for example, to support more vocationally oriented courses as opposed to ones with an academic emphasis) and communications legislation (whether or not it encourages liberalisation). In addition, it has fallen to the state to take responsibility for maintaining social order in circumstances that are frequently dislocating. Thus for example during the present period of industrial restructuring when resources are being shifted away from 'sunset' industries such as coal and steel towards 'sunrise' businesses such as electronic engineering and computer programming, it is government that must try to ensure the readjustments are managed adroitly. It could well be the case, for instance, that civil disobedience resulting from policies aimed at creating an 'information economy' could have economically deleterious consequences. Inner city riots, or even an intensification of crime in urban centres, are not propitious for investment. In these circumstances government must take upon itself to instigate various strategies (regional programmes, youth employment policies, additional policing etc) designed to mitigate or at least contain the harsher effects of economic relocation.

What this intervention amounts to is that a prime responsibility of the state is economic planning that entails ordered change. A requisite of this is that the state systematically monitors economic and other matters so that planning might be effective and reliably grounded. In consequence, state organisations invest considerable resources in gathering economic and industrial indices (production levels, wage rates, skill distributions, training resources etc) and devising policies on the basis of analysis of such data. By the same token, the state must amass relevant information on obstacles to its economic intervention and planning, such as dissident political groups, social movements and even trade union activists.

Economic planning insists that the state continuously draws together detailed information on conditions in the nation. It also requires the state to dissemble information to those engaged in business that they might proceed with adequate knowledge of the prevailing economic climate, hence publications flow from HMSO with titles like *British Business*, *Employment Gazette*, *Energy Trends* and *Economic Trends*. All in all, these roles underline the fact that economic performance has heightened the import of information collection and distribution to the modern state.

(iii) *The state and political management*

The state in liberal democracies is the main sphere of contestation between different political parties and interests, the most significant of which still divide on lines of class today. This has been so for the bulk of this century in Britain and often the conflicts entered into, conspicuously in and around Parliament, have been acute and open. Nonetheless, the contest has never been one between equal antagonists. One reason for this has been that the influence of the need for a 'healthy economy' has told heavily against political programmes that might want to break with the *status quo*. The dull compulsion of 'confidence in sterling' has long been a major obstacle to radical politicians and this is a pressure which if anything has built up in post-war years with the increased integration of the international economy making domestic industry especially vulnerable to outside influence. A related factor curtailing those who would disturb the equilibrium has been the web of alliances and international agreements into which the state has entered to assure its own and others' sovereignty. This issue – broadly the question of national 'security' – has meant that state agencies have been predisposed to believe that non-radical politicians are more 'reliable' and 'trustworthy', having greater 'loyalty' to the 'national interest' than those who propose to break with established allies. It even appears that reforming governments, at least at the highest levels, have had to have been committed to retention of these alliances (and their associated procedures and secrecy, notably in nuclear matters) as the price of co-operation from key state personnel.

A second reason stems from the fact that politics is about much more than voting at elections and decision-making in Parliament. Influence from interested parties can be exercised in many ways, from attempting to shape what the electorate believe, to lobbying at Westminster, to direct representation in the Commons. In this domain the power of commercial interests has been pre-eminent and has increased of late, with some commentators observing a political 'mobilisation of business' since the 1970s that has manifested itself in much more intensified lobbying, support for conservative think tanks, sponsorship, grooming of leading personnel for media presentation, advocacy advertising and the like (Useem, 1984). These are forces intervening between, yet reaching, people and politicians, and their

major resource is *information*: on politicians' predisposi-
tions, government procedures, media operations, public
opinion, intellectual ideas and leaders, corporate priorities
and so on.

These two reasons can coalesce, the former impelling
governments of the day towards conservatism in key policy
areas which requires the management of public opinion in
order to quell possible dissatisfaction or disquiet. Politicians
in office, the record shows, quickly give way to information
manipulation to persuade the populace of the rectitude of a
policy, or even recourse to secrecy to keep decisions from
the public eye – the sphere of nuclear power and weaponry
providing notable examples of the latter (Jungk, 1979).

In times of crisis, as the Falklands War dramatically
illustrated (Harris, 1983) and Northern Ireland constantly
reveals (Curtis, 1984), information control is the order of the
day. Since present conditions of Cold War mean that we are
in a state of constant crisis, the information manipulation of
all things nuclear is to be expected, something confirmed in
recent NATO moves to formalise and normalise censorship
procedures for the reporting of war and 'periods of tension'
(Beach, 1983).

Behind this information management is an array of civil
servants and security services which monitor trends, groups
and individuals for signs of 'subversion', systematically
gathering information on trade unionists and socialists who
might be involved in extra-parliamentary activities unpalat-
able to the stomach of the market economy, peace activists
and anti-nuclear movements. It is difficult to come across
reliable information in this murky area of state surveillance,
but occasional exposés and sustained investigative journalism suggests that GCHQ, MI5, Special Branch and 'intelligence' sections of local police forces have collected substantial, and have increasingly computerised, files on several
million British citizens (Leigh, 1980). Occasionally it is
revealed that information from these files finds its way to
employers vetting people who have applied for work with
them, though there are usually no aspects of the work
concerned with national security (Campbell and Connor,
1986, pp. 285–91). One can be certain that information

released from these files can have important consequences for unsuspecting citizens, a point illustrated in 1985 when the *Observer* issue of 18 August detailed how all BBC personnel on current affairs and news were vetted prior to appointment, a process that had cost some candidates their jobs. Presumably this cost the public something of the diversity of views that might be expected from public service broadcasting.

(iv) *The state and the military*

Mention of the state's search for 'subversives' in the interest of the nation's security leads one to more direct discussion of the military's generation and use of information. Chapter 8 of this book deals at some length with I.T. and defence, but in a general review of the state's informational role we may emphasise that today military capability hinges on effective command, control, communications and intelligence (C3I) systems. Information is at the core of modern military preparation and mobilisation, and it is evident in satellite systems, missiles, battlefield communications, worldwide communications networks and a wide variety of electronic measures and counter-measures for use in war. Indeed, it is no exaggeration to say that electronics – I.T. in the widest sense – permeates all modern weapons in the advanced nations (Barnaby, 1986).

Together these technologies constitute an awesome array of intelligence gathering and communications equipment that demand prodigious human resources and which underline that the maintenance of military superiority depends upon the capacity to monitor, observe, predict and act upon enemy and potential enemy movements. America's Strategic Defense Initiative, with its aspiration of C3I technologies being able to supply a protective shield capable of thwarting a Soviet nuclear attack and with its $30 billion investment over five years as initial expenditure only, is testament to the critical importance information holds for all defence activities.

We would stress a number of features in the military use of information:

Most striking of all is the sheer quantity and diversity of information that must be utilised by the military machine. C3I technologies handle, store and transmit immense amounts of information ranging from weather reports, flight schedules and troop and weapon deployment, to the political complexion of a particular country or region. Indeed, so vast is the body of relevant information to be garnered that a one-time deputy director of the US Central Intelligence Agency recently complained that: 'The danger today is less with the paucity of information than it is with the difficulty of comprehending all of the information' (Cline, 1978). Dr Cline continued to list areas that the 'military machine' felt obliged to draw upon for 'intelligence'. It included 'the national intelligence system' that must review

> Newspaper accounts of foreign events, periodical literature on economic, political and scientific trends, foreign broadcasts of speeches and news, the proceedings of scholarly conferences

US diplomatic reporting from foreign sources, CIA monitoring of overseas broadcasting and documents, often undertaken covertly, and the mind-boggling data that emanates from the National Security Agency which, according to James Bamford, is the 'eavesdropping equivalent of the H-bomb' (Bamford, 1983, p. 4) with its classification of between 50 and 100 million documents a year (p. 65).

But it must be stressed that these are only one element of the defence establishment's information needs, omitting consideration of its role in guidance of weapons within and across continents, co-ordination of worldwide armed forces, and such mundane matters as salary payments in several currencies.

Such is the vast scale of the military involvement in information that it has an important effect on the information technologies that are manufactured, notably through defence's weight as a market for I.T. corporations (in the UK it typically accounts for 20 per cent of corporate sales, though in some cases it rises to in excess of 50 per cent) and because defence takes the lion's share of government research and development expenditure.

While the military generates and draws upon immense amounts of information, little of this is publicly available for reasons of state security. Indeed, recent proposals for further CIA vetting of research in cryptography and related I.T. developments (Inman, 1982) suggest that military participation in the informational sphere is inversely related to public access (Shattuck, 1986). In Britain the security services MI5 and MI6 do not officially exist, neither, one presumes, do its computer files that contain details of some 500 000 citizens (Davies and Black, 1984). Therefore the prospects of their resources being subject to Parliamentary scrutiny are slight indeed. What Paul Bracken describes as a 'wartime information regime' is, he believes, intrinsically beyond democratic control (Bracken, 1983, pp. 201, 233), such is the chaos that will ensue from the launch, or even the build up to launch, of nuclear weapons and the strategic advantage to any side of keeping military secrecy as regards its options for activating weapons.

Conclusion

We are indeed living in an age when information is of vastly more significance than before. It is axial for corporate and state functioning, with their aggrandisement its centrality to social order has become evident, and its burgeoning development has called forth numerous computer communications technologies to make it manageable. But the coming of an information society has not been the upshot of technological innovation. Rather, it has emanated from the need of corporate and state agencies to regulate what have been their inexorably enlarged domains:

> What is called the 'information society' is, in fact, the production, processing, and transmission of a very large amount of data about all sorts of matters – individual and national, social and commercial, economic and military. Most of the data are

produced to meet very specific needs of super-corporations, national governmental bureaucracies, and the military establishments of the advanced industrial state. (Schiller, 1981, p. 25)

Information gathering, analysis and communication have been key ingredients allowing for the organisation and systematisation of social relationships in the twentieth century, stamping our society with its well-policed character which, while not necessarily repressive, has drawn the public deeper under the influence of corporate capitalism and state agencies.

3

Recession and Restructuring

'If the social changes now upon us seem necessary, it is because they follow not from any disembodied technological logic but from a social logic – to which we all conform.'
(David Noble, 1984, p. 324)

Introduction

In our first chapter we argued that technology is best understood not as an extra-social phenomenon which 'impacts' from without, but rather as an integral part of society. We developed this perpective in Chapter 2 by offering a sketch of the origins of the 'information society', outlining the major social, economic and political forces that have resulted in a heightened importance for information and for technologies capable of managing and incorporating its various forms.

Historical trends may provide an explanatory framework, but what of the present? On all sides we are told that the changes we are living through – and the many more that are coming – result from the unanticipated arrival of the microchip in the late 1970s. Prime Minister James Callaghan's language during that period is revealing. Speaking in December, he advised the public that 1978 'has proved to be the year when Britain woke up to microelectronics' and that, once alerted, we must make ready for what looks set to be 'the most rapid industrial change in history' (Callaghan, 1978).

Mrs Thatcher played the same tune still more energetic-
ally. To shake the British from their slumbers an expensive
publicity campaign, Information Technology Year 1982
(I.T. '82), was launched with a programme of travelling
exhibitions, advertising, demonstrations and conferences.
I.T. '82 harried people with the rhetoric 'Has the revolution
started without you?', as it chronicled ways in which technology was 'transforming old industries, taking away boredom,
removing danger, making factories cleaner, more pleasant
places to work'. It urged them to embrace this 'once-in-a-
century chance to create new wealth, higher standards of
living and a world in which routine and drudgery are
alleviated and in which all of us have more time, freedom
and ability to pursue our interests'. No doubt about it, I.T.
had arrived and it promised to re-make the world.

We have already criticised this technological determinism
which serves to impose social, economic and political
changes without having to go to the trouble of debating
them. In this scenario, everything of consequence follows
from the advent of I.T. and, while the immediate impacts
may be unsettling, the long-term outlook is good. It has no
space for political debate because technology is beyond such
issues and, moreover, such is the haste with which we must
adjust that there is no time for political conjecture.

We believe that a survey of conditions prevailing in
Britain undermines the assumptions of the technoboosters.
In this chapter we want to look more closely at the circumstances in which I.T. is being introduced and, perhaps more
important, at those which are influencing the development
of I.T. in some directions rather than in others. Our aim is
twofold. First, to show more clearly that it is folly to extract
I.T. from society and only then to ascribe to it an overwhelming social significance: to understand the social consequences of I.T. we would argue that one must at the outset
consider the social construction of technological innovation.
Second, as we pursue this, it will become evident that we
find the neologism I.T. somewhat misleading. The term is of
use as a shorthand, but such a generic concept too readily
leads one to conduct debates about it at an unreal level. The
question posed tends to be 'What do you think are the likely

effects of I.T.?' Given the enormous compass of the term –
anything from video games to guided missiles, from kitchen
gadgets to transworld communications – it is difficult to
provide a retort that is not banal. It is rather like asking what
one thinks about SOCIETY – at the general level it is
impossible to say anything that is not trite. But shift discussion to substantive social relations such as schoolroom
interaction and family activities and much more meaningful
analyses can result.

Similarly, we believe it is a better way of coming to grips
with the significance of I.T. if discussion is brought down to
earth, to a level of more particular forms of I.T. such as
domestic technologies, military applications and financial
databases. After all, this is the level at which real technologies are found. If we can examine them in this way we can
then begin to see how technologies bear the imprint, often in
complex and intricate ways, in their design, development
and implementation, of social, political and economic relations.

Escape from recession?

I.T. is at the storm centre of changes presently engulfing
Britain. But those who contend that it is I.T. that is causing
these changes are in error, as can be seen by reflecting on the
single most telling factor in the UK today. It is the brute fact
of recession and everything associated with it that is most
decisively shaping social developments and it is this which
above all else is exercising a hold on I.T.

All observers appear to agree that recession has brought
about mass unemployment, has hastened industrial decline
and brought fear of still further collapse. There is also an
extraordinarily widespread consensus about how to escape
the malaise which runs along the following lines: Britain is
failing to produce goods and services that can compete
effectively in price or quality with those offered by other
nations, and it is this which is maintaining high unemployment and threatening more. To rectify matters British
industry must rapidly restructure by, above all else, taking

aboard the latest technologies in order that productivity and quality can be improved. The message is that, if we can increase our competitive edge in this way, then British companies will win markets fought for by the Japanese, French and Americans. By extending the market share then, industry will be able to take on more workers from the unemployment register or, perhaps more likely, having restored profitability, to enable companies to pay higher wages to their employees and bigger dividends to their shareholders, who will spend the extra on more services, hence creating additional service sector jobs. In sum, re-structuring British industry to heighten its competitive standing is presented as the way out of recession and into boom, with competition-induced growth leading back to full employment.

I.T. is certainly at the heart of this strategy because it is a key means of increasing competitive position. High technology promises a cheapening of production in 'smokestack' industries and, even more desirable, it portends entirely new businesses in the 'information sector' that will thrive in a market environment and generate additional jobs. However, it must be emphasised that the determinant of policy here is recession, how to escape it and how best to respond to the intense competitive squeeze that is its concomitant. To be sure, technology is granted a privileged role in plans for recovery, but I.T. does not lead the response. On the contrary, it is firmly subordinate to the imperative of success in the international market economy. The agenda has been set by the conditions of recession; I.T. has a place on the list, but how it will be considered and decided upon is in the hands of others (cf. Dickson, 1984, Chapter 1).

I.T. initiatives in education have been conceived according to the same logic. It has not been that we are about to be engulfed by the 'Information Technology revolution' which has induced the call for 'computer literacy' in pupils, for dramatic increases in I.T. graduates, and a general 'steer' of funds away from the arts and humanities towards science and technology. Bluntly, education is undergoing decisive changes because it is being conscripted in the war against recession. With the sights set on capturing foreign markets, everything possible must be done to ensure that the army is best equipped to move fast and effectively. There are many things that education can do to facilitate this operation. One, of course, is to survive on less income, and this reduced ration it has shared with most other recipients of public funds. This sacrifice is being made in the name of bolstering the efficacy of industry, which has been hampered too long by excessive taxation. A complementary role is that education is to be geared more closely to industrial practices. Here a recurrent call is for education to supply appropriately trained personnel – hence the 'I.T. initiatives' and cognate programmes which we discuss at length in this book.

The bipartisan character of responses to recession, and the identification of I.T. as central to its resolution, ought to be stressed. The strategy of escape through growth achieved by gaining market advantage is endorsed by Conservative, Labour and former Alliance parties. To be sure, there are differences of approach: Labour, true to its traditions, believes that a state plan is the best guarantee of the smooth and rapid innovation necessary to rejuvenate the economy. The Tories place more faith in private capital's ability to develop products that will be successful in the marketplace. The social democratic groupings steer a middle course between state guidance and *laissez-faire*.

Nonetheless, all aspire to progress by revitalising the market economy and it is this goal which decisively shapes technological innovation. It is generally the case that strategies for recovery are couched in the language of technical necessity, it being suggested that a technological discovery makes inevitable our readjustment to new circumstances. But a moment's thought leads one to realise that we must adapt not because of a technological breakthrough, but because of the consequences for our competitive position in the world market. Across the spectrum politicians shroud this brutal truth by announcing that 'the inevitable logic is that we must accept the technologies' (Baker, 1980), but at the back of such technocratic reasoning lurks the economic exigency: 'Automate or Liquidate.' If Britain does not rapidly accommodate the new technologies, then the Japanese, French, Germans, Americans, even the New Zealanders and Malaysians will, and thence they will steal remaining markets, leaving the British helpless to stop the slide down the league table of prosperous nations.

Some may agree that the climate of recession dictates that we adapt to I.T., but continue to argue that the technology remains a determinant factor. Having been discovered, it has rewritten the economic agenda and it brings its own imperatives to bear. This takes us back to the reasoning which assumes technology is a *deus ex machina* that imposes itself. Against this we insist that the exigencies of the market remain predominant and initiatory of the new technologies. Further, we would support this argument by contending that the particular forms of I.T. that are developed – as opposed to the generalised concept of I.T. – are almost always products of the commitment to increase or at least retain competitive position. I.T. finds application in certain ways, by performing certain tasks, because particular priorities have been established favouring this function rather than that one. Primary among these priorities is the recession and its logic of marketability as the determinant of innovation.

For instance, we are struck by evidence which suggests that the introduction of I.T. into workplaces has been guided rigidly, and of late frenetically, by the query 'How can we beat our competitors?' (Webster and Robins, 1986, Part 2). Of course it would be madness for an employer to strive to develop forms of I.T. which enhanced the work experience of his employees without being justifiable in terms of greater productivity. But it must be stressed that such 'madness' can only be diagnosed because of a market determination of normalcy. An ecological, as opposed to a technocentric point of view, as the Green movement has reminded us, goes far to redefining the bases of such diagnoses with its prioritisation of 'good work' above the doctrine of greater output for least cost (Pepper, 1984, Chapters 2–4). If there was really a widespread commitment to ennoble work experiences, then it is surely hard to doubt that fundamentally different technologies would have been developed. Conversely, because the overriding reason to innovate is to cut costs, then we cannot be surprised that new technologies are so often regarded as threatening to workers who must accommodate themselves to usually alien designs and dangers of redundancy.

Moreover, because a central element of industrial relations has been the struggle for control over work, and because the outcome of this has invariably influenced costs, it is to be expected that in the present period technologies are being adopted which take power from employees. For instance, Barry Wilkinson's studies of the introduction of microelectronics into West Midlands factories revealed time and again that managers adopted I.T. with a view to cheapening costs and gaining ascendancy over employees. A plating company Wilkinson visited was revealing: there controls were placed behind a wall and employees prohibited from the area 'for no other reason than to prevent workers tampering with them, and management made no secret of the fact that the intention is to wrest control of the plating process out of the hands of a problematic workforce' (Wilkinson, 1983, p. 36). Still more illuminating, because exceptional in its pursuit, was an optical plant which strove to retain the skills of its workforce when technologies were available that made these unnecessary. Nevertheless, this considerate employer eventually had to capitulate and introduce machinery which deskilled his lens makers becaue his competitors had introduced them and could now undercut him on price – a case which highlights the power of the market imperative and underscores our point that innovation is a value-laden process. Far from it being the upshot of an autonomous technology, technological change is steered by the firm hand of the market. Where that requires the workforce to suffer this is an expression of a social priority, not the self-driven motor of technological progress (cf. Noble, 1984).

I.T. and market principles

If it is recession that determines the viability of introducing particular types of I.T. into the workplace, then it is equally the case that market principles shape the production of most forms of I.T. A startling example of these values – startling because it was an overt expression of what must be a generally tacit reasoning – was given in 1980 by the Chairman of Thorn–EMI when he announced that his company's 'decision to withdraw from medical electronics was [because] there appeared little likelihood of achieving profits in the foreseeable future' (Thorn–EMI, 1980). In this instance the operative value was that medical scanners, essential in the early and accurate diagnosis of cancers, were of less importance than Thorn–EMI's commitment to pop music, leisure stadiums and feature films. The Lucas Aerospace workers who devised an alternative plan for the production of socially useful rather than commercially attractive technologies revealed the same values in action. The Lucas Aerospace Combine Committee's suggestions that the expertise of their members be put to the manufacture of medical equipment (portable kidney machines, sight substitution aids for the blind, artificial limb control systems, and so on), alternative energy technologies (solar-cell technology, a flexible power pack etc), road-rail vehicles and other technologies were not rejected by management because they were technically infeasible. In fact, the company's retort had nothing at all to say about the viability of these ideas as technologies. Its considerations were singularly commercial when it announced that

> it intends to concentrate on its traditional business which involves the development of aircraft systems and components for the aerospace and defence industries [because] the only way to secure jobs in the market economy is to manufacture the products which the Company is best at producing efficiently and profitably. (quoted in Wainwright and Elliott, 1982, pp. 114–15)

As we shall see, the corporations which dominate the I.T. industry operate unabashedly on market principles, and to this end they tailor their production to those areas which hold out the prospect of greatest rewards. At the moment great promise lies in large corporate and state endeavours to save costs and secure better control of their enterprises by automating as much of their affairs as is possible. Since these are the big spenders, IBM targets its annual multi-billion dollar research and development programme towards the creation of technologies that will find appeal there. That IBM already accounts for 70 per cent of the world market for the mainframe computers which get installed and net-worked in large organisations, is testament to the fact that it has long worked on the assumption that it is best to follow the big budgets. As for the lower end of the computer market – that occupied by the 'general public' – IBM for years was unconcerned. Its priorities meant that it did not decide to manufacture a personal computer until 1981, and then it was not available for sale in Britain until 1983. Even when it got round to marketing a PC it was oriented to the business segment of the market rather than to the hobbyist. In fact, IBM has never cared to offer a machine to a public able to spend less than a thousand dollars on a computer. As for this sector, the impoverished groups of the I.T. world, IBM felt able to leave it to the supporting players such as Sinclair, Commodore and Amstrad.

The information commodity

It is characteristic of futurism that an 'information society' is envisaged that will be created by the I.T. explosion. Yet little attention is given to the substance of the information that will become available. It is simply assumed that there will be more of it in a 'post-industrial society' and that this of itself will be an advance. Our view is that, just as the I.T. hardware is infused by social values, so too will be the information that will swirl around in the 'wired society'. In the here and now principles are being established and organisational arrangements being developed that allow us to assess something of the type and quality of information coming on stream.

   Most important, the scramble to escape recession and the increased importance of information management in the advanced societies have combined to place an emphasis on information as a commodity. Although for centuries in-formation has had a price and a great deal has been proprietary – publishing and the news media are obvious examples – there has long been a countervailing view that much information should be generated by and/or made available through the public purse. Thus, for example, in Britain there has been a commitment to gather information on social and economic developments by government agencies which would then disseminate statistics and reports on health, income distribution, household expenditure and so forth as a necessary component of a mature democracy.

Similarly, the extensive network of some five thousand public libraries in Britain was created not least because of a commitment to the principle that information should be paid for out of general taxation and then made available to everyone on the basis of expressed need. Education itself has been fundamentally shaped by this sort of commitment: it is commonly felt, for instance, that research findings should be freely available to interested and able scholars and that financial barriers to knowledge should be reduced to a minimum. To be sure, these public service ideals have never worked as they proclaim – there is a weight of sociological evidence to show that these resources are used disproportionately by the middle classes – but they have nevertheless significantly affected organisations and their operation. There is, indeed, something still not quite respectable about restricting information on grounds of money: fee-paying education, for instance, is regularly disapproved of in opinion surveys. Those major information commodities, books and the press, retain this form largely because it is known that libraries can supply them free of charge and the press are, for most people, available at very cheap prices.

The institutions that have been established to make available information to the public as a whole operate on principles at variance with market criteria, which insist that information will be developed only if it is saleable and will be made available only on a basis of ability to pay. However, in recent years recession has been met by a vigorous attempt to reassert market principles in social relations that, on the one hand, has resulted in sharp reductions in the budgets of public service organisations and, on the other hand, has promoted the application of commercial values to these and other informational domains. Peter Golding and Graham Murdock correctly observe a new trend that leads to there being 'across the range of information, advice, and leisure facilities, a reduction in public sector provision and an increased use of market mechanism' (Golding and Murdock, 1986, pp. 74–5). What we are witnessing in the area of public information agencies is a squeeze on services provided free to the public and a simultaneous increase in the application of commercial tenets.

An influential report, *Making a Business of Information*, signalled this shift towards handling information as a commodity. The Information Technology Advisory Panel identified

> an expanding 'tradeable information sector' which encompasses the supply of financial and business information, printing and publishing, on-line technical information, consultancies etc. We consider that the entertainment industry and aspects of education and training services fall within this sector. (ITAP, 1983, p. 7)

Urging that 'Both private and public sectors in the United Kingdom . . . [should] pay much more attention to information as a commercial commodity' (p. 8), the ITAP team recommended that entrepreneurs be allowed to enter previously excluded terrain and that those already in position should become entrepreneurial. Obviously, it added, these changes might require that public service ideals and practices be reviewed. For instance, with the development of on-line information delivery systems, government statistics could, when appropriately 'packaged' and given 'added value', appeal to a burgeoning sector of the information market – that catering for corporate clients with a need for such detailed data for marketing strategies. Of course, for this to be effective Government Statistical Services might have to jettison the practice of making this information available irrespective of the user's ability to pay (see below). Similarly, as new technologies were being introduced into public libraries, ITAP-type people could be expected to examine possibilities of raising revenue from on-line search activities, although this might conflict with the public service goal of free access to information.

The culmination of these trends is the intrusion of commercial tenets into territories where previously their entry had been restricted. As an astute observer of these developments has noted:

> What is unique in this period is the effort to extend the commercialization of information into every existing space of the social sphere. No longer restricted to publishing and broadcasting, market criteria for information now are being applied to public information facilities and processes. Universities, libraries, and the Government's information activities are being seized by private information entrepreneurs. (Schiller, 1987, p. 25)

Let us review some of these developments in key areas of the public information domain.

(a)   Museums and art galleries

Britain's national museums and art galleries have been seriously affected by the new philosophy of information. For the past decade they have had to cope with reductions in income from government funds and in consequence have sought to recoup losses by other means. The major result is that charging for access is rapidly becoming the norm. This shift from the principle of free access is expected to bring about a significant fall in visitors, 65 million of whom entered in 1986. Indeed, the Victoria and Albert Museum, which imposed a 'voluntary' levy in 1985, experienced a 40 per cent drop in its visitors as a result and the Natural History Museum anticipated a similar fall when it introduced entry charges in 1987. Clearly we may expect the shortfall in attendances to come from the poorer (working-class, single parent families, children) sections of society – those, incidentally, who require most encouragement to visit such places anyway because they find the social and cultural ambiance off-putting – for whom free admission had been instigated in the first place because the 'palace(s) of enlightenment' (as the Victoria and Albert was described at its foundation) were regarded as national educative assets that should be made available to the whole public, without regard for income.

But the effects of a forced switch to a market-oriented regime are more extensive. At the Natural History Museum complaints about noisy school parties (always in evidence at this sprawling educational institution and at present exempt from charges) has led to the imposition of limits on the numbers allowed to visit at any one time, not because of problems of size but because it is felt that visitors who pay for admission require a more reverent setting.

Further, with a market ethos established museums and galleries must compete for customers with out-and-out commercial ventures such as Madame Tussauds. This requires a constant search for the exotic, unusual and dramatic exhibit that will lure the public and highlights the growing tendency to mount 'entertainment' in places dedicated to housing art treasures and historical artifacts. There is, of course, a thin line to be drawn between making exhibits accessible and trivialising artistic and cultural works. In addition, the plethora of shops, restaurants and purveyors of mementoes and trinkets that has sprung up and expanded in our museums and galleries are derived from an entrepreneurial ethos.

Finally, these institutions come to rely increasingly on sponsors for revenue – and sponsors do not get involved for altruistic reasons. As an art critic, angry at the spectacular rise of sponsorship in the 1980s that has turned 'London's public galleries ... into shop windows and sumptuous advertising malls for arms manufacturers and credit salesmen' (Januszczak, 1986), recently observed:

> Sponsors see the art gallery as a relatively cheap, high profile advertising hoarding and they go there only to launder their reputations. They naturally support the kind of art which they calculate will reflect well on them; as their influence grows so does the power of their censorship. (Januszczak, 1985)

(b)   Public libraries

The public library system in Britain is one of the great legacies of the commitment to the view that knowledge should be available to all. There are few if any sizeable towns and villages in Britain without a library and all are connected through the inter-library loan scheme. The service is impressive to any observer and its centrality to the nation is recognised in the 1964 Public Libraries and Museums Act, which stipulates that libraries should offer a comprehensive and efficient information service for all citizens desiring to make use of it. However, over two hundred public libraries have been closed in Britain since 1979, opening hours have been reduced in the majority of them, and purchases have slumped because price rises have far exceeded budget allocations. This will be a familiar story to many readers since libraries are very extensively used (annually there are in Britain almost 650 million loans – about a dozen book issues per head of population) and one can scarcely fail to notice the cancellation of newspapers and periodicals, early closing and fewer volumes on the shelves. The reason is obvious: funding from government and local authorities has been squeezed.

In reply to complaints Ministers have urged that

> Librarians should look beyond their traditional sources of funds and consider whether some costs may be recovered from users, or whether private sponsorship, or even private investment in new services, is possible. (*Report by the Minister for the Arts on Library and Information Matters during 1983*)

More recently, an influential think tank, the Adam Smith Institute, has published a report which has charged that 'the fundamental concept of providing libraries free at the public expense has seldom been challenged or its consequences examined' (Adam Smith Institute, 1986, p. 1). Arguing that present circumstances mean that the need 'is long overdue for the most thoroughgoing reform in the history of public library provision in the United Kingdom' (p. 42), the report deplores the way in which free loans drove commercial lending libraries like Smiths and Boots out of business and advocates the introduction of full-blooded commercial principles. To the fore are recommendations for user charges and a move towards the privatisation of the library world. *Ex Libris* beats a drum that is heard in influential political circles.

Public libraries have not travelled quite so far down this path, but 'the levying of charges is gradually becoming more widely accepted' (Lewis and Martyn, 1986, p. 32). Striving to recoup lost revenues, librarians increasingly charge for everything except basic book loans; hence inter-library loan requests carry a charge, non-book materials are at a price, and the reservation of books is costed to the user. Characteristically, the British Library admitted in its 1985–86 report that 'all divisions and departments are considering ways to generate more revenue, including charging for premium services', to which end a 'corporate marketing manager' had been appointed. In addition, sponsorship is sought by librarians as a means of mounting exhibitions and to provide additional services to the community, with predictable dangers of censorship of materials.

As for on-line information services in public libraries, a Department of Education and Science report starkly notes that 'The advent of computer based systems means that information is increasingly accessible only for payment' (DES, 1982, p. 34). Because these services are expensive, with connection fees rarely below £60 per hour, librarians feel compelled to charge the users. Moreover, librarians have tended to regard on-line as different from other kinds of information. A consequence was that as I.T. permeates the public library the 'ability to pay' principle rises in prominence. As Roberta Lumek observes:

> the failure to perceive I.T.-based information as an intrinsic part of the library service led to the introduction of charges for what was thought to be a 'frill' . . . Thus a precedent was established . . . it will soon be impossible to run a self-respecting reference, community information or indeed current awareness service on the basis of paper-based information. But although the principle of 'Agatha Christie on the Rates' is even now sacrosanct, the

principle of a free public library service is in danger of being tacitly abandoned. (Lumek, 1984, p. 43)

Witnessing the decline in services and the encroachment of commercial practices, we cannot think either that public libraries will flourish in the 'information age' or that their users will reap the rewards of I.T. (cf. Schiller and Schiller, 1988). Indeed, we concur with the view that the escalating commoditisation of information is likely to leave public libraries unable to stay in the race. As I.T. develops it will go increasingly to those who can afford the associated and expensive equipment and access costs, and with it will go large areas of publishing material delivered direct to the customer. In this scenario

> it is possible that the public sector could find itself obliged to assume the role of dumping-ground for low-appeal, economically unviable publications, and provider of services in only such areas as are financially unattractive . . . the public library could find itself in an exposed position, with its remit and capabilities increasingly curtailed to the point at which extinction became inevitable. (Cronin and Martyn, 1984)

(c)   Government information services

The 1981 Rayner investigation of Government Statistical Services recommended that:

> information should not be collected primarily for publication. It should be collected primarily because government needs it for its own business. Information of value to business should be made available with a timeliness which maximizes its value and should be charged for commercially. (Government Statistical Services, 1981, pp 14–15)

Rayner paved the way for 25 per cent cuts in the government statistical services and a decisive shift towards charging market rates for what would be made available. This led to large increases in the price of HMSO materials, two and three times the retail price index, such that reports of but a few pages generally costs several pounds, and commenced a generalised move towards ministerial departments charging for information previously distributed gratis. This can mean the exclusion of vital information from many individuals and groups.

Connectedly, plans for a mid-term census in 1986 were abandoned, less regular information on such matters as take-up rates of means-tested benefits was released, and the Economic and Social Research Council underwent a swingeing cut in its budget, severely curtailing investigation of contemporary Britain. In addition, the Royal Commission on the Distribution of Income and Wealth was abruptly brought to a close in 1979. One commentator has noted that:

> knowledge about the taxable capacity of the rich is vital if really fair tax policies are to be developed and an efficient system of taxation and of the allocation of public resources is to be devised. (Townsend, 1981)

This sort of knowledge could not be commercially (or ideologically) justified.

Finally, there has been a commitment from government to hiving off information services to private organisations whenever feasible, and the progressive privatisation of government computer operations. High-tech information companies have been to the forefront of these developments, promising to cheapen costs to the Exchequer and to 'value-add' to the raw data to make it more vendible. It is increasingly the case that government is contracting with private companies to make information available in electronic form. This can give a rapid service (to those who subscribe), but there are fears that it will result in making hard copies of some information difficult to obtain. In the United States this process is most developed, and the American Library Association sounds a warning about a trend which

> has resulted in the increased emergence of contractual arrangements with commercial firms to disseminate information collected at the public expense, higher user charges for government information, and the proliferation of government information available in electronic format only ... Will public access to

government information be further restricted for people who cannot afford a computer or pay for computer time? (American Library Association, 1986; cf. Smith, 1985)

It is surely beyond dispute that democratic societies need to be informed about themselves in order that reliable decisions may be made about social, economic and political priorities. Government is in a unique position to collect, assemble and disseminate information about the state of the nation without which the citizenry are seriously disenfranchised. As an 'information society' comes upon us we seem to be seeing government information services – which are far and away the major providers of society's self-knowledge – reducing in quality and becoming less readily available to all.

(d) Broadcasting

Broadcasting, especially television, is arguably the public's major informational resource, far more central than newspapers and a facility which occupies many hours of almost everyone's time. We are promised that I.T. will expand this role: cable, satellite, video disc and cassette herald more and better information via the television console.

These new technologies are being introduced on commercial premises with the result that they offer a stolid and restricted diet of sport, sex and movies. Entertainment of an escapist and action-packed kind is, as ever, the predominant commercial mode. The reason why is obvious: pioneered to achieve maximum commercial return, these services aim to reach the largest possible audience, either to reap optimum subscriptions or to appeal to advertisers. Mass market TV is unavoidably lowest common denominator stuff: oriented to that which reaches the most people most of the time, it has little if any space to cater for the diversity of social groups or even the individual. Certainly, I.T. will bring more information into the home as cable and other media become available, but these will be urging us to 'Watch all the time, learn nothing': a surfeit of disinformation, 'information that creates the illusion of knowing something but which in fact leads one away from knowing' (Postman, 1986, pp. 141, 107).

Moreover, as these services develop they pose an alarming threat to public service broadcasting in Britain and its aim to 'inform, educate and entertain'. Already the philosophy of the market has been established as a model for future developments: 'British broadcasting should move towards a sophisticated market system based on consumer sovereignty' (Peacock, 1986, para. 592).

Where the starting point is the individual consumer, more tedchnology does seem to promise more programming choice. But where it is the real world of concentrated media corporations eager to maximise their return on capital, then new delivery systems presage more of the pap the uncontrolled media market already supplies. If one seeks an example, then look to the United States' television system (see Barnouw, 1978). It is, revealingly, the model for the British government's information policy. Where the ratings determine programme content provided by media conglomerates such as those owned by Rupert Murdoch, public service television will be pressed to survive. Neither the ethos of the BBC – to provide high quality comprehensive services to audiences who are to be regarded as diverse minorities – nor its subsidy from the public purse accords with advertising-oriented or subscription-based viewing. Even the Peacock Commission recognised this and offered to ghettoise the BBC:

> There will always be a need to supplement the direct consumer market by public finance for programmes of a public service kind supported by people in their capacity as citizens and voters but unlikely to be commercially self-supporting in the view of broadcasting entrepreneurs. (Ibid)

Our view is that a public service channel restricted to a small minority will not long survive in the 'information age'. It will be superseded by a surfeit of 'entertainment' programmes which will denude news and current affairs, valuable culture, challenging documentaries and the like.

If we argue that the undermining of public service information is likely to lead to a diminution of meaningful information coming to the public, we should also make it clear that new forms of information are fast becoming available. Particularly important in this respect is the exponential growth of on-line information agencies dedicated to supplying clients throughout the world. By 1985 there were already 3000 data bases available on-line with numbers increasing weekly (Williams, 1985). They are the very stuff of the 'information age': at the touch of a button information can be accessed in Los Angeles, Nice, Tokyo or Oslo by the user living in Scunthorpe. Gone are the days when one had to wait weeks for the article to arrive from Boston Spa; today a few tapped digits on the telephone, several strokes of the keyboard, and it is there at one's terminal.

The concept is impressive, the reality of these types of I.T. markedly different. It is important to recognise that the data bases contain particular sorts of information. Financial information, which represents more than half of the electronic information now sold in the United States, has become 'the driving force of the industry' (Snoddy, 1986, p. 13). Typical data base holdings are credit checks, price listings, energy reports, mergers and acquisitions, precious metals and world insurance. This information is not only specialised; increasingly it is targetted at particular segments of the market. So, for example, Lloyd's Maritime Data Network tracks the cargoes and movements of every commercial ocean-going vessel, compiling an awesome data base, but the information is aimed at but a few hundred clients – shippers. Further, there is a trend emerging towards specification of the information with the customising of data bases. For instance, Reuters sells software that lets currency and commodities traders spot opportunities based on their own strategies when drawing on Reuters' data base (Field and Harris, 1986, p. 49).

The designers of on-line information services have endeavoured to appeal to corporate clients since these have an identifiable need for real-time business information and they have the ability to pay the premium rates that have fuelled the rapid rise of 'information factories' like TRW, Telerate,

Quotron and Datastream. Herbert Schiller's comment is to the point:

> In a market economy, the questions of costs and prices inevitably play the most important . . . roles in what kind of base will be constructed and the category of user the base is intended to service (and by which it is to be paid for). The selection of material that goes into a data base is closely linked to the need for, and the marketability of, the information service. (Schiller, 1981, p. 35)

On-line information is scarcely addressed to the wider public. In fact, less than 37 per cent of it goes to the non-business consumer (*Business Week*, 25 August, 1986, p. 52). Moreover, even if John Smith were interested in accessing data bases (and there are several text retrieval systems likely to appeal to those interested in socio-economic and political affairs), he would find them far beyond his pocket. Average access costs are £75 per hour (plus transatlantic phone bills) and the typical user spends almost £200 per month on searches. At these rates the idea that computer installation in each home will offer the public unrestricted entry to a world repository of information is risible.

The fact that I.T. will lead to there being more modes of information delivery and virtuoso ways of analysing it has led many observers to the premature conclusion that this of itself must lead to better information. Looking at the commoditisation of information, we cannot but be sceptical of this vision. In truth, we are likely to see the increasing scarcity of information that is not considered commercially viable. There are already strong indications of a diminution in the social availability of information simultaneous with quantities of disinformation increasing for the many and quality improving only for those with the ability to pay. In future, as now, available information will be differentially distributed: financial, commercial and scientific data for the wealthy corporate sector; a glut of garbage information for the mass of the public limited to enhanced television I.T. Most important, the principle of public knowledgeability, of the availability of information as a public service – an ideal imperfectly realised at the best of times – will be undermined.

The information technology business

Information Technology is more than a technology: it is also a global business that is dominated by a few privileged transnational corporations, the influence of which is felt on the entire range of computer communications technologies now available and still emerging. The information business is a fluid and fast-growing phenomenon about which no-one agrees, except that it will surpass energy as the most lucrative market of all in the near future. The chief of AT&T (the leading telecommunications company) estimates its value at over 500 billion dollars per year (Olson, 1987) and IBM believes it will grow to three times that by 1992. Everyone realises that the potential is stupendous and all the significant players are engaged in intense competition over markets, standards and product innovation, each major participant offering proprietary ranges of complementary and compatible technologies. Although their focus is mainly on computer communications systems for the office, the I.T. industry is so vast, rapidly integrating and converging that many enormous corporate bodies in media, telecommunications, electronics, computing and information supply are entering the arena to struggle for mastery over the emerging 'information grid' (Webster and Robins, 1986, Chapter 7).

At the forefront of the industry stands IBM (1986 revenue 52 billion dollars) which dominates world computing. It is followed by AT&T (1986 revenue 34 billion dollars) which has for long been restricted in its operations to the United States, but in recent years has been freed to enter foreign markets. These are followed by a clutch of multi-billion dollar earners such as Philips, Hitachi, Nippon Electric Company, Siemens, Digital Equipment and ITT. It is these behemoths which possess the vast resources needed to survive the fierce competition taking place in the I.T. market and, as important, the financial weight to keep usurpers at bay. They also have the funds to purchase important wings of the business when it suits. Indeed, buy-outs are increasingly the norm as the key I.T. players consolidate by vertically and horizontally integrating their affairs, pushing towards the day when we shall have an overarching information/communications industry under the control of a handful of elite mega-corporations. Significantly, the booming on-line information companies to which we have referred are already being absorbed by larger units: Telerate by Citicorp, Quotron by Dow Jones, Datastream by Dun & Bradstreet. IBM and AT&T, sensing big profits, have now entered that market.

On a wider scale IBM could afford in 1985 to buy out MCI Communications, a multi-billion dollar telecommunications business, and to take sole charge of Satellite Business Systems when its partners withdrew after over a billion dollars of investment had brought little return. Meanwhile, AT&T has bought 25 per cent of Olivetti (1986 earnings 5.5 billion dollars), one of Europe's leading data processing operators, and has entered a co-operative deal with Philips to present a 'global challenge' to IBM's ambitions to be the major force in I.T. In this arena even leading manufacturers have had to merge: thus in 1986 Burroughs and Sperry came together in a 4.4 billion dollar deal which catapulted the new firm into second place in the computer business (with about 10 per cent the sales of IBM). The only serious new entrants in this industry are equally wealthy transnationals, vividly illustrative of which is General Motors (1986 revenue 103 billion dollars) which paid a staggering 5 billion dollars for Hughes Aircraft in 1985, a purchase soon after matched in scale by General Electric's (1986 revenue 35 billion dollars) payment of 6.3 billion dollars for RCA, a powerful I.T. Company in its own right.

The conclusion of any description of the I.T. industry is inescapable: to get involved on any significant scale it is not enough to have a marvellous technological breakthrough, because a requisite is to have available the multi-billion dollar organisations that can support sales outlets, research and development facilities and a worldwide marketing network. In Britain there is a habit of lauding I.T. entrepreneurs like Clive Sinclair and Alan Sugar of Amstrad fame as if these were leading us into the 'information society'. These are minnows that have found – temporarily – a pool ignored by the heavyweights. Should they get fatter and venture out, they are swallowed like plankton by the whales of the industry who spend their time in the deep waters.

The architects of the 'information age' are involved in I.T. not for love of technological advance, but because it appears a sound commercial investment. In pursuit of the goal of profit maximisation they tailor their development strategies towards the production of the most marketable technologies. Broadly speaking, the richer the client the higher is the priority of the I.T. industry to meet his or her requirements. AT&T openly advertises that its 'gospel is that business strategy dictates system design' (AT&T, 1985). For this reason the concerns of the industry are, in descending order: large, especially transnational, corporate clients, the defence agencies, and – far behind – the general public (and with this latter the lion's share goes to entertainment and a minute portion to education).

The priority of market principles means that the likes of IBM targets its annual research and development budget of 2 billion dollars to generating technologies that have most potential for profitable return. It is that, rather than any logic of technological progress, which results in the major computer communications systems being applied in large corporate organisations with massive informational needs, a large proportion of white-collar workers currently employed to handle and process this information, and an appetite for reducing the costs of these people and procedures. Computer terminals in banks and finance houses, communications networks linking disparate corporate sites, data processing centres and the like have been pioneered, produced and marketed for identifiable needs and predominantly for those of large commercial enterprises.

No-one who is aware of the rise of the transnational corporation can be ignorant of the need of these global companies to have sophisticated and reliable computer communications networks that tie together their operations (see D. Schiller, 1982). Indeed, two scholars have appositely noted that 'The essential communications infrastructure for the information economy . . . is being created by and for the transnational corporations' (Goddard and Gillespie, 1986, p. 384). Moreover, encountering the global recession of the past decade, it has been I.T. that has been to the forefront of the response of these transnationals by helping to effect the restructuring strategy of 'productive decentralisation' which we mentioned in Chapter 2. Robin Murray describes it succinctly:

> In the USA it is referred to as 'flexible specialisation', in France as 'neo-Fordism'. It consists of applying computer technology not only to each stage of the production process, from design to retailing, but also to the integration of all stages of the process into a single co-ordinated system. As a result, the economies of scale of mass production can now be achieved on much smaller runs, whether small batch engineering products, or clothes, shoes, furniture and even books. Instead of Fordism's special-ised machinery producing standardised products, we now have flexible, all-purpose machinery producing a variety of products. Computers have been applied to design, cutting down the waste of materials, and to stock control. Distribution has been revolu-tionised, as has the link between sales, production and innova-tion. (Murray, 1985, pp. 29–30)

A *Financial Times* report on Ford's 'global strategy' to manufacture a 'world truck' is illustrative. Ford's 'world truck' will have

> a European cab and panels shipped out from Europe as well as using the European name, Cargo. It will have a North American chassis, a diesel engine developed from one used by the group's agricultural tractor division. And it will be assembled in Brazil for the domestic and North American markets. (Gooding, 1984)

This new international division of labour, which does much to overcome the hitherto intractable contraints of time and space, is leading to the increasingly centralised control of consciously diversified operations. While it is most drama-tic at an international level, it is evident within a given

nation too (Goddard and Gillespie, 1986). Especially convenient for corporate planners, Ford's

> new system (orchestrated as it is by detailed computer control)
> gives them an added flexibility. To begin with, it lessens their
> dependence upon particular groups of workers. Ford got beaten
> in 1941 because all of its eggs were in the basket of the Rouge.
> No longer is this true. Today, Ford's main assembly plants
> replicate each other, and production can be switched with some
> ease from one to the other. (Beynon, 1984, p. 327)

I.T. and political power

The development of computer communications networks to
suit an extensive transnational empire undoubtedly bolsters
the power of participating corporations. The hardware and
software of the data networks that string together their
activities enable them to manage what AT&T describes as
'global markets for the movement and management of
information' (Hall, 1985). This puts them in an advan-
tageous position compared to poor countries that cannot
afford a similar informational infrastructure and gives them
a decisive edge over employees located in isolated plants
around the globe.

This is not a narrowly economic issue. The interest of
transnational capital in information networks has been a
major factor shaping the American doctrine of the 'free flow
of information'. An integrated global economy demands the
movement of text and data across geographical boundaries
between corporate locations and financial centres. National
interests or decisions that obstruct this are an anathema.
However, in recent years many nations have come to the
conclusion that the 'free flow' policy, while (like technology)
admirable as an abstract concept, in practice means freedom
for the mighty (chiefly US) corporations to continue their
domination of international trade. Moves have been made
accordingly to establish a 'new world information order' that
intends to redress the balance in favour of the poorer
nations. At the United Nations and UNESCO efforts have

been made to reverse the present imbalance by, for example, limiting and/or insisting on scrutiny of the movement of economic, political and cultural information across national frontiers. The result has been sustained US pressure to retain the 'free flow' principle in face of widespread opposition – pressure which ended in US withdrawal from UNESCO in 1984 when it found it could not get its way.

There is a similar US enthusiasm for a 'free market' in I.T. that stems from the fact that the manufacture of equipment and software is the monopoly of the rich nations. Typically, American corporations are world leaders, followed by Japanese conglomerates and a cluster of European electrical and electronic groups. It is in the interest of most of these to have open markets since they start against any opposition with the advantage of present dominance. Thus, for example, America alone accounts for almost 50 per cent of the world telecommunications equipment market, and with Japan and a half dozen European companies commands 90 per cent of world trade in such produce (Department of Commerce, 1983).

The dominant nations, desperate for growth, are keen to continue their supply of I.T. to the rest of the world, but can do so only if they subscribe to market precepts. In the area of telecommunications a good many countries, including some affluent nations themselves, have been perverse enough to establish nationally owned services that are answerable, in some way at least, to politicians who might favour purchase of equipment supplied by indigenous industries, who might place conditions on orders that do not suit the commercial interests of foreign competitors, and who frequently insist on there being public service clauses attached to the operation of communications (for example, subsidy of uneconomic services to remote rural areas by more lucrative business traffic).

Such presumptions threaten to diminish the ability of US corporations especially to continue and extend their role as suppliers of equipment and services. In consequence American politicians have been called upon to act by the business lobby:

The future well-being of its [telecommunications] supplier industries will depend critically upon their ability to perform in the
international marketplace. At present foreign restrictions
seriously constrain this essential type of growth and development. It is imperative that the US government makes full use of
both bilateral channels and multilateral frameworks to minimize
such interference, with the objective of affording American
producers equitable opportunities for competition and growth.
(Eckelmann, 1983, p. 13)

The US government has prodigious powers at its disposal
(foreign aid, trade embargoes, investment allocations and so
on) to make dissident nations fall into line. Europe and
Japan have bowed to pressure to liberalise their telecommunications and other nations are set to follow suit. Certainly, Third World nations will have considerably less power to
resist American conditions.

The role of the state

The state today is involved in a great many spheres of society
– as legislator, as market, provider of education, administra-
tor of social security and so on – and it is also doing its
utmost to aid economic recovery. The key role of I.T. in this
is well known and the state acts to ease its introduction in
myriad ways: in special educational programmes, in training
enterprises, research support, grant-aided initiatives, astute
placing of government contracts, and so forth. We devote an
entire chapter of this book to the state's participation in I.T.
via its defence programmes and our subject of education
vividly illustrates its involvement in high technology, but
here we would lay emphasis on the deep commitment of the
state to restore the health of the market economy.

Look where one will at government policies towards I.T.
and one finds at their root a commitment to support the
creation of goods and services that sell and/or facilitate
selling. This is the fulcrum of all policy, from liberalisation
of telecommunications to apportionment of research
awards. In the present period, extreme anxiety of still

further industrial decline has led to frenetic endorsement of market values in the I.T. sphere. The *raison d'être* of I.T., as far as government is concerned, is that it will reinvigorate the economy; as such, it is prepared to support only commercially-oriented developments and it works assiduously to ensure that I.T. which is produced succeeds on the market.

Nevertheless, government is well aware that the I.T. market is not a free one and it is therefore unwilling to get too carried away by its own rhetoric. Its prime responsibility is to achieve success for Britain *vis-à-vis* other countries and to this end it seeks national champions to spearhead the I.T. attack. Recognising the dominance of the I.T. industry by transnational giants, this translates into a policy of encouraging the consolidation of domestic I.T. industries into groups large enough to withstand the challenge of Japan and America. To this end it has smiled on the merger of strategic businesses (Thorn and EMI, Racal and Decca), urged GEC and Plessey to get together, and has intervened frequently with preferential purchases to bolster companies such as GEC and Ferranti (Arnold and Guy, 1986, Chapter 6).

Moreover, government knows that the spread of I.T. cannot be left solely to individual corporations since their particular interests may not be the same as those of the collective economy. For this reason the state must orchestrate the 'I.T. revolution', acting to ensure the overall health of the British economy. Hence here it pressurises an established company to innovate; there it protects a vulnerable industrial sector from bullish overseas competitors; elsewhere it nurtures embryonic companies that later may be able to compete on their own. Always, note, the endeavour is to establish success as measured by market criteria. Nothing else will be permitted while the nation wallows in depression.

Finally, a central role of the state is to achieve social order amidst what is presently unsettling change: steelworkers made redundant, manufacturing plant automated and job opportunities curtailed, industry relocated leaving communities bereft of work – all these consequences of recession and restructuring impose grave obligations on the state to maintain social stability. It may try to do this by the heavy disciplines of mass unemployment, legislative action, and deployment of police, as well as by persuasion in schools and through the mass media.

It is well known that in the present period the Thatcher government has been guided by the philosophy of a 'strong state/free market' (Gamble, 1979) and that, while the cushion of the welfare state remains to catch the losers, the constraints of an interventionist state, notably through a strengthened and technologised police force, anti-trade union laws, and a more punitive allocation of social security benefits, have been prominent (Schwarz, 1987). An important facet of this strategy has been the use of I.T. to better monitor the population, the better to maintain social order. As we mentioned in our previous chapter, the state has an insatiable appetite for information on its citizens. In recent years it has collected this even more assiduously than before and its agencies have adopted I.T. to make the task much more effective. An index of developments is that the Police National Computer is now accessed some 34 million times annually for its criminal and vehicle registration indexes. Plans are in hand whereby state data banks will be inter-linked so that 'total portraits' will be able to be drawn from files such as Inland Revenue, Health and Social Security, Immigration and Education records using National Insurance Numbers for purposes of identity (Campbell and Connor, 1986; cf. Laudon, 1986). As a resource for attaining social order, the data bases being established by the state – most of which the public will not have access to – will be of inestimable value.

This signals an important feature of the emerging 'information society': people themselves will be increasingly relegated to the status of data; their actions and transactions will be recorded as digits and ciphers by ubiquitous and always watching information machines. Already credit agencies, finance houses, advertisers and retailers are constructing data bases on customers and potential customers, categorising them, analysing them, scrutinising their movements that they may be used to optimum benefit of corporate or even political clients. There are on-line links giving instant access to buying patterns, demographic traits, bank balances, individual spending records and other characteristics. People's lives are becoming routinely monitored and everyday activities (telephone calls, use of utilities, shopping) are recorded, stored and analysed.

'Transactional information', a 'new category of information that automatically documents the daily lives of almost every person' (Burnham, 1983, p. 50), is created every time we use electronic terminals, not just in the home with the TV and telephone, but also in banks, shops, offices and restaurants. The consequence is that it becomes possible to 'pinpoint the location of an individual at a particular moment, indicate his daily patterns of work and sleep, and even suggest his state of mind' (ibid, p. 56). In this way the individual becomes routinely watched and studied – without even being aware of it. Paradoxically, with this erosion of privacy goes the spread of an increasingly privatised style of life; as people are more and more individuated by anonymous users of I.T., so there has grown an ideology of individualism (Abercrombie *et al.*, 1986, Chapter 5).

The collection and storage of information is important to corporate agencies who aim to practice 'precision management', just as it is to ambitious politicians who decide upon direct mailing to target their electorate and to state departments which intend to hone the administration of their affairs. Above all, what it underlines is a crucial aspect of I.T.: its development – for whom, in what circumstances, in what form – hinges on power, on the power to buy, to define, to initiate, and to design technological innovations. Those who promise that an 'information society', courtesy of I.T., will bring us all unimagined benefits construct their Cockaigne in profound ignorance of power. It is our conviction that, seen from this point of view, the 'information age' will be one best understood in terms of Jeremy Bentham's Panopticon: an all-seeing authority without need of physical walls. Thanks to the creation of the 'wired society', we are fast approaching a time in which the individual 'is seen, but he does not see; he is the object of information, never a subject in communication' (Foucault, 1979, p. 200).

Part II
The Industrialisation
of Education

4

Education, Utopia and Crisis

'It is ... neither Luddism nor ivory-tower arrogance to suggest that the prescriptions of industrialists and technologists can never be more than a partial element in debates over curriculum reform. What should be taught is at bottom a matter of moral and political discussion for it is a function of the kind of society we wish to live in.' (Ruth Jonathan, 1986, p. 141)

In Part I we have criticised the wishful speculations and anticipations of post-industrial and futurological seers. This silicon utopianism, we have suggested, is but the latest version of the ideology of technological progress which has characterised Western societies for two centuries. As before, science and technology are at the heart both of what is possible and what is desirable. However, in the late 1980s this idealisation of the future should be rooted in the context of recession and crisis, factors which are implicated in the shift from what we describe as one regime of accumulation (Fordism) to a possible new regime (neo-Fordism). Our opinion is that at present we are undergoing a process of restructuring which is leaving behind the mode of ensuring profitable production that has dominated the post-war world and entering into a new era. The latest futurology reflects the imperatives and priorities of this transformation, but it simultaneously denies and obscures the nature and significance of this upheaval in its invocation of an evolutionary progression into a post-industrial future. Our opposition to the likes of Daniel Bell and Alvin Toffler is centred on the significance of this broader context of crisis for understanding the meaning of the 'information revolution'.

In this part of the book we turn to an examination of the role of the education system in this transition from Fordism to neo-Fordism. As before we begin with the futurological and post-industrial accounts of, in this case, a 'technological revolution' in education. Just as the 'information revolution' in general cannot be understood outside the broader context of recession and restructuring, so too, we shall argue, is this the appropriate framework for comprehending recent developments in education. The real significance of the 'computer revolution' is not revealed by looking simply at the use of the new technologies in the classroom. What is needed, rather, is a perspective which relates the microworld of the school to the more general economic, technological, industrial and social transformations associated with the emergence of the neo-Fordist system. Just as we have argued that the new information technologies, far from being the neutral phenomena that futurists would have us believe, tend in fact to express and reinforce the prevailing relations of power, so, we shall argue, are the new computer technologies and curricula implicated in relations of power and profit.

Computers and classroom utopianism

The technological utopianism that we described in Chapter 1 has its counterpart in the sphere of education. Thus Frederic Golden writes of a new wave of 'microkids' who are 'part of a revolutionary vanguard: the computer generation' (Golden, 1985, p. 219). 'Where their parents fear to tread', we are told, 'the microkids plunge right in, no more worried about pushing incorrect buttons or making errors than adults are about dialling a wrong telephone number' (ibid, p. 221). According to another speculator, 'the world is facing a period in education similar to the introduction of the printing press five hundred years ago' (Dede, 1985, p. 257). The author of *The Mighty Micro* tells us that 'teaching as it is presently carried out, has changed very little in millenia', but that a new 'wave of highly advanced super-miniaturised technology' will 'lead to major changes and advances in the teaching process itself' (Evans, 1979, pp. 126, 118).

The truth is, according to Evans, that 'the world is about to move on from the era when knowledge comes locked up in devices known as books' (p. 128). In the brave new world of instantaneous access to information resources we are likely, for the first time, to see the development of 'a true Science of Education, and with it a real understanding of the nature of learning' (p. 125). Will we remain 'wedded to the haphazard ignorance of the past', or will we put our faith in a new generation of children 'who have amplified their own brain power with that of the computer'? (p. 127).

Perhaps the most sustained account of the post-industrialist utopia is that put forward by Tom Stonier, particularly in his book *The Three Cs* (written with Cathy Conlin). According to Stonier and Conlin, 'we now live in a post-industrial economy' and 'for better or worse, we have moved into an information age' (Stonier and Conlin, 1985, pp. 189, 166). The consequence is that 'the first genuine revolution in over a century is beginning to overtake the education system' (p. 3). The engine of this drama is the computer, which will come increasingly to 'provide access to incredible amounts of information' and to be 'a personal tutor par excellence' (p. 6). 'We have', the authors argue,

> devised an artificial intelligence external to our brain, potentially of incredible power. Computers will not only help solve problems by extending our brain power outside our heads, they will also vastly improve the information-handling processes going on inside! (p. 7)

Stonier and Conlin believe that 'the entire education system will begin to revolve increasingly around the computer [which] will become part of a genuine cradle-to-grave education system' (p. 10, 9). 'Undoubtedly', we are assured, 'the expanding use of computers as a learning aid will provide new insights into the learning process and will, by early in the next century, increase the efficiency of the learning process to undreamed-of levels' (p. 48).

Stonier and Conlin go so far as to project the coming of a 'new sub-species: *Homo sapiens cerebus*' (p. 195), thereby integrating high tech and post-industrialism with Social Darwinism:

> In human history it is always those who were able to develop and use new technologies adroitly who in the long run not only survived better, but also came to dominate others. Homo sapiens cerebus will survive, prosper, and in due course dominate all those who do not partake of the new intellectual technology. Among higher organisms, new behaviour patterns, rather than new anatomical features, set the stage for a revolution as profound as the hominid revolution of a half a dozen, or so, million years ago. Will we be able to cope with it? (p. 196)

Such examples, if exaggerated, are typical of a large and growing literature on computers in education and we need not parade more here. Within this genre what we are aware of is the fundamental acceptance of a linear and upward movement of history, one characterised in the late twentieth century by a qualitative transformation from an industrial to a post-industrial, or information society. At the core of this process of social and economic amelioration is the driving force of technological innovation. As such, post-industrial scenarios represent just the most recent variant of a long-standing belief in 'progress': a way of seeing which regards science and technology as the arbiter of economic and social improvement, to the increasingly rational management of society, and even to the evolution of the human species (Robins and Webster, 1988).

Invariably, as Lewis Mumford has argued, technology is idealised as 'a way of reaching Heaven'; it paves the way for social harmony, in so far as 'the promise of material abundance on earth, through exploration, organised conquest and invention, offer[s] a common objective to all classes' (Mumford, 1967, p. 283). Along this route technology is the prime mover. Everything is predicated on the productivity of the technological enterprise, the very ethical and moral basis of society depending on technology's ability to deliver more and better commodities. Of course, the utopia of ultimate abundance always remains elusive. What is important, however, is the promise, for on this basis inequalities in the here and now may be held in dynamic tension.

Also fundamental to silicon utopianism is an ideal of rational social management. This represents a particular rendition of the Enlightenment belief that knowledge and reason were the root of human progress and happiness. In practice this belief has become a philosophy of instrumentalism: knowledge has been reduced to technique and rationality to rationalisation by a technocratic expression of the Enlightenment ideal. Cornelius Castoriadis refers to it as the 'rationalist ideology':

> the illusion of omnipotence, the supremacy of the economic 'calculus', the absurdity and incoherence of the 'rational' organisation of society, the new religion of 'science', and the idea of development for development's sake. (Castoriadis, 1984/85, p. 35)

It is through this rationalist ideology that silicon prophets like Bell, Toffler and Stonier write. For them I.T. promises to realise a dream of control through knowledge and reason that was only glimpsed by the eighteenth-century philosophers of Enlightenment. As we have suggested, this doctrine of rational progress readily translates into an evolutionary idiom. This may be invoked not only in terms of a theory of social development which contends that greater quantities represent a qualitatively higher stage. What may also be at stake is the evolutionary development of intelligence itself – a development now centred around the transition from a carbon-based to a silicon-based stage. 'The human mind is an exquisite information processing device reflecting the evolution of intelligence over a period of a billion years' (Stonier and Conlin, 1985, p. 194). Through the new technologies of the 'information society', this evolutionary process will move to a higher and purer level.

Crisis and the new instrumentalism

One stimulus to writing this book was the despair and gloom we experienced when we read Stonier and Conlin's declamations. It might be asked, however, why we should ever bother to take their missionary paeans seriously. Well, we believe that it would be quite wrong to underestimate the power of this futurological discourse. Many people accept the kind of arguments put forward by Stonier and Conlin as an appropriate, if exuberant, account of the 'information revolution' in education. They do so in large part because their own way of thinking draws, often implicitly, upon similar ideals of progress and growth that form the dominant imagery. They perceive change in terms of the common-sense categories of our time, those which seem to be self-evident and incontestable. All the more reason to contest them!

In pursuit of this we would turn attention to a subordinate theme of educational futurology which, if pursued, can take us to an alternative, and in our view more realistic, analysis of what the 'computer revolution' is about. As we have said, it is the productive potential of I.T. which underwrites all other premises. However, for over a decade now, growth and expansion have not been satisfactorily sustained in the Western economies. It is alleged that the cause of this has been both the failure to develop and exploit new technologies and an inability or reluctance to compete with our major economic and industrial rivals. Fundamental to both of these problems are the shortcomings of the education system. In the words of futurologist Fred Williams, 'our schools, with their assembly line instruction and even their bells, are a holdover from the industrial age . . . Yet we are depending on them to train our youngsters for life in a clearly developing postindustrial era of high technologies' (Williams, 1982, pp. 187–8). Education must come to develop the new skills, competence and expertise necessary for economic renaissance and the transition to post-industrialism. According to two recent commentators, 'this major revolution in the structure of society can be characterised as the move from an energy-rich to an information-rich economy'. It is, however, 'one to which schools are making little or no contribution and which, as the offspring of the old society, they are barely capable of understanding' (Meighan and Reid, 1982, p. 356).

An index of the present crisis in the condition of education is the frequent public lamentations of industrialists and politicians. according to Graham Day, chief executive of the Rover Group, current educational methods and policies 'are not producing the stream of managerial talent which business and industry currently requires'; 'the nation's pool of skills must be renewed, enhanced and expanded if the UK is to be successful in the current process of industrial regeneration' (*Financial Times*, 25 February, 1987). As for the Chair of Unilever, 'the educational sector at many levels is out of touch and does not meet industrial needs' (Durham, 1984, p. 15). It follows, of course, that education must be brought into line with the needs of industry, on terms set by industrialists.

Such reproaches are not specific to the 1980s. The argument of writers like Martin Wiener and Corelli Barnett has been that the rift between education and industry dates back to the early days of the Industrial Revolution (see Chapter 5). The charge against the universities has been that 'the more practically useless a subject, the higher [have been] its claims as an instrument of mental discipline'. The consequence of this, it is argued, has been a long-standing 'prejudice against vocational education' (Allen, 1976, p. 40).

This is not to say that the British education system has not functioned in the interests of capitalist enterprise. The encouragement of mass literacy, the development of compulsory education, mechanics' institutes, the founding of civic universities and the growth of technical colleges and universities have in their different ways been oriented around the needs of business and industry. All bear witness to the economic functionality of education: 'Education may contribute directly to industrial performance by improving the technical quality of the labour force. Or indirectly, it may, for example, induce a sense of discipline and peaceful order within which industrialisation can thrive' (Sanderson, 1983, p. 9).

To be sure, such accommodation between education and the industrial order has never been given. There have always been a liberal and critical dimension to education that resists subordination to the market and aspires to other – intellectual, imaginative and aesthetic – truths and values. The historical development of British education can be seen in terms of a continuous tension between forces working towards the autonomy of education on the one hand, and the pressure for the incorporation of education to the needs of industry on the other.

The present period represents an important moment in this struggle between liberal and functional aspirations, one in which it is felt that education and industry have drifted too far apart. In the context of recession, when the restoration of productivity, profitability and competitiveness has become the order of the day, education is being reined in. What we are now seeing is a new emphasis on scientific and technological education and a restructuring of the relation between training and education. This 'new orthodoxy' (Grubb, 1987) aims to make the education system conform to the 'needs of society'. It is a question of 'adapting the education system to the rapidly changing pattern of economic activity which has been spurred by the extraordinary advances in technology of recent years', and of establishing that 'only those in touch with, and particularly those who have experience of, the world of industry, commerce and services, can appreciate the challenge to the education system presented by these charges' (Peacock, 1984, p. 10). As Ruth Jonathan makes clear, the new vocationalism 'assumes that, in an industrial society, the needs of society are to be conflated with the needs of industry, and that, moreover, the needs of each individual are best served by preparing him/her to serve the needs of society, understood in economic terms' (Jonathan, 1986, p. 136).

Neo-Fordism and flexible accumulation

So far we have argued that the 'education debate' in the 1980s is but the most recent episode in the long history of encounters between industry and the education system. After a period, in the 1960s and early 1970s, when egalitarian, liberal and critical principles came into the ascendancy, the pendulum is now swinging back in favour of an instrumental and utilitarian approach. Ideals of equal opportunity and individual development have been relegated by an emphasis on the processing of 'human capital' and what Ken Jones calls 'the ticking of economic calculation' (Jones, 1983, p. 19).

However, the new vocationalism is not just the reassertion of a more functional relation between industry and education, but its reassertion at a particular historical period. This is the transitional period between the era of Fordism, which has characterised much of the century to date, and a new economic and social system referred to as neo-Fordism. Whilst this process is represented in the dominant social imagery in terms of technological evolution and post-industrial utopianism, what is in fact occurring is a transformation in the nature of capital accumulation and of the social relations necessary to sustain and reproduce this.

Regulation School scholars (see Aglietta, 1979; de Vroey, 1984) describe this transformation in terms of a restructuring of the dominant regime of capital accumulation and its concomitant mode of regulation. The regime of accumulation is the prevailing organisational, technological and sectoral strategy for economic growth. By the mode of regulation is meant the 'norms, habits, laws, regulating networks and so on that ensure the unity of the process [of accumulation]' (Lipietz, 1986, p. 19). The present period marks a period of structural and mutational crisis, where the system cannot be adequately stabilised around the old coherence of production and regulation. It represents a 'crisis regime' (Lipietz, 1987, p. 199) in search of a new coherence which must find a resolution for what is both an economic crisis and a crisis of regulation through the establishment of both a new model of development and new ways of living (Lipietz, 1982). We may speak of a dual crisis, then: a crisis of *accumulation* and one of *control*.

We discuss the control dimensions of neo-Fordism further in Chapter 7. For the moment, we want to concentrate on transformations in the form of accumulation and the implications this has for education. Ron Martin (1987) has provided an overview of the transformation from the 'post war [i.e. Fordist] expansionary regime of accumulation' to an 'emergent regime of flexible accumulation' dating from the mid 1970s. Adapting the terminology of Regulationists, Martin describes the changing 'accumulation regime' and what he calls the 'socio-institutional structure of accumulation', 'the matrix of market mechanisms, institutions, social relationships, forms of state intervention and political legitimation, and social and physical infrastructures, that are shaped by and which facilitate and mediate a particular regime of accumulation' (ibid, p. 5). What he identifies is a shift from a monopolistic regime of mass production (see Table 4.1) to a new regime (see Table 4.2) 'in which the accent is increasingly on flexibility of production, capital investment and disinvestment, of consumer markets, production, labour processes and work practices' (p. 11).

From other perspectives several writers have made contributions to our understanding of the present crisis of accumulation. Michael Piore and Charles Sabel (1984) have described a 'Second Industrial Divide' that marks the transition from a system of mass production to one of 'flexible specialisation'. Philip Cooke sees this process as the shift from what he calls the 'modernisation era' (1945–1975) to a new post-modernisation paradigm 'characterised by the unleashing of market principles, the rolling back of the "nanny-state", and the growth of flexible production' (Cooke, 1987). In the terminology of Scott Lash and John Urry (1987), we are now seeing the transformation from a period of 'organised capitalism' to one of 'disorganisation' (though 'reorganisation' might be a better term). Again, the account centres around the shift from the centralised and concentrated organisation of accumulation to a more decentralised and flexible system.

These various accounts have important commonalities and convergences. In contrast to the celebrants of a coming 'post-industrial' society, all these writers identify changes as shifts in the character of twentieth-century capitalism. What they all focus on is the crisis of (Fordist) mass production

Table 4.1   *The post–war expansionary regime, late 1940s to early 1970s*

Characteristic	Key features
	Accumulation regime: monopolistic
Industry	Monopolistic; increasing concentration of capital; steady growth of output and productivity, especially in new consumer durable goods sectors; secular expansion of private and especially public services.
Employment	Growing and near-full; shift in structure from manufacturing to services; decline of male employment growth of female work; de-skilling of traditional craft labour.
Consumption	Rise and spread of mass consumption norms for standardised household durables (especially electrical goods) and motor vehicles.
Production	Economies of scale; volume, mechanised (Fordist) production processes; functional decentralisation and multinationalisation of production.
	Socio-institutional structure: collectivistic
Labour market	Collectivistic; segmented by skill; increasingly institutionalised and unionised; spread of collective wage bargaining; employment protection.
Social structure	Organised mainly by occupation, but tendency towards homogenisation. Income distribution slowly convergent.
Politics	Still closely aligned with occupation and organised labour; working class politics important; regionalist.
State intervention	Keynesian-liberal collectivist; regulation of markets; maintenance of demand; expansion of Welfare State; corporatist; nationalisation of capital for the State.

Source   adapted from Ron Martin (1987)

(and mass consumption) and the emergence of a new regime of flexible production (and consumption).

What is flexibility? At one level – and this would be the pre-eminent focus of the post-industrialists and futurologists – it is a question of industrial and organisational decentralisation made possible by the new information technolo-

Table 4.2 *The emergent regime of flexible accumulation, mid-1970s onwards*

Characteristic	Key features
	Accumulation regime: flexible
Industry	Rationalisation and modernisation of established sectors to restore profitability and improve competitiveness; growth of high output high tech and producer service activities, and small firm sector generally.
Employment	Stagnant followed by hesitant growth; persistent mass unemployment; generalised contraction of manufacturing employment, growth of private service sector jobs; partial de-feminisation (in manufacturing); flexibilisation of labour utilisation; large part-time and temporary segment.
Consumption	Increasingly differentiated (customised) consumption patterns for new goods (esp. electronics) and household services.
Production	Economies of scope; post-Fordist flexible automation; small batch specialisation; organisational fragmentation combined with internationalisation of production.
	Socio-institutional structure: competitive-individualist
Labour market	Competitive; de-unionisation and de-rigidification; increasing dualism between core and peripheral workers; less collective, more localised wage determination.
Social structure	Trichotomous and increasingly hierarchical; income distribution divergent.
Politics	De-alignment from socio-economic class; marked decline of working class politics; conservative individualism; localist.
State intervention	Keynesianism replaced by free-market Conservatism; monetary and supply-side intervention rather than demand stabilisation; de-regulation of markets; constraints on welfare; self-help ideology; privatising the State for capital.

SOURCE   adapted from Ron Martin (1987)

gies. What we are seeing is the development of flexible manufacturing systems (FMS) (Jaikumar, 1986) and 'just-in-time' (JIT) manufacturing and sourcing systems. This development of high-tech, computer-governed systems, not just in manufacturing, but also in retailing, design, service provision and managerial activities, provides the rationale for the current enthusiasm for computer literacy. There are, however, other dimensions to the new flexibility that lead us to conclusions quite other than those of the silicon utopians. First, it is increasingly clear that neo-Fordist flexibility applies not only to high-tech sectors of the economy, but also to low-tech and no-tech areas (which, as we observe in Chapter 6, are likely to be the most significant growth sectors of the future). 'Flexibility' will be associated not only with computers and robotics, but also with various forms of sweated and household work. Indeed, the most consequential aspect of flexibilisation is the creation of new and the elaboration of existent economic and social divisions.

Flexibility may assume three distinct forms:

• numerical flexibility, 'or, the ease with which the number of workers employed can be adjusted to meet fluctuations in the level of demand';
• functional flexibility, 'or, the ease with which the tasks performed by workers can be adjusted to meet changing business demands';
• financial flexibility, 'or, the extent to which the structure of pay encourages and supports the numerical or functional flexibility which the firm seeks' (Atkinson, 1985, p. 26).

These categories of flexibility help explain the innovations in economic and industrial management and organisation associated with neo-Fordism. Within the neo-Fordist enterprise there has increasingly developed a segmentation of the workforce between a core of high-waged, functional – or skill – flexible employees, on the one hand, and a low-waged, numerically-flexible periphery, on the other. The former group has security and status; the latter exists on a much more precarious level as casual and sub-contracted workers (cf. Hakim, 1987). Charlie Leadbeater notes still more complex segmentations and graduations. In his view, there is a fivefold segmentation of the labour market: the long-term unemployed; those who suffer short term unemployment; the peripheral workforce, 'a growing army of part-timers, temporary workers, home-workers and the self-employed who are suspended in the grey area between unemployment and full-time employment'; unskilled and semi-skilled workers; and, finally, 'genuinely core workers, permanent skilled workers, with stable employment prospects' (Leadbeater, 1987, pp. 18–20).

These differentiations, which have begun to replace the old distinctions between manual and non-manual with a core/periphery polarisation based on relevant skills, are central to the new regime of accumulation. Accordingly, the Thatcherite road to neo-Fordism depends on 'legitimising a society where roughly two-thirds have done, and will continue to do, quite well while the other third languish in unemployment or perpetual insecurity' (ibid, p. 21).

Education and Neo-Fordism

Neo-Fordism is, at the present time, only an embryonic and tentative strategy for accumulation. Its eventual nature and also its viability remain uncertain. Nonetheless, in this period of upheaval, it does seem that segmentation of the workplace along lines of skill, security and status are evolving as a key feature of a developing strategy. As the Confederation of British Industry has put it, 'many companies [have] come through the recession with a deep commitment to improving their business performance by becoming leaner, fitter and more flexible in their organisation of work'. To this end, they continue, such companies have 'maintained a small group of workers, highly trained, with their remuneration and security linked to the performance of the enterprise' and, 'to support and service this nucleus', 'they have encouraged the development of a peripheral workforce of non-regular employees' (CBI, 1985, pp. 12–13).

The objective of the Thatcher government is to ensure

that the education system should both adapt to and reinforce this new strategy. But, of course, this throws up certain problems. The new functionalism goes against the grain of long-standing liberal ideals and principles and hence meets considerable resistance both within and without educational institutions. At a more pragmatic level, it is difficult for educationalists actually to predict what the 'needs of industry' might be in the 1990s – particularly in a context where 'industry itself has found it difficult to articulate a clear statement of its needs and has no effective mechanism at its disposal for making its views felt' (NEDC, 1983, p. 1).

Nonetheless, education is being called upon to serve the new regime. Already we are seeing the emergence in secondary education of a new tripartism selecting and processing future workers for their core and periphery destinies. 'Able' pupils take a grammar school-type course, leading to higher and professional education; a middle band 'reincarnates the old technical streams and schools of the past'; and, below them, there is a 'new and prevocational education for the "practical"', to be followed by 'vocational courses combining life "skills" and "work experience"' (Chitty, 1986, p. 83). Stewart Ranson argues that the new politics of education combines vocationalism, rationalisation and also an explicit stratification. For Ranson there is a new tripartism emerging in the tertiary sector, dividing a tertiary grammar group from a tertiary technical group and a tertiary modern group (Ranson, 1984, p. 240). In this respect it is responding to the claims of industrialists that 'different talents and aptitudes can only be nurtured by different types of education' (Peacock, 1984, p. 10). 'The time has come', we are told, 'for selection to be restored as a pre-eminent principle in education . . . different abilities require different types of education and different approaches to talent-stimulation' (Goldsmith, 1984, p. 25).

Whilst we should emphasise again the still embryonic nature of many of these developments, it would be wrong to underestimate the clarity of purpose that is forming around the new strategy for education. There are distinct indications of an emerging specialisation in education which services and supports changing employment patterns. Moreover,

there are signs of an increasingly co-ordinated and integrated approach to all levels of education. This is apparent,
for example, in the elaboration of a national school curriculum and in the move towards a cohesive national system of
vocational qualifications (MSC/DES, 1986). All this reflects
an increasingly centralised and *dirigiste* management of the
education system. As Stewart Ranson points out, 'the
complex, often ambiguous, traditional framework of decision-making [in education] – with its assumptions about who
should be involved, whose values count, how decisions
should be arrived at – is being clarified, concentrated and
centralized' (Ranson, 1985a, p. 103). This centralisation,
moreover, has assumed a decisively managerial, technocratic and instrumental character (Hall, 1985).

   We cannot attribute these developments to the manipula-
tive imagination of the Thatcher government alone. As
Denis Lawton (1984) argues, the 'tightening grip of centralisation certainly dates back to the mid 1970s. And so, too,
does the new vocationalism and the urgent attention to the
needs of industry. Already, in his now legendary Ruskin
College speech of 1976, James Callaghan was 'concerned . . .
to find complaints from industry that new recruits from the
schools sometimes do not have the basic tools to do the job
that is required'. He went on to voice his unease about the
'insufficient co-ordination between schools and industry',
about basic literacy and numeracy, and about the general
standards of education. Callaghan also put his support
behind a core curriculum and emphasised the need for 'a
more technological bias in science teaching that will lead
towards practical applications in industry rather than towards academic studies' (Callaghan, 1976, pp. 332–3). This
'speech of trenchant commonplaces' (Hopkins, 1978,
p. 105) set the agenda for the so-called Great Debate
around the issues of control and vocationalism. As Shirley
Williams' Green Paper, *Education in Schools*, formulated it:

   Teachers lacked adequate professional skills, and did not know
   how to discipline children or to instil in them concern for hard
   work or good manners. Underlying all this was the feeling that
   the educational system was out of touch with the fundamental

need for Britain to survive economically in a highly competitive world through the efficiency of its industry and commerce. (quoted in Moore, 1984, p. 74)

Callaghan's speech 'marked, at the highest political level, the formal end of the long post-war phase of educational expansion' and 'a public redefinition of educational objectives' (Education Group, 1981, p. 218). As such, we can take the date of its delivery, 18 October 1976, as marking the inception of the neo-Fordist strategy for education. But what more precisely is the relation between the last gasps of Labourism in the 1970s and the battle cry of Thatcherism in the 1980s? Writing about neo-Fordism more generally, John Holloway has identified three phases in its evolution. An initial, still Keynesian and social-democratic phase sought, through corporatist mechanism, to co-ordinate the efforts of managers, government and workers towards growth and productivity. Recognition of the cumbersome and less than satisfactory nature of this policy resulted in a second phase, characterised by a 'macho' approach of industrialists and politicians alike (Edwardes, MacGregor, Thatcher), aimed at reasserting managerial power and forwarding a new strategy for growth.

This second phase, Holloway argues, should be seen as a transitional period, 'well suited to destroying the vestiges of Fordism/Keynesianism but not suitable for establishing the . . . patterns of the brave new world' (Holloway, 1987, p. 158). This latter objective is the project of the third phase in the development of neo-Fordism. It aims to build upon the defeats achieved in the second phase in order to construct a new consensus and new forms of integration based on the new divisions between core and marginalised workers: 'The emphasis is moving towards the construction of a new consensus, not a consensus that will cover everybody, but a consensus among the responsible moral majority' (ibid, p. 161).

These same phases can be discerned in the attempts to elaborate a neo-Fordist strategy for education (though not in a neat sequential order). During the period of Callaghan's Great Debate, the problem is diagnosed and a social-democratic remedy sought. Whilst there is a 'pre-monetarist tone' in Callaghan's pronouncements, their vocational nostrums are subordinated to a common vision which integrates the citizen within a shared purpose and community' (Moore, 1984, pp. 75–6).

A more divisive, instrumental and militant approach comes with the 'macho' second phase strategies of Thatcherism, aimed at 'nothing short of dismantling a whole epoch' (Hall, 1983, p. 2). Initial 'softening-up moves' appealed to parent and governor power, sought the re-establishment of 'standards' and put an emphasis on market forces. But these have been followed up by more aggressive moves aimed to 'break local authority monopoly over public education provision, devolve power from administrations to heads, and prescribe a nationwide core curriculum' (Jessop *et al.*, 1987, p. 114).

The third phase, aiming at the construction of a new social consensus, now seems to be rising out of the fire. It is centred around the image of the new model pupil/student/ worker committed to 'such goals as team work, flexibility and the desire to learn'. The objective (as we shall argue in Chapter 7) is self-motivation and adaptability: 'The encouragement of self-reliant behaviour is foreign to British traditions, but becoming recognised as essential to modern conditions' (NEDC/MSC, 1984, p. 86, 6). Rather than driving education 'back to the stone age' (Hall, 1983, p. 2), or turning the clock back, the Thatcherite attack is intently directed to the development of an educational consensus fitted to the new regime of flexible accumulation.

The industrialisation of education

In the remainder of this chapter, we want to look at some of the key developments that have shaped the emergence of a neo-Fordist education strategy under the Thatcher government. Rather than a detailed chronological account, we are aiming to draw out some of the major events and documents that have contributed to the new education for flexibility. We seek, however, to cover all levels of education, since we believe the essence of current developments is their comprehensive range and scope.

In this section we focus upon the vocational and technological dimensions of the educational 'revolution'. Generally, transformations in education are associated with, and indeed often seen as a consequence of, the 'information technology revolution'. Whilst we argue in this book that the issue is more complex, and that it is a matter of broad political economic shifts rather than simply technological innovations, it is no doubt the case that I.T. is playing an important facilitating role in the emergence of the hallowed 'enterprise culture'. These new technologies are being introduced extensively at all levels (Centre for Education Research and Innovation, 1986; DES, 1987) and they do enable significant moves towards the neo-Fordist paradigm.

Thus, they offer the possibility of 'removing formal education from its position at the centre of our educational programme' because potentially they could allow home-centred learning systems. This, of course, 'makes the concept of education as a consumer product a real possibility'. The new technologies are also valued for the way they facilitate 'a shift in the traditional balance of the teacher/ student relationship' (ITAP, 1986, pp. 32, 34, 37). As Roland Meighan and William Reid (1982, p. 356) argue, 'for the first time new technologies have challenged the schools and their curriculum at a time when the schools themselves are suffering budget cuts, and when the conditions which have guaranteed their stability are changing fundamentally'. The real significance of I.T. initiatives is a consequence of their ability to engage with and to reinforce broader transformations in the structure and character of education. It is to this developing neo-Fordist alliance between I.T., vocationalism and the 'needs of industry' that we now turn.

(i)   Better schools?

The campaign against 'dysfunctional' attitudes in education necessarily begins with schools. Schools, according to the government, have tended to devalue the central role of business and industry, and consequently have failed to equip their pupils for later training and the world of work. Its strategy for combatting this state of affairs, and for creating a functional relation between schools and industry, is most clearly set out in the White Paper *Better Schools* (1985) which, according to its architect Sir Keith Joseph, aimed to 'secure the best possible return for the resources invested in school education', and thereby 'promote the nation's ability to seize the challenging opportunities of a technological and competitive world' (*Hansard*, 26 March 1985).

Conscious of 'the demands of the modern world' (*Better Schools*, 1985, p. 1), this policy statement is fully aware of the evolving socio-economic context with which the education system must engage. In the context of 'rapid technological change in an increasingly competitive world', the government's educational policies, and also its broader economic programme, 'place a premium on enterprise, personal versatility and national cohesion' (ibid, p. 8). The emphasis is undoubtedly on adaptation to changing economic 'realities'. To this end four areas of policy initiative are introduced:

● pursuing broad agreement on the objectives of the curriculum.
● introducing reformed examinations together with records of achievement.
● improving teacher quality in all of its aspects.
● harnessing the energies of parents and others in a reformed system. (p. 90)

In combination, these represent a range of strategies for breaking down old inflexibilities and rendering the education system more manipulable and responsive, especially to the needs of business and industry.

The overriding objective is that the curriculum should be 'relevant' and that there should be a 'practical dimension' to learning. 'It is vital', the document stresses, 'that schools should always remember that preparation for working life is one of their principal functions ... Britain's work-force should possess the skills and attitudes, and display the understanding, the enterprise and adaptability that the pervasive impact of technological advance will increasingly demand' (p. 15). 'The linking of education and training', it is made clear, 'should have preparation for employment as one of their principal functions' (p. 16). It is also made explicit that pupils, as they move through the school system, should come to recognise their place in the order of things: 'there should be careful differentiation: what is taught and how it is taught need to be matched to pupils' abilities and aptitudes' (p. 15).

In line with the emerging neo-Fordist consensus, there is also an emphasis on self-motivation and self-direction: 'the development of personal qualities and skills, including motivation and commitment, self-discipline and reliability, confidence, enthusiasm and initiative, flexibility and the ability to work both individually and as part of a team' (p. 15). The government's objectives require that it intervenes in the curriculum to ensure that pupils are introduced to a wide range of areas of experience, knowledge and skill. This external shaping of the curriculum – which has subsequently resulted in plans for the national curriculum (DES/Welsh Office, 1987) – aims at 'a broad, balanced and suitably differentiated programme until age 16', but it is, nonetheless, a vocationally-oriented project: 'All the elements of a broad 5–16 curriculum are vocational in the sense that they encourage qualities, attitudes, knowledge, understanding and competences which are the necessary foundations for employment. But only the programmes which prepare directly for a specific vocational area are strictly vocational' (*Better Schools*, 1985, p. 16).

What we have here is an index of the dissolving frontiers between education and training, between the vocational and liberal aspects of schooling. Some programmes are more vocational than others, but all are geared to the 'real' world of work, business and industry. What further characterises education for neo-Fordism is that it should not be too narrow a training, but, rather a broad grounding that will support later flexibility and adaptability. As the House of Lords Select Committee on Science and Technology puts it, in a context of rapid industrial and technological change:

> it makes little sense to introduce specialised teaching at school
> for most technologies . . . the pattern of education which best
> suits the demands of new technology is one offering a broad
> base of scientific and technological knowledge and deferring
> detailed specialisation to as late a stage as possible. At schools
> future employment options should not be closed by premature
> specialisation. (House of Lords, 1984, pp. 25, 46)

A major development in harnessing education to neo-
Fordism has been the Technical and Vocational Education
Initiative (TVEI), first introduced as a pilot scheme in 1983
and extended into a national programme in 1986. Its clear
objectives were to establish a vocational orientation in
schools and to ensure greater collaboration between schools
and industry and, moreover 'to ensure that such activites are
integral and not merely peripheral to the main stream of
educational development' (Waddington, 1987, p. 17). In
line with the new orthodoxy, it aims, according to the
director of the programme, at 'encouraging initiative, problem solving and other aspects of personal development', and
at equipping pupils to 'cope with change' and 'adapt to the
changing occupational environment' (Woolhouse, 1984, pp.
73–4).

What characterised the introduction of TVEI was the
centralist and *dirigiste* manner with which it was imposed on
schools by the then Manpower Services Commission (MSC).
Its origination and also its mode of operation, in fact,
by-pass the conventional forms of educational innovation.
TVEI has sought to 'move the centre of gravity away from
the academic, rooted in the university-controlled GCE
domination of the secondary curriculum, to the vocational.
It is a means of working through the practical curricular,
pedagogic and assessment implications of that attempted
shift from the expressive to the instrumental, the intrinsic to
the extrinsic' (Dale, 1986, p. 28). Whilst apparently progressive in its student-centred approach – its focus on 'experiential' learning and 'problem solving', on competences and
skills – TVEI in fact operate to differentiate and segment
various categories of learners; it undermines the comprehensive principle and replaces it with 'separate classrooms,

separate teachers, separate streams, separate curricula, separate exams, separate papers and separate course assessment according to prejudgements about what kind of "ability" different pupils possess' (Chitty, 1986, p. 82).

More recently, such divisions have been reinforced and extended with the development of city technology colleges – business-oriented, selective schools, described by the *Times Education Supplement* (10 October, 1986) as 'Mr Baker's cuckoos'. With their emphasis on 'self-discipline and positive attitudes', on work experience, and on collaboration with industry (DES, 1986a), these colleges offer a more privileged vocational education than TVEI. If such initiatives are about education for flexibility in the 'information age', they are also about 'Knowing Your Place' in the order of things.

The new vocationalism in schools is hyped as preparation for the coming 'information society'. It is mystified in the rhetoric of 'computer literacy' and the glamour of high tech. Greasing the wheels of the 'computer literacy' bandwagon has become an important enterprise of journalists and many academics, giving rise to a sub-genre of publishing (see, *inter alia*, Chandler, 1984; Chandler and Marcus, 1985; Hawkridge, 1983; Wellington, 1985). Through such programmes as the Micros in Schools Scheme and the Microelectronics Education Programme, computers have assumed a high profile in schools (DES, 1986b). In our view, 'computer literacy' reflects an infatuation with high tech scenarios for the future and a naive faith that computers will form the basis for additional employment, competitiveness and economic revival (see Chapter 6). The discourse of 'computer literacy' embellishes and simultaneously clouds the real issue on the government's agenda: *work* literacy.

(ii)   'Watch Out, Japan, Here Comes Spikey Dodds'

Better Schools makes clear the integral relation between education and training and also the importance of bridging the transition between the broad programmes which are required up to age 16 and those post-16 programmes which are explicitly vocational. The key focus here, it argues, must be on the 14–18 age range, and it must 'embrace the work of the schools and of colleges of further education, and the needs of industry and commerce' (*Better Schools*, 1985, p. 16). The introduction of TVEI into schools represents part of this programme, but by far the most important development has been the MSC's (now TC) Youth Training Scheme (YTS), which has sought to impose a co-ordinated training programme – initially one year, and now two – on all unemployed school leavers. In August 1987 there were 398 700 trainees on YTS, including 142 700 in their second year of training (*Youth Training News*, 41, November 1987, p. 17). Spikey Dodds is just one of these young people who are being trained, supposedly to advance the cause of British industrial competitiveness. According to the advertisement that features him, Spikey 'is a typical British sixteen-year-old leaving school this year. But to Japan, and our other industrial competitors, he's a big threat'.

YTS is the most prominent component of the government's strategy to 'refunctionalise' education in line with the requirements of neo-Fordism, and many detailed accounts have been written of it (see, *inter alia*, Edwards, 1984; Benn and Fairley, 1986; Finn, 1987; Chapman and Tooze, 1987; St John-Brooks, 1985). Our aim here is not to duplicate these accounts, but to relate YTS to the emerging 'education for flexibility' strategy. The initial objective of the MSC was to clear away what had become a deficient system of training, geared to the needs of Fordism and now increasingly anachronistic. Vocational education became 'squeezed between a school system informed by liberal ideals, geared to academic standards and inadequately funded, on the one side, and an industrial system attuned largely to the immediate needs of employers, on the other' (Ryan, 1984, p. 35). What became evident to the major architect of the new vocationalism, Lord Young, was a need to 'modernise' training in order to provide a basis for flexibility (Young, 1984). In order to loosen up the old order, Young by-passed the existing agencies and also introduced commercialism into further education through the encouragement of private training agencies. 'The voice of business, large and small, must be heard', he declared, adding that 'deregulation is not a panacea, but . . . too many regulations is one of the ills' (Young, 1985b).

His overall strategy aimed then to move through a process of creative destruction to a new business ethic and a remoralisation of the young workforce. Young (1985b) referred to it as a 'cultural revolution' that would 'inculcate enthusiasm and enterprise' in the troops of neo-Fordism. The system that has come to be established, which has been called 'the manpower service model of education', aims at 'forming those personal characteristics – resourcefulness, adaptability, social conformity – envisaged as appropriate for members of a rapidly changing technological society' (Jonathan, 1983, p. 3).

Of course, this manpower service model did not emerge wholly developed and operational from the ruins. It has, in fact, developed out of some considerable degree of jostling between the DES and the MSC – for example, over whether the new training scheme should be employer based or college based (Parkes, 1985). There has also been a process of negotiation and trade-off over the balance of liberal and vocational elements between the MSC and the DES-funded Further Education Unit (FEU) (Seale, 1984). Robert Aitken has identified three periods in the development of the MSC and the manpower services model of education. In the first, from its inception in 1974 up to 1978, the MSC worked alongside or through existing agencies. The second period, from 1979, saw a 'more thrusting intent to reshape the training and apprenticeship systems' and an attempt to restructure secondary education. At present, we are entering a third period of development in which 'the political intent is now less evident or aggressive' and a new consensus is being built (Aitken, 1986, pp. 231–2). The parallels with John Holloway's account of the broader development of neo-Fordism – from its corporatist phase, through the transitional ('macho') phase towards the elaboration of a new consensus – are striking.

The manpower services model has been defined and refined through a series of important documents (MSC, 1981; *Training for Jobs*, 1984; *Education and Training for*

Young People, 1985; *Working Together – Education and Training*, 1986). Within these various papers, four main objectives of YTS are addressed: the reduction of unemployment; manpower development; enhancing individual employability and personal effectiveness; and social purposes and personal development (Eraut and Burke, 1986, pp. 9–11). During the course of the 1980s, the latter tasks have assumed greater importance as the aim of achieving a new consensus and remoralisation has become more central. The needs of industry remain paramount, but YTS is now proactive rather than simply reactive. The old approach of training for 'an immediate and limited job' is to be 'replaced by training for competence' (*Working Together . . .*, 1986, p. 15). Account is taken of 'individual initiative, innovation and competence across the whole spectrum of skills and aptitudes', and it is recognised that 'people – with their knowledge, learning, skills, intelligence, innovation and competence – are our most important resource' (ibid, p. 1). The emphasis is now on integrating the responsible worker-citizen: 'positive attitudes', 'motivation', and 'initiative and enterprise' all have a premium put on them.

If the new enterprise culture appeals to the aptitudes and potential of trainees like Spikey Dodds, then the 'new realism' sets firm limits on their expectations. Throughout the second phase of neo-Fordism, the government has waged a war of attrition on trade unions to make labour more submissive and adaptable to the needs of industry. Such gains are not to be given up. As Andy Green argues, the new emphasis on 'relevance' and on experential learning may sound progressive, but what has happened is that 'progressive techniques have been pressed into the service of reactionary ends': 'Thus relevance is unduly restricted to "work-oriented" learning, experiences are carefully selected so that they involve mainly experience of work, and counselling and group dynamics are used for social control, and so on' (Green, 1986, pp. 113–14). Education is subordinate to training or, rather, the distinction is seemingly abolished as vocationalism comes to demand not merely job-skills but also 'life skills' and, almost, existential commitment. As one approving commentator notes: 'The pointless attempt to distinguish between education and training is one of the snobberies of British culture, and the MSC has made a great contribution to breaking down the distinction in recent years' (Collins, 1986, p. 236).

The apparent new progressivism must also be seen in the context of new educational castes. Skills and competences are distributed in line with the new segmentations of the neo-Fordist labour force. Further education is, thus, characterised by a new tripartism of those taking GCSE or B/TEC examinations and headed for managerial-type work; those taking craft courses and junior clerical courses; and those who, via YTS and TVEI, will move into the more precarious world of unskilled and semi-skilled jobs (Gleeson and Hopkins, 1987; Green, 1986). The new consensus is to be built on the firm foundation of 'knowing your place' and abandoning 'unrealistic' expectations.

(iii) Beyond the ivory tower

The third area of education that must be reconstructed and reconstituted is higher education. The Thatcher government is attacking this problem with particular vigour, for the universities are regarded as the breeding ground of the 'English disease' of 'anti-business snobbery' and of ivory-tower gentrification. Universities and polytechnics are crucial, not only for the processing of future core workers, but also to the production of that scientific and technological knowledge which will (supposedly) keep us at the front of the race for competitiveness and growth. To this end there have been strenuous efforts to tie the knot between higher education and industrial and business concerns, and to tie it tightly.

In 1970, Edward Thompson felt justified in attacking Warwick as the 'business university', condemning 'a new type of intimate (and subordinate) association with "industry"', a 'symbiotic relationship with the aims and ethos of industrial capitalism, but built within a shell of public money and public legitimation' (Thompson, 1970a, pp. 301, 307; cf. Thompson, 1970b). The anomaly has, in 1988, become the norm. Collaboration is firmly on the agenda

(Pearson, 1983). The regulatory body for public sector higher education produces a report on 'Partnership in Progress' (NAB, 1986a). The Council for Industry and Higher Education, set up in 1986 to 'encourage industry and higher education to work together and to represent their joint thinking to government' produces a report, *Towards a Partnership: Higher Education–Government–Industry* (CIHE, 1987). An OECD report gives details of 'long-term national and international "megabuck" research deals, close integration of industrial and university teams, new demands for university initiatives in the diffusion and application of research results', and so on (OECD, 1984, p. 9). Even so, higher education has, we are told, failed to adapt:

> The corner shop has become a supermarket; the bespoke aristocratic tailor is now turning out readymades for the mass market. It is the failure of the universities to think through the implications of this transformation that explains their present situation. (Klein, 1987, p. 10)

The world has truly turned upside down.

To a large extent, the new pressures of industry derive from the changing needs and demands of high tech industry. While the relationship between industry and higher education goes back into the nineteenth century (Sanderson, 1972), it is with the growth of large corporations that its autonomy becomes eroded. As J. D. Bernal noted in the 1930s, 'the influence of big commercial corporations and of Governments closely linked to them is tending to dominate Universities, particularly on the scientific side' (Bernal, 1935, p. 952). Scientific and technological innovation under advanced capitalism demands an even more functional and subordinate relationship of universities to industry. As higher education institutions (HEIs) become increasingly science and knowledge factories, so it becomes necessary to move beyond the ivory tower (Bok, 1982). In so far as higher education has been recalcitrant and resistant to complete instrumentalisation, however, the old liberal traditions have persisted as frictions to the new 'enterprise culture'. It was in large part to humble and discipline the ivory tower academics and to assert the primacy of business and industry that the Thatcher government began its attack on higher education in the early 1980s (Kogan and Kogan, 1983).

The campaign has been undertaken through two complementary strategies. The first is that of centralisation, which aims to overcome the 'lack of accountability' of HEIs and to turn them into a co-ordinated and efficient force for economic and technological progress. To this end the National Advisory Body (NAB) was set up in 1982 to co-ordinate and regulate public sector higher education and, particularly, to engineer a shift towards science, technology and business education. At the same time, the University Grants Committee (UGC), in its new *dirigiste* guise, has become the agent for plans to 'modernise' and rationalise the universities and, according to its chair, to 'bring industry and higher education closer together' (Swinnerton-Dyer, 1985, p. 12). The UGC and NAB have also been involved in consultative exercises to develop a co-ordinated national policy for higher education as a whole, covering such issues as student numbers; the level and sources of funding; the shift to science, technology, engineering and business studies; and the movement to a greater degree of earmarking and selectivity in research allocations. These various moves towards centralisation and political orchestration are consolidated in the organisational, management and financial strategies set out in the White Paper, *Higher Education: Meeting the Challenge* (1987).

Alongside this explicit centralising thrust, there is a second strategy being used to undermine and reconstruct HEIs: the withdrawal of government finance and the introduction of market forces (Price, 1984/85). Since 1981, this cutting of budgets has been used as a disciplinary instrument, but the longer term belief is that more money should come from industry, and that on this basis the objectives and destinies of HEIs and of capital will be enmeshed. A favoured lesson is that of Salford University, which after suffering a 40 per cent cut in its recurrent grant from government in July 1981, went on to develop a new entrepreneurial élan (Ashworth, 1982; 1984). What the Thatcher government also sought was a more 'efficient', cost-effective and business-like manner in the organisation and running of HEIs (Peston, 1985). As part of this general campaign to impose business criteria, the Jarratt Committee was appointed to undertake an efficiency study of the universities. Its conclusion – that universities should be more efficiently managed in the manner of private corporations – must have been music to the ears of the Education Secretary, Sir Keith Joseph (Committee of Vice-Chancellors and Principals, 1985).

Education and industry are to be manoeuvred into a marriage of convenience:

> The Government and its central funding agencies will do all they can to encourage and reward approaches by higher education institutions which bring them closer to the world of business. The Government will correspondingly encourage industry and commerce to recognise the value, to themselves, and more widely, of working closely with education. (*Higher Education*, 1987, p. 2)

The government is resolved to subvert what it sees as the unworldly ethos of higher education and to assimilate it into the new enterprise culture. In the words of Sir Keith Joseph:

> It will be wise for universities and other higher education institutions to inch . . . towards a larger contribution of their funds from the private sector . . . Every step that [they] can take to increase contributions from the private sector will be a step towards the greater reality of academic freedom and real independence. (*Hansard*, 26 October 1984, col. 912, 918)

The new instrumental philosophy of education has become *de rigeur*. The shape of things to come has been mapped out in a report from the Butcher Committee: contract education for industry; training partnerships; academics as business consultants; loans and gifts of equipment by industry to education institutions; and 'greater interchange of views between industry and education' (Information Technology Skills Shortages Committee, 1984). This is the 'new realism'.

Within HEIs, teaching and research activities alike are

being transformed in keeping with the new utilitarian and instrumental outlook. As far as teaching is concerned, there is, in the longer term, a need to restructure curricula in line with changes occurring in secondary education. Sir Peter Swinnerton-Dyer (1985, p. 10) believes that 'outside pressures . . . will be for more general degree courses, establishing a wider intellectual base on which graduates can thereafter build a greater variety of ways'. There has also been a substantial counter-attack against the 'academic drift' towards the humanities and social sciences (Gombrich, 1985), and an assertion of the importance of science, technology and engineering courses which are assumed to be more important for the country's economic renaissance. Thus, in December 1982, the government launched an initiative to increase provision for I.T., providing for about 2500 extra students in the first year of operation (1983/84). At the same time, it created some 240 'new blood' posts, primarily in scientific and technological subjects, and 70 new 'information technology' appointments. Increasingly, I.T. is permeating all areas of the curriculum. According to the Council for National Academic Awards, the body responsible for validating courses in public sector higher education, 'there will be virtually no area in industry, commerce, administration, knowledge or learning which will not be affected by the information technology revolution' and, accordingly, colleges should attend to 'the development of information technology for education in general . . . no course, in any subject area, should be thought immune from such developments' (CNAA, 1982, pp. 1–2). There is also a growing emphasis on the importance of 'personal transferable skills' (for example, communication, problem-solving, teamwork, interpersonal skills) and upon motivation, flexibility, adaptability and initiative, to equip students for their future places in the world of industry (NAB, 1986b).

If teaching and curriculum development are increasingly oriented to (information) technological literacy and enterprise culture, this is no less the case in the research area. Already, from the government's point of view, there have been encouraging signs of links between HEIs and industry in the form of research programmes, science and technology parks, and entrepreneurial activities aimed at marketing technological expertise. A major example of such collaboration is work undertaken in the Alvey Programme, which covers research into the development of computer software engineering, knowledge-based systems, man (sic)-machine interface and very large scale integration in silicon chip design, and which entails co-operation between industry and HEIs in order to qualify for government funding. At Salford University, flagship of the new high tech spirit of free enterprise, the proud boast is that 'we are dismantling our Ivory Tower' and that 'a better and deeper relationship with industry is a high priority' (Ashworth, 1985, pp. 31, 36). Collaboration with industry and business funding are now fundamental to Salford's very existence.

One important development in this symbiotic relationship between industry and universities is the burgeoning, since the mid-1970s, of science parks, technology parks and research parks (Lowe, 1985). It has been argued that:

> Since the potential growth in new technologies is phenomenal
> . . . it is vitally important for universities to make their tech-
> nology and information transfer mechanisms as effective as
> possible . . . Hence, the urgent search for ways and means of
> creating new kinds of linkage between higher education and
> industry to initiate research and promote its application. In the
> UK, science parks are the latest in an evolutionary line of such
> linkages. (Roberts, 1987, pp. 16)

Following the American model, some twenty of this evolved species have been established in Britain. The intention is for the 'provision of a site very close to a HEI, where science-based firms can easily interact with the scientific community. The park can also provide "nesting boxes" for new small enterprises set up to develop and exploit academic ideas' (ACARD/ABRC, 1983, p. 18). It seems that the claims for science parks have been somewhat exaggerated and that few university-industry initiatives are generating significant income (Turney, 1987). But what is more important, perhaps, is their symbolic value. The ivory towers are giving way to new expanses of steel, glass and chromium.

The subordination of academic research to the priorities of the market is reflected in an increasingly commercial and entrepreneurial outlook among researchers (Leyland, 1986). Academics are now being encouraged to exploit their work commercially, through the development of companies and consultancies for example. As Dorothy Nelkin (1984, pp. 2, 4) has it:

> the application of knowledge today is often immediate and direct, and research scientists themselves are personally involved in commercialising their work ... The pressures on researchers to produce results with the potential for commercial or military exploitation are transforming scientific data and even the research process itself into 'intellectual property' – property which can be owned or possessed and is therefore subject to competing claims.

The consequence is that universities' responsibility for open communication conflicts with the commercial imperative to maintain proprietary secrecy. What we are seeing in the increased commercialisation of research is the intensification of industry's grip and the weakening of broader social and political responsibilities. The new enterprise culture blurs the distinctions between corporations and universities, between profit and the public good.

(iv)   Enterprise culture

The industrialisation of education has occurred not only through state initiatives, but also through the activities of industry and various pressure groups. James Callaghan's Ruskin speech was important in generating what has been called the schools-industry movement:

> a diverse collection of employer and trade union groupings; specially constructed educational or quasi-educational 'projects'; government agencies and government statements and exhortations – all designed to put pressure on the education system to change the content of what is taught, how it is taught, and how it is assessed and examined. (Jamieson, 1985a, p. 27; cf. Jamieson and Lighfoot, 1982; Jamieson, 1985b)

Among the various pressure groups can be numbered such organisations as the Schools Curriculum Industry Project, Understanding British Industry, Young Enterprise and Project Trident (Ball and Gordon, 1985). Young Enterprise, for example, which publishes a magazine called *Achiever*, aims to encourage young people to become familiar with the organisation, methods and practice of commerce and industry (E. Smith, 1985). Understanding Industry, which has been in operation since 1976, is another representative organisation and aims to 'change the anti-industry culture of this country' and 'to change the poor perceptions which many teachers and students have of Industry and Commerce' (*UI News*, no. 2, June 1986).

The objectives are broadly threefold. The first is to provide young people with work experience (Watts, 1983), and to introduce them to the work ethic. This applies even to primary schools, where many industrialists have sought 'a chance to influence the children's attitudes before they become set against the world of industry' (Jamieson, 1985b, p. 30). The second is to promote the spirit of enterprise and entrepreneurship (Smith and Wootton, 1986). The third, and most general, is to publicise on behalf of British industry and its high tech future.

Justifications of this new instrumentalism tend to be banal:

> All we need to assert is that the economic environment, which includes industry and commerce and the supporting infrastructure of services, is a vital one for us all . . . If the purpose of a school is to educate young people for life, and if large areas of life are dominated by the operation of industry and commerce, then it follows that schools must take the industrial world seriously. (Jamieson, 1986, p. 6)

It is the ignorance of substantive political, economic and social pressures which make one wince at this sort of statement. For the bulk of the schools-industry movement the assumption is that skills for life amount to little more than the skills necessary to fit into the world of work. If children can see the challenges and excitement of the world of industry, the argument continues, then they will be queuing at the factory gates when they leave school.

One further organisation must be referred to, and in our view it is the leading lobby group for the consensus phase of neo-Fordist education policy. It is the 'Education for Capability' movement, sponsored by a broad range of politicians, academics and industrialists, and intellectually led by such figures as Tyrell Burgess, Corelli Barnett, John Raven, Patrick Nuttgens and Charles Handy. In its 'Manifesto for Change' the movement argues that

> the motivation problem which plagues many schools, the anti-social attitudes found among some young people, and a great deal of under-functioning in industry and commerce, are consequences of a hiatus between one traditional secondary system, and what we need as the outcomes of secondary education.

It advocates a fundamental restructuring of education, centred around the acquisition of 'capability' and competences, 'not only the familiar basic skills, but also practical ability, the ability to get on with others, skill in solving real-life problems, and such necessary attributes for a full and effective life as judgement, responsibility and reliability'. Also prized is the 'ability to adapt to the constantly changing situation' which 'calls for openness of mind, flexibility, and imagination' (*Times Higher Education Supplement*, 30 January 1981, p. 18).

The context and strategy of the movement are set out most clearly in a book, *Education for Capability*, edited by Tyrell Burgess in 1986. It is firmly rooted in Corelli Barnett's crusade against the 'anti-business culture' and for future grandeur: 'Education for capability alone can keep Britain an advanced technological society and save her from becoming a Portugal, perhaps even an Egypt, of tomorrow' (Barnett, in Burgess, 1986, p. 23; see also Chapter 5 below). In his contribution to the book, Patrick Nuttgens is critical of a 'dislike and fear of technology – and therefore of the modern world' (p. 24). Charles Handy looks to the coming 'communications revolution' and the 'new industrial society' as the context within, and for which a new educational philosophy must be elaborated. This 'creative revolution in learning' should, according to Burgess, be organised 'at all levels explicitly round the formulation of problems, the proposal of solutions and the testing of these solutions' (p. 70). It is all about moving away from the traditional subject-based and content-based curricula to a new focus on processes, skills and competences. Traditional forms of grading are to be replaced by individualised student profiles covering capability, interest and progress, which require 'the co-operation of the student in planning and monitoring his [sic] course of study' (Elizabeth Adams, p. 81).

Education for Capability is about motivational disposi-tions, about correct attitudes, about flexibility and enter-prise, and about active and practical learning (Raven, 1982; 1984). As such it is a variant – albeit an impoverished one – of progressive education. It is also about developing a new consensus and sense of motivation, by adapting elements of the progressive tradition, to what its proponents see as the high tech, post-industrial future, and what we prefer to call the emerging neo-Fordist regime of flexible accumulation. In our view, it constitutes an important element in the building of a new moral majority. It is not coincidental that the objectives of the Education for Capability movement have been endorsed by the MSC as 'totally central to the aims and objectives of the Commission' and as indicating 'the way in which . . . the world of education should face' (quoted in Thompson, 1984, p. 212).

Postmodern education

In this chapter we have given an overview of growing subordination of education, at all levels, to the needs of industry, and we have situated this in the context of emerg-ing neo-Fordist structures. Many other critics have lamented that an instrumental philosophy of training has come to prevail over liberal traditions. Thus, Maurice Holt, a critic of 'vocational pressures and employment-led skills', argues that 'a fundamental decision we have to make about educa-tion is whether it should transform the mind so as to equip it for independent judgement and rational action, or whether it should be directed towards practical skills for particular ends' (Holt, 1983, pp. 84–5). We agree with the spirit of Holt's critique of the new functionalism, but there are, now, real problems with his attempt to bolster and defend liberal principles. The necessary critique of utilitarian education has to confront the reality of an increasingly rationalised and technocratic world, where the space for liberal thought has been effectively reduced.

In his book on 'the postmodern condition', Jean-François Lyotard has discussed these transformations specifically in the context of developments associated with the 'information revolution'. In his view, this and the new technologies with which it is connected are bringing about a transmutation in the nature of knowledge. Liberal traditions, Lyotard argues, have been replaced by power as the motive for seeking knowledge. The question now asked is not 'is it true?', but 'what use is it?' and 'is it saleable?' (Lyotard, 1979, p. 84). In the postmodern context, education based on the principle of emancipatory humanism seems anachronistic. Humanism and liberal beliefs have been displaced by the instrumentalisation and commodification of knowledge, its subordination to the principle of 'performativity'. Writing of higher education – though his argument can be generalised to all levels – Lyotard suggests that educational institutions are

> required to produce competences, and no longer ideals . . . The transmission of knowledge is no longer destined to produce an elite capable of guiding the nation towards emancipation, but to provide the system with players capable of acceptably playing their role in the pragmatic positions required by the institutions. (Ibid, pp. 79–80)

With Lyotard's account of the industrial mobilisation of knowledge, we have moved a long way from the information utopia of Tom Stonier and his fellow-travelling post-industrial visionaries with which we began this chapter. What we have in Lyotard's position is an understanding of how knowledge begins to relate to the emerging neo-Fordism – or, in his terms, the post-modern condition – and also a recognition of the interrelations between power and knowledge: 'the growth of power, and its self-legitimation, is now taking the path of data production, storage, accessibility and operationalisation' (Lyotard, 1979, p. 77). What Lyotard forces us to confront are the difficulties this raises for critical reason. When knowledge and education cease to be ends in themselves, and when the systematic production of operational skills and competences has become the objective of the socio-technical system, then the appeal to liberal and emancipatory truths and values can seem to be out of its time.

5

The English Disease?

> 'My contention is that as our society became more structured
> and ordered in the aftermath of the Industrial Revolution –
> particularly in the latter part of the century – attitudes were
> developed which were antipathetic to the entrepreneur. In-
> deed in our very approach, in the skills we desired and in our
> whole economic life, we moved towards the gentrified corpo-
> rate cossetted State – and the entrepreneur was left out in the
> cold.' (Lord Young, 1985c, p. 5)

Introduction

No one could dispute that Britain has undergone a relative
decline *vis-à-vis* other countries: from occupancy of the
premier position in the nineteenth and opening decades of
the twentieth centuries, the nation has tumbled out of the
top ten richest nations as measured by income per head. To
be sure, this is a *relative* decline and the standard of living of
those of us in contemporary Britain is far in excess of that of
our parents, let alone that of our grandparents, but no one
can be complacent about a situation where the country
appears set on an irremediably downward course. The deep
recession which we have experienced since the mid-1970s,
the reliance on North Sea oil, and the seemingly intractable
problem of the economy's falling competitiveness compared
with that of Japan, West Germany and America make for
widespread pessimism.

Nonetheless, there are an increasingly combative and
increasingly influential number who refuse to be downcast.

They do not deny the seriousness of the situation, but contend that this is reason to look at the underlying causes of the British demise and to seek for radical solutions. For the tough-minded and determined 'it marks at least some progress that it is now so generally acknowledged that there is something peculiarly and profoundly wrong with our economic and industrial affairs' (Barnett, 1975, p. 900). This quest takes them rapidly to education and to the new technologies. Their analysis invariably concludes that education has played a major role in bringing about the decline of British competitiveness due to its inability to produce a workforce and technology capable of matching the rest of the world. Further, and following from this, it is their prognosis that it is change in the sphere of education which will be decisive in bringing a halt to the national decline if it can be induced to help the country with skills and research appropriate to advanced technology. At once education is identified as the reason for the collapse of the British economy and as its only hope for regeneration. Richard Knight, President of the Society of Education Officers, voices a wisdom that is rapidly becoming dominant:

> Without the contribution of the education system in developing the attitudes and skills which make up technological capability, the economic future must be in serious doubt. The slow response in this country to opportunities which have already appeared and been lost can be attributed in large part to deeply inbuilt social forces and to the shortcomings of education itself. (Knight, 1983)

In the previous chapter we discussed demands that education must adjust to the 'second industrial revolution' by adopting I.T., creating 'I.T. awareness' and orienting towards vocational needs. To achieve this shift without too much resistance it has been essential that the public, and educationalists themselves, be convinced that schools and universities have been failing in what they have been doing for some time. It is this issue, the accusation that education has been a cause of the decline of Britain, which is the subject of this chapter.

A 'non-industrial industrial society'

For decades commentators have sought to explain why Britain has been overtaken by foreign competitors. Indeed, concerned commentators were issuing warnings shortly after the 1851 Great Exhibition in London (Barnett, 1979; 1986a, Chapter 11). The question has become more urgent as decline has accelerated in recent years and the country has experienced the consequences in mass unemployment, urban riots and threats to law and order. Coincidental with this heightened degree of crisis, the one-time variety of explanations for the cause of decline has narrowed decisively. During the 1960s and 1970s a number of accounts vied with one another for supremacy (see Coates and Hillard, 1986; Gamble, 1981, pp. 23–6): Britain had overstretched herself by trying to maintain a world presence, economically, militarily and politically, with profound costs for domestic industry; there was a lack of planning for strategic industries as in France and Japan, which meant Britain missed the boat for key technological innovations; pluralist democracy was placing such demands on economic processes that it was interrupting efficiency; successive governments had neglected industrial investment in search of financial balances (Pollard, 1982).

Today, however, one argument above all others has emerged to dominate debate about the 'English disease'. The view that features of culture, as opposed to economy or empire, have been the primary cause of Britain's decline has become ascendant. This has it that the peculiarities of English history and class structure have led to Britain having odd attitudes which are at once anti-industrial, anti-capitalist (usually coded as 'anti-enterprise') and anti-technology. The thesis is that there is something about British culture, about our national character, attitudes and institutions, which is antipathetic to industry, that it is a living contradiction in being what Ralf Dahrendorf has called a 'non-industrial industrial society' (Dahrendorf, 1982, p. 44). By this he means a society which, in spite of industrial success in the past, never came to terms with it, preferring the ideal of rural life, idealising the countryside, and gravitating towards a retrospective nostalgia (see also Newby, 1979; Williams, 1973). It has been possible to construct a superficially convincing case from literary anecdotes, political comment and industrial personalities that this 'anti-industrial culture' has been the cause of Britain's relatively poor economic performance over the last century or so. Let us sketch major elements of the argument.

The role of the aristocracy

In most accounts the aristocracy is taken to be the major cause of this peculiarly anti-industrial culture. It is the strange history of the aristocracy, notably the singularity of its survival of the Civil War and the upheavals consequent upon rapid industrialisation, that explains the persistence of values which are thought to be antipathetic to success in business. In essence what we have inside – and decisively affecting – the society is a group which no longer belongs.

The argument has it that the aristocracy (an imprecisely – indeed rarely – defined collection, including, certainly, the peerage, but embracing other landed interests such as the gentry and the more affluent squires) in England was never successfully done away with; that, in fact, the nation's capacity for compromise and conciliation ensured that many of these emerged from the internecine struggles of the seventeenth century more or less intact – in the words of Trevelyan, the aristocracy 'had not been destroyed as a class, but had been put into cold storage' (Trevelyan, 1944, p. 254; cf. Hill, 1967, Part Three) – to play a significant role in the agrarian revolution that preceded industrial capitalism. Indeed it can be argued that it was this early conversion to the application of commerce to land by the aristocracy that led much of it to side with the regicides against feudal restrictions. As historian Lawrence Stone has observed, 'the older nobility showed a surprising readiness both to develop new resources on their own estates and to take a prominent part in industrial, commercial and colonising projects' (Stone, 1965, p. 380). Thereby it played an important role in the development of the Industrial Revolution. Thus Barrington Moore:

> The strong commercial tone in the life of the landed upper classes, both gentry and titled nobility, also meant that there was no very solid phalanx of aristocratic opposition to the advance of industry itself . . . the most influential sector of the landed upper classes acted as a political advance guard for commercial and industrial capitalism. (1966, p. 30)

Other historians contend that the aristocracy upheld this progressive attitude towards business up and into the eighteenth century. Indeed, Harold Perkin believes that the characteristics the aristocracy stamped upon English society were expecially conducive to the successful birth of capitalist endeavours. By providing social stability with prospects of upward mobility for the entrepreneurial,

> Britain had in the fullest degree the right kind of society to produce it [the Industrial Revolution]. An open, dynamic aristocracy based on absolute property and linked vertically by patronage was the ideal society for generating a spontaneous industrial revolution. (Perkin, 1969, p. 63; cf. Thompson, 1974, 1978)

It had certainly survived, but if the aristocracy had helped weaken absolutist monarchy, had pioneered commercial agriculture and provided the right environment for industrial capitalism in its early days, how can writers see it as 'anti-industry'? Martin Wiener answers that this was because the 'capitalism of the aristocracy . . . was basically rentier, not entrepreneurial or productive' (Wiener, 1981, p. 8), so when the industrial capitalist arrived on the scene he had to accommodate himself to the lifestyle and aspirations of a rentier aristocracy.

This was not, in the opening decades of the nineteenth century, a comfortable process. For one thing, by that time emergent industrial capitalism had effective ideologues who regarded those who gained their living as landlords as parasites. Ricardo and like-minded industrial capitalists distinguished parasitic capital from active capital, the former unproductive, the latter ever-concerned to reinvest and expand wealth in the form of factories and trade. In addition, those committed to a *laissez-faire* doctrine could no longer stomach the paternalism of the aristocracy, countering *noblesse oblige* with ideals of self-sufficiency, individualism and the justness of the market. Behind these beliefs were substantial issues such as free trade (favoured by capitalist industrialists) versus protectionism (favoured by the landed interests), parliamentary reform, and – pressing in the opening decades of the nineteenth century – what to do about the industrial proletariat.

However, if during the opening decades of the century there appeared to be an irreconcilable gulf between aristocratic ideals, interests and way of life and thoroughgoing capitalist ethics, it is believed that by around 1850 the aristocracy had realised it could not retain its pre-eminence if it persisted in holding to an aristocratic creed that opposed *laissez-faire*. Its capacity to compromise – and thereby to ensure its survival – resulted in the conversion of the aristocracy to industrial capitalism and the need for a measure of reform sufficient to incorporate the middle classes.

It is at this stage where most commentators on the 'English disease' commence their accounts, arguing that, in truth, the aristocracy gave up less than they retained of their way of life. While they did effect significant reform, the aristocracy retained a powerful presence in politics, the civil service, the church and other professions. Still more important, there are questions asked as to what degree the aristocracy sincerely did adopt capitalist ethics. Indeed, it is the view of those who believe that the aristocracy is disproportionately responsible for industrial decline that they continued with values that were antipathetic to commercial success. That is, the charge is that the aristocracy held to a belief in paternalism, in caring for the less fortunate, in the responsibility of the privileged to cultivate an organic community, in a chivalric code (of manners, honour and conduct of affairs), in placing the quality of relations and environment prior to questions of cost and production – all of which are said to have reduced business efficacy. Integral to this is the charge that the aristocratic creed presented a disdain for science, technology and trade, something which also weakened the nation's commercial standing. In brief, the landed aristocracy may have tactically retreated in the face of industrial capitalism's rise during the nineteenth century, but it never really changed its ways, preferring the life of the country squire to that of combative manufacturer.

Emulation of the aristocracy

It must be said that the accusers do not lay their charges solely at the door of the aristocracy. This is such a small percentage of even the elite of modern Britain that in themselves, try as they might, it is hard to see how aristocrats could bring about industrial decline. The argument of 'English disease' theorists is that the survival of the aristocracy in Britain has infected other institutions and groups in such ways as to incapacitate them.

In part this was a willing contamination. Thus it has often been remarked that industrialists had at least an ambivalent attitude towards the aristocracy. As F. M. L. Thompson observes, 'while denouncing it [the aristocracy] as functionless, privileged and parasitic, [industrialists] envied and sought to emulate it as the embodiment of all that was admirable in taste, manners and civilized living' (1963, p. 3). This outlook connects with that Walter Bagehot, writing in the mid-nineteenth century, perceived as the *deferential character* of English society. Bagehot was convinced that in Britain the majority willingly 'abdicates in favour of its *elite* and consents to obey whoever that *elite* may confide in' (p. 265), continuing to note that:

> The apparent rulers of the English nation are like the most imposing personages of a splendid procession: it is by them the mob are influenced; it is they whom the spectators cheer. The real rulers are secreted in second-rate carriages; no one cares for them or asks about them, but they are obeyed implicitly and unconsciously by reason of the splendour of those who eclipsed and preceded them. (p. 268)

It is not difficult to understand the ambition of those occupying the 'second-rate carriages' to enter the first. Moreover, when one recalls that by the late nineteenth century a good many industrialists were living off the capital they had accumulated in manufacture and trade, and as in effect a business aristocracy were thus in conscience scarcely able to continue to berate 'parasitic' landed interests who lived on much the same basis as themselves, it is hardly surprising to witness much apeing of the aristocracy by the newly arrived rich. A major expression of this was in the peerage itself: between 1886–1914 there were over two hundred new nobles created and as much as a third was composed of industrialists (F. M. L. Thompson, 1963, p. 294). The prestige of a title – indeed the retention of a House of Lords itself – the panoply of ceremony associated with it, and the disproportionate presence of peers on company boards (*Labour Research*, December 1985) testifies to the continuing impulse of many industrialists to emulate the aristocracy.

The same desire is evident in the practice of successful industrialists evacuating the town in favour of a stately home in the countryside where, thanks to the 'peculiar flexibility' of the English aristocracy which accommodated the *nouveaux riches*, they 'became landed gentlemen, JPs, and men of breeding' (Wiener, 1981, p. 14), a process that drew upon and impelled the growth of 'ruralism' as a distinctive feature of a British culture (cf. J. Marsh, 1982). They bought up titles, even married into the aristocracy, and built themselves mansions:

> The subscribed to local charities, sent their sons to the right schools and hunted, shot and fished with enthusiasm. After relatively few years, and as long as they kept the rules, they generally were accepted. (Girouard, 1978, p. 268).

This process, centering around the concept of the 'gentleman', effectively harmonised relations between industrial capitalist families and the aristocracy:

> The new image of the gentleman provided a magical means of dissolving much of the antagonism between middle and upper

classes which had been such a conspicuous feature of the early nineteenth century. By the end of the century thousands of middle-class Victorians, if asked their social rank, would have unhesitatingly answered not that they belonged to the middle class, but that they were gentlemen. As gentlemen, they identified with the upper classes and joined with them in running the country. (Girouard, 1981, p. 262)

Education

However it came to be expressed, the argument is that aristocratic emulation incapacitated the nation's industrialists and their descendants in so far as endorsement of values of the elite undermined the cut and thrust and calculation required of twentieth century industry. In no sphere was this more important than in education. A predominant theme of 'English decline' theorists is that the rapid growth and establishment of public schools in the mid to late nineteenth century played a major part in the incapability of future industrial leaders. The contention is that public schools, new and old, were subservient to aristocratic ideals and modelled on them. Thus the descendants of factory owners were sent to institutions where they were taught to emulate aristocratic rather than utilitarian models. As such, they were schooled to be 'gentlemen' rather than 'players' (Coleman, 1973), to be people who put values on loyalty, chivalry, tradition, becoming conduct, friendship, community, sportsmanship and character above those of economic individualism, money-making, competitiveness and industrial efficiency.

The generation that grew up during the high summer of English capitalism was, ironically, encouraged to distance itself from the grubby world in which their fathers and grandfathers had created wealth, to be 'so bred that it did not acquire the taste, nor possibly the aptitude, for the world of business' (F. M. L. Thompson, 1963, p. 132). In such schools young gentlemen would be taught that authority ranked over ability, that the team took precedence over the talented individual, that good fellowship was more important than any number of trophies, that engagement in trade was morally inferior to being a gentleman farmer, that the 'practical' was not the vocation of a 'cultured mind' (Girouard, 1981, pp. 163–76). No technology and but little science would be allowed, such that, inevitably, the graduates of such institutions emerged incapable of effectively taking over the reins of industry from their forefathers. According to Austen Albu, 'Of the 5 percent of Cambridge undergraduates who came from business families . . . *none* went into business themselves. To be classical dons, doctors, orchestral conductors, or simply country gentlemen – these were their aspirations' (Albu, 1963, p. 46). Even such an engineering giant as Brunel, the lament goes, felt obliged to send his sons to Harrow, where they would learn that a gentleman 'worked at play and played at work' (Landes, 1969, p. 336).

Worse, continues the story, this situation, found preeminently at the upper levels of society, came to shape profoundly much of the rest. English cultural values, class outlooks, behaviour and aspirations, as well as educational ideals, expressed a *general* disdain for business and technology. Higher education, at the premier levels of Oxford and Cambridge, consistently closed the door, or at the most opened it only reluctantly, to anything smacking of utility (Halsey, 1961), thereby endorsing the aristocratic spirit of the public schools. From the domain of Oxbridge the entire university and school system was polluted by an ethos that relegated practical studies. Most importantly, the 'mere practicality' of technical skills and education came to be identified as the domain of the artisan. Since aristocrats did not produce but ruled, and the role in life of the lower classes was to labour obediently, so it followed that endeavours to establish educational programmes that aspired to give prestige to the technical encountered a powerfully resistant elite culture. Not surprisingly, the Mechanics Institute and provincial universities that did include technical instruction found disdain and unacceptance from the dominant personages and institutions (Simon, 1974).

A corollary of this was the conviction that the arts and humanities were the pinnacle of intellectual endeavour and the necessary accoutrements of the educated 'amateur'. Such aspirations received their theoretical embodiment in the writings of J. S. Mill and of J. H. Newman, for whom 'the purpose of the universities should be a liberal education which he defined as knowledge "which stands on its own pretensions, which is independent of sequel, expects no complement, refuses to be informed (as it is called) by any end, or absorbed into any art"' (Sanderson, 1972, p. 4). University education was not to be functional and in-strumental; its purpose was to incubate the civilised values and beliefs that would act as a cultural beacon for society as a whole. The university was the home of the 'pure' disci-plines (classics, literature, mathematics, philosophy) and the practitioners of the applied disciplines, the technologists and engineers, were looked upon as unwelcome and unworthy intruders.

As the university became an ivory tower, a refuge from the stresses and strains of industry and the market, and a place where the pure cultivation of the mind was to be pre-eminent, so its products emerged into the world of work with particular dispositions. For a tiny few schooled at Eton and Oxford, they were well trained to fulfil the aristocratic role they had been born into. For the rest who had to earn a living their choice of career was stamped with an over-whelmingly negative feature: almost anything except indus-try and technology. For many the orientation was directed by an aristocratic sense of *noblesse oblige*, notably in the form of a (paternalistic) public service ethos (Coleman, 1973, p. 98). The BBC, civil service, even schoolteaching, are popular choices for the university graduates; the sphere of manufacturing still holds few attractions.

The cult of the practical

The aristocratic infection of education was spread, paradox-ically, by forces from another direction which were hostile to education for technical expertise. A result of the fact that the first Industrial Revolution was achieved by practical and uneducated men such as George Stephenson and William Arkwright was the conviction that results could be achieved only by those 'trained to the job', by those prepared to 'get their hands dirty'. A recent historian has described how this mentality was transformed into the

> immutable faith of self-taught ironmasters, coal owners, engine-builders and masters of textile mills that the native British genius of the 'practical man' had put Britain in her place as the world's greatest industrial power, and would keep her there . . . From boardroom to workbench this was the British way; this was seen as the secret of British success. (Barnett, 1986a, p. 210)

From industry there was a marked resistance to allow training to take place off-site and widespread belief that the gulf between the 'academic' and 'practical' was unbridgeable. Gordon Roderick and Michael Stephens make the point that 'Education played no role in the attainment of [Britain's] industrial pre-eminence but could have had a key role in the maintenance of the pre-eminence as the favourable circumstances disappeared one by one' (1978, p. 172). Because those who created the factories and plant were unschooled but successful, there was encouraged in them a profound scepticism towards the value of education, a blinkered vision contrasted with developments in Europe and the USA where technical institutions were being founded of equal status to universities and were being supported and used by industrialists (Roderick and Stephens, 1982).

Moreover, when these practical men did encounter education they brought to it an excessively utilitarian outlook which fed the prejudices of Classics and History dons and made it that much more difficult for science and technology to thrive at the higher levels. On the one hand it led to confirmation that what technical instruction there was should be restricted to tutoring the labouring classes; on the other, it resulted in science itself, and technology especially, having a strained existence where it got inside education. Although 'pure scientific research is akin to other kinds of scholarship [being] disinterested, pursued for its own sake, undeterred by practical considerations or popular opinion', one former Cambridge master observes that the utilitarianism of many who supported scientific education meant it was not endorsed by 'British universities [which] have never quite surrendered the idea of Renaissance Man to the idea of the Research Worker' (Ashby, 1963, pp. 49, 66). Since

> teaching and research in technology are unashamedly tenden-tious today the crude engineer, the mere technologists . . . are tolerated in universities because the state and industry are willing to finance them. Tolerated, but not assimilated; for the traditional don is not yet willing to admit that technologists may have anything intrinsic to contribute to academic life. It is not yet taken for granted that a faculty of technology enriches a university intellectually as well as materially. (Ashby, 1963, p. 66).

Consensus

This explanation of the British malaise is not new, though circumstances have promoted it to greater heights over the last decade. However, what is perhaps most striking about it is not so much that it is a well-rehearsed account of economic decline, but that it finds adherents across the political spectrum. This is so much so that, while presently it is announced and acted upon as a truism by Mrs Thatcher, the leader of the Labour Party parrots that

> the inadequacy and long-term decline of British manufacturing industry is a result of a cultural hostility towards industry, and towards the 'practical man' and the engineer, that originated in the Victorian public schools and older universities. These in-stitutions elevated the classicist at the expense of the tech-nologist, the 'pure' academic . . . at the expense of the practical innovator, and the administrator at the expense of the specialist. The disdain of the public school educated son of the Victorian entrepreneur for industry thrust him into the realms of the Civil Service and the professions (Kinnock, 1986, pp. 133–4)

This is readily accepted on the Left doubtless because it attacks the aristocratic – the privileged – elements of our society. For much the same reasons it is endorsed by Thatcherite radicals.

It echoes too the impatience Harold Wilson showed towards those 'amateur' forces which proved obstacles to Labour's goal of 'modernising' the British economy by way of 'the white heat of technological revolution' in the 1960s. Mr Wilson's irritation found accord with bad-tempered contributors to an *Encounter* symposium in 1963 where the editor raged about:

> The cult of amateurishness and the contempt in which proficiency and expertise are held [which] breed mediocrats by natural selection; the too-keen, the too-clever-by-half, are unfit for survival and are eliminated from the race in which the last to pass the post is winner. Old Struthonians are Amateurs and Gentlemen; they fight rearguard-actions in the merry civil war between Eggheads and Engineers; and they see to it that their sons are educated in the same spirit, by becoming thoroughly immersed in Homer's universe, but not in the universe of Newton. (Koestler, 1963, p. 8).

But the account from the Left which is most congruent with Conservative explanations of the 'English disease' came from Perry Anderson, arguably the leading New Left voice of the 1960s, in an influential and polemical essay published in 1965. Anderson decried the 'amateurism and nepotism' that had spread 'from the councils of state to the inner sanctum of the bourgeoisie itself' (Anderson, 1965, p. 48), had infected British capitalism with a 'universal dilettantism' (p. 49) that was incapable of matching foreign competition, and had meant that 'science and technique went by the board' (p. 50). 'The English bourgeoisie', continued Anderson, 'had never been outstanding for its devotion to technological and scientific education . . . [because] In the mid-nineteenth century, the burgeoning middle class sold its birthright for the accent of a gentleman' (pp. 49–50). This apeing of the aristocracy by the bourgeoisie meant that the 'highly skilled technocrats' (p. 49) demanded by 'neo-capitalism' were not produced. At the head of the corporation and state remained a 'ruling bloc [which] was trained to rule, and did so; but a century later its skills had become mere manners, and its manners, increasingly, affectation' (p. 50).

The last extract identifies the cause of Britain's anti-industrial ethos, the emulation of an aristocracy which had survived from the seventeenth century. In his most recent essay, Anderson iterates his 1960s theme, that in the late nineteenth century there was secreted

> a deeply conformist and conservative cult of countryside and club, tradition and constitution, as a predominant outlook among the intelligentsia, repudiating bourgeois origins and miming seigneurial postures in a synthetic gentility and ruralism extending far into the 20th century. (Anderson, 1987, p. 41)

To explain the continuity of the aristocracy Anderson is entirely in agreement with the orthodoxy: the Civil War was 'primarily fought *within* and not *between* classes' (Anderson, 1965, p. 15). So while it did away with feudalism, it 'left almost the entire social structure intact' (p. 15) and 'landed aristocrats, large and small, continued to rule England' (p. 16). The eighteenth century agrarian revolution was led and facilitated by the 'landed aristocracy [which] had . . . become its own capitalist class' (p. 17), one eager to pioneer commercial farming, so much so as to make 'Britain the most agriculturally efficient country in the world' (p. 16). Manufacturers and the nobility clashed in the early days of the Industrial Revolution, but the 'late Victorian era and the high noon of imperialism welded aristocracy and bourgeoisie together in a single social bloc' (p. 29). The consequence is an educational system incapable of matching the technical expertise of the Germans and French, blockage of meritocrats by an old-boy network cemented in privileged school and university where is produced an 'unspecialised, gentlemanly elitism' (Adelstein, 1969, p. 63) which wallows in 'the suffocating traditionalism of English life' (Anderson, 1965, p. 22).

Kinnock, Wilson and Anderson's analyses unavoidably push them towards the advocacy of science, technology and 'modernisation' as the antidote to Britain's economic decline and they identify, inescapably, education as the key means by which this will be brought about. An endeavour to combat patrician values has been tried on several occasions in the post-war years, always the aim being to harmonise business needs and education; always the policy being premised on the view that education to date has been diverted from valuable work by 'pseudo-aristocratic' pretensions. Anthony Crosland, the minister responsible for creating technical universities and vocationally-oriented polytechnics, was sensitive to the role of education for adaptation to the then latest 'technological revolution' (Crosland, 1956, pp. 258–77). As Dick Atkinson has argued,

> each succeeding wave of politicians and governments has sought to increase control over all levels of education. It has done so with the purpose ... of relating education to economic and technological development. (Atkinson, 1972, p. 43)

The objective has been to break with elitist and impractical attitudes in favour of a 'modern' technocratic and managerial ethos.

Over the last decade, however, the most significant definers of the 'English malaise', those who have had the opportunity and will to act upon their diagnosis, have been on the political Right. The intellectual origins of their position are worth tracing to highlight the affinity of Left and Right as regards identifying the problem.

Sir Keith Joseph was a leading architect of the New Right that has come to be known as Thatcherism and he commenced his design with a dramatic announcement. Although he had joined the Conservative Party in the early 1950s, 'it was only in April 1974 that I was converted to Conservatism' (Joseph, 1975, p. 4). After the defeat of the Heath government a month or so earlier, members of the Conservative Party were willing to reconsider their postulates and Sir Keith tried to convert them to his way of thinking. In the aftermath of electoral failure emerged a new Conservatism which took its stance not only against the traditional socialist enemy, but also against long-standing members of its own ranks. As Sir Keith endorsed monetarist economics and commenced an unabashed 'campaign for capitalism' (p. 63) that found virtue in the market, in the self-striving entrepreneur, and opposition to the 'nanny state', he announced a new populist Conservatism that, distinctively individualist and go-getting, was scornful of the 'gentlemanly' creed of one-nation Conservatism that had held sway for so long.

He went on to identify six 'poisons' that were stultifying economic progress, one of which was an 'anti-enterprise culture'. Expressive of this creed, one which put the emphasis on community stability rather than competitive advantage, were paternalistic Conservatives that a few years earlier had been admired; later their successors were to be scorned as 'wets'. Sir Keith was sure that the English malaise had its roots deep in a history of emulation of the British aristocracy:

> Britain never really internalised capitalist values, if the truth be known. For four centuries . . . the rich man's aim was to get away from the background of trade – later industry – in which he had made his wealth and power. Rich and powerful people founded landed-gentry families; the capitalist's son was educated not in capitalist values but against them, in favour of the older values of army, church, upper civil service, professions, and land-owning. This avoided the class struggle between middle and upper strata families for European history – but at what a cost? (Joseph, 1975, pp. 60–61)

Mrs Thatcher won office in 1979 and 1983 determined that this 'gentlemanly' culture at last would be assailed. An attack long since encouraged by the Left was now to be led by a Radical Right which was 'smiting Toryism hip and thigh' (Beer, 1982, p. 178). Sir Keith Joseph occupied the Industry ministry for a while, but he moved soon to Education where he could make inroads into institutions largely responsible for inculcating attitudes and values. Having long endorsed the argument that the privileged in Britain were a halter to 'modernization', the Left had no credible response to the New Conservative endeavour to purge education of its 'anti-enterprise' values and reshape it to suit the needs of an economy deep in crisis.

Sir Keith's policies in education were helped by a changing intellectual climate to which he himself had contributed. His input had been centred in the political arena, but academics were active in elaborating his argument. Defending his Green Paper to the Commons the Education Minister could justify his policies by observing that 'The criticism of many historians has been that this country has failed to provide technical education in schools and higher education' (*Hansard*, no. 139, 21 May 1985, col. 870). Two historians in particular – Martin Wiener and Corelli Barnett – had been prominent in giving intellectual credibility to the thesis that British culture, through its distain for the practical and admiration for the aristocratic, had created an education system incapable of producing economically effective results. Let us review arguments they forwarded that have become the conventional wisdom of the 1980s.

Martin Wiener and Corelli Barnett

Martin Wiener, an American academic, identified what he terms 'pseudo-aristocratic' attitudes and values as hostile to economic growth. He argues that because England 'never had a straightforwardly bourgeois or industrial elite' (Wiener, 1981, p. 8), what developed in the nineteenth century was 'a new dominant bourgeois culture bearing the imprint of the old aristocracy' (p. 10) which choked off the 'industrial spirit' essential for success in an epoch of growing international competition and technological sophistication.

Wiener believes that it is suspicion of change – especially of technological innovation and commercial adaptation – that has brought us to our present predicament of decline and stagnation. This is the disease that lies at the heart of the ailing condition of the nation. 'For a long time', writes Wiener, 'the English have not felt comfortable with "progress" . . . The English nation even became ill at ease enough with its prodigal progeny to deny its legitimacy by adopting a conception of Englishness that virtually excludes "industrialisation"' (p. 5). Country retreats, anti-American sentiment, the poetry of Blake and Betjeman, Dickens' novels, World War Two songs, suburban growth, the mellow Conservatism of Baldwin and Macmillan, Tudor-style housing estates, Priestley's distaste for advertising, Churchill's choice of metaphor, Kipling's eulogies on Sussex . . .

all are drawn together, assembled for inspection and arraigned with the same charge – voices and expressions of an industrial nation that has failed to accommodate to industrial advance.

From the outset of industrialisation, contends Wiener, there were forces inside British society working to subvert its logic and blunt its consequences. Nowhere were they more powerfully ensconced and determined than in the education system where they transmitted assiduously an image of true England as a pastoral antithesis to urban industrialisation and where they functioned to produce scholars gentlemanly in learning and manners. It was, says Wiener, 'particularly the rooting of pseudo-aristocratic attitudes and values in upper-middle-class educated opinion [which] shaped an unfavourable context for economic endeavour' (p. 10). From the playing fields of Eton, Westminster and Rugby seeped out a poison which has been drunk with profound consequences for economic standing by the entire state education system. Because the 'ancient public schools' were estabished as '*the* model of secondary education for all who aspired to rise in English society' (p. 17) the state schools that followed in their wake 'developed a curriculum, an outlook, and forms of organization in line with the education of the gentry' (p. 22). The need for reform via education was perceived by many but, continues Wiener, the 'pseudo-aristocratic' grip has remained firm:

New institutions have been created – universities, polytechnics and so on – which have been meant to educate people into a much more technological and competitive ethos. But they have gradually turned into copies of the old ones, with the same anti-materialist values. (Wiener, *in* Allison, 1983, p. 275)

Wiener, whose book has been 'widely quoted by people prescribing educational reform' (ibid), considers that the real 'obstacle to British economic "redevelopment" may well be the continuing resistance of cultural values and attitudes' (Wiener, 1981, p. 161). 'It may be,' he concludes, 'that Margaret Thatcher will find her most fundamental challenge not in holding down the money supply or inhibiting government spending, or even in fighting the shop stewards, but in changing this frame of mind' (p. 166).

Wiener's review was followed by a more scholarly and sustained book by Corelli Barnett (cf. Anderson, 1987, pp. 46–7). *The Audit of War* (1986) was also considerably more polemical, condemnatory and strident in tone. It recited much the same theme as Wiener, but in a more urgent and less tolerant tone that harmonised well with the increasing assertiveness of those convinced that the 'English disease' stemmed from defective values. The unmistakable reason for decline, feels Barnett, is that 'too much of British private enterprise simply lacks enterprise' (1975, p. 901) which itself stems from there being 'something deeply amiss with the British character, British national attitudes, British institutions' (Ibid).

Barnett claims that even during the 1939–1945 war Britain was a less industrially efficient country than Germany or America. Despite the 'people's self-congratulation' (1986a, p. 51) about the achievements of planning and the harmonization of science and technology during the struggle, Britain 'even in the crisis of total war had manifested the classic symptoms of what was later to be dubbed the "British disease"' (Ibid). Worse, the nation in 1945 went ahead and rewarded itself for victory by establishing the Welfare State – without having the industrial base to pay for it. The National Health Service, Social Security and the like came into being too early, destined to become 'a prior charge on the national income of ever monstrous size . . . uncontrollably guzzling taxes which might have gone into productive investment' (p. 241). The folly was that the British opted for the Welfare State before it had been earned: 'Instead of starting with a new workshop so as to become rich enough to afford a new family villa, John Bull opted for the villa straightaway – even though he happened to be bankrupt at the time' (pp. 246–7).

Barnett argues that a certain type of person was responsible for this financial madness, a type that was active especially during the war, spurring on the populace with wild promises of a 'New Jerusalem', a genus Barnett collectively labels 'the "enlightened" establishment' (p. 11). The 'romantics' who pioneered the welfare state – chiefly Labour Party adherents but all 'evangelists' – were *privileged* (Barnett insistently names leading figures, adding in parenthesis their private schooling and Oxbridge college), *impractical* ('not one of them had ever had experience of running any kind of operation in the real world in which Britain competed commercially in peacetime and fought for its very life in wartime' (p. 18)), and *elitist* (Barnett asserts that the public did not want the Welfare State which was the 'highminded gift' that the likes of Beveridge 'proceeded successfully to press on the British people between 1940–1945' (p. 19)).

Our military historian sees the Welfare State as symptomatic of Britain's demise, but he traces the causes further back. First he castigates the predecessors of the likes of Sir William Beveridge ('the Field Marshal Montgomery of social welfare' (p. 26)) whom he regards as unworldly moralists, unduly tainted by Christian ethics which fly in the face of sound business sense. These people had an especial influence on education as a whole, an influence motivated by attitudes they had acquired at their own public schools. Barnett repeats the familiar refrain:

> it is in the nature of the Victorian public school that we find the other key factor explaining why Britain was so low and so inadequate in educating for industrial capability. The Victorian public school was inspired by the religious and moral ideals of the Romantic Movement. It turned away from the realities of the industrial world of the era and from such topics as science and technology. (Barnett, 1979, p. 121)

Good enough for turning out 'Christian gentleman able to govern the Empire and ornament the ancient professions like the Church and the Law' (p. 122), the public schools were hopeless in producing really useful people.

From these institutions 'the Victorian crusade against a useful or technical education' (1986a, p. 214) spread and its 'victory . . . for a "liberal education" must be accounted one of the crucial factors in Britain's loss of technological leadership' (ibid, p. 220). It led to a willingness to 'manipulate money' (Barnett, 1975, p. 908) in the City, and to enter 'public service' with enthusiasm, but it engendered the habit of despising technology and industry. Worse, the ethos was carried throughout state-funded elementary and secondary education, concluding with a system entirely impractical where

> Every 'failure' who left school at sixteen or seventeen – with a smattering of Latin or English literature, a smidgin of religious knowledge, some history learned by heart and a few dry morsels of the laws of physics and the formulae of chemistry was therefore a living tribute to the success achieved . . . by the evangelists of an academic 'liberal education'. (Barnett, 1986a, p. 227)

Barnett does not restrict himself to lambasting the privileged. He also turns on the philistine in the shape of the practical man whose very engagement with the nuts and bolts 'carried with it a positive mistrust of the application of intellectual study and scientific research to industrial operations; a deep suspicion of the very kind of theoretically grounded professional for which Britain's rivals looked right from the start' (1986a, p. 210). The self-made men carry responsibility for the 'English disease' because they were unwilling to train their workforce or to be trained themselves in advanced technological skills.

If on one side we see the privileged distorting education by designing it as an unworldly escape, and if on another we witness philistine industrialists refusing to provide the sort of education their businesses required, then Barnett sees on another the negative contribution of the proletariat whom he regards as an unskilled, uncooperative and recalitrant group. Peering with the unsympathetic eye of the 'military historian' (p. 188), he proclaims that the British working class is one of the most grievous handicaps to efficient industry because it is 'too largely composed of coolies, with the psychology and primitive culture to be expected of coolies' (p. 187).

Barnett believes that the British working class was created in times so harsh that, without an ameliorating state, its formative experience embittered it, exacerbating class consciousness and helping to develop an oppositional culture that echoes the lifestyle of 'the Bantu coolies of South Africa still alive today' (p. 189). Indeed he avers that

> It is impossible to exaggerate the long-term consequences . . . of the experience of the workforce in the factory towns of late Georgian and early Victorian Britain under conditions of ferocious competition and uncontrolled exploitation. (1975, p. 904)

Developing the 'mentality of a self-contained tribe' (Barnett, 1986a, p. 70) has incubated inward-looking values in its members. For this reason Barnett indicts the British working class for restrictive practices, shoddy work, high rates of absenteeism, lack of ambition, and unwillingess to adapt. He even blames their 'tribalism' for poor health and high mortality rates which result from 'housewifely incompetence and unwise priorities' (p. 193) reflected in the 'ignorant choices' of 'unskilled mothers' whose 'tribal' upbringing led to 'domestic incapability' that only came into the open with the mass evacuations during 1939 and 1940. Any attempt to raise the skills and expectations of this 'coolie' class was going to meet with surliness; that given by the elites 'concerned itself as much with religious indoctrination as with the basic skills of the three R's' (p. 224). Education adequate to produce a workforce capable of matching the Germans failed yet again.

Barnett considers that where state officials did intervene in education they applied the tenets of the gentlemanly ideal to the lower orders and, perhaps worse, were unwilling and incapable of creating a coherent and integrated national education system. Burdened by a suspicion of centralisation, the architects of British education moved only at a piecemeal and dilatory pace to establish what were, on the whole, anti-industrial schools. Moreover, looking at leading civil servants within and even beyond the education office, Barnett detects the 'Whitehall mandarin' (p. 215) whose characteristics did much to hinder business efficacy. Aloof from the discipline of the market and assured of a knighthood, it was possible for civil servants to at once despise industry's 'box-wallahs' (p. 221) and themselves to favour the temperament of the 'academic rather than the man of action' (p. 215), to be 'more redolent of the stateliness of the striped trouser than the dynamism of the rolled-up sleeve' (p. 267). These state bureaucrats, their 'minds judicious, balanced and cautious rather than operational and engaged' (p. 215), signally failed to produce the determined, industrially and commercially sound policies a Britain in decline required.

Thus concludes Corelli Barnett's prosecution. The privileged, the practical, the proletariat and the patrician have conspired, unwillingly perhaps, to bring about the malaise we see all around. Today our historian snorts at the failure of the New Jerusalem to establish even effective welfare services, their shortcomings revealing 'a dream turned to a dank reality of a segregated, subliterate, unskilled, unhealthy and institutionalised proletariat hanging on the nipple of state maternalism' (1986a, p. 304).

This is a language most appropriate for Thatcher's Britain with its determination to break with the flabby consensus that remained in place from 1945 to 1979. Barnett's recommendations also strike a chord. Thus in a recent piece for *Management Today* he contends that 'Japanese, American and German technological growth has not merely *depended* on a superb national education and training system at all levels, it has been *driven* by it' (Barnett, 1986b, p. 139). Conversely, British education has hindered technology and commercial success. The advocacy follows ineluctably: Barnett urges government to 'thrust a stake through the living corpse of Victorian education' (quoted in *THES*, 26 September 1986) since 'it is upon our national education that largely depends whether our hundred-year-old decline is to be reversed, or whether it will continue, and not merely continue, but continue to accelerate' (Barnett, 1975, p. 914). Education for the market, spearheaded by a shift to disciplines that are technologically advanced and commercially applicable, is Barnett's order. Our military man wants a decisive assault mounted on the education system led by a resolute government that will rise to the challenge to grasp central command, will ignore the advice of vacillating and faint-hearted civil servants, and will issue directives for deep

cuts in 'liberal education' in order to reinforce the vocationally relevant. Alongside must come drastic reductions of
the burden of the Welfare State in order to support 'productive investment' (1986a, p. 241). Nothing less than this –
centralisation, instrumentalism, vocationalism – will be required if Britain intends to be a world-beating industrial
country. Nothing less than this is the ambition of the
Thatcher government. Corelli Barnett has found his Com-
mander-in-Chief.

The failure of education

In recent years, as politicians have struggled to revive the
fortunes of a badly ailing economy, the view that these
attitudes and the institutions which ensure their continuation
have caused the decline of the economy has taken a powerful hold. Invariably responsibility for the 'English malaise' is
laid at the door of the education system. The *Financial
Times* avers that Britain's 'state education system has always
been biased against practical subjects in favour of "liberal"
ones' (Lorenz, 1982) and it joins a chorus of corporate
leaders who complain of a 'cultural environment' in which
'the educational bias against the business community insidiously colours the attitudes of those entering the Civil
Service, the professions and, more especially, the academic
world so the prejudice is recycled' (Porter, 1984, p. 45).

The values and ideals of liberal education (à la Newman),
it is argued, are not conducive to the industrial spirit and the
commercial ethos. Before the gaze of those who aspire to
make Britain great again, the schools and universities are
seen as corrupting and debilitating forces. They are what is
wrong with society, and it is the unworldly humanities that
are singled out for abuse. 'Schools still impel children to the
liberal arts and pure science and not enough towards technology' (Kennaway, 1981, p. 17). It is education that is
responsible for the loss of English economic supremacy
because 'while English education remained sterile, deliberately detached from possible application to everyday life, it
was different in the countries destined to become our chief

industrial competitors' (Ibid). Education today remains hopelessly impractical: 'in the post-war era we have seen the prestige of the liberal arts triumph again in the new Lego universities of the 1960s – as if Britain were to be saved by sociologists any more than by classicists' (Barnett, in *THES*, 26 September 1986, p. 8). It follows that this 'entrenched' system must be reformed root and branch that industry may thrive.

To be sure, attempts to break with education's 'pseudo-aristocratic' pretensions have been tried before, notably in the 1960s when the Labour government created the polytechnics and new universities. But now, in the eighties, the stakes are higher. The suffocating pressure of a deep depression and overwhelming market competition on a global scale threaten to push Britain into 'Third World status' (NEDC, 1984). The Thatcher government, aware of the magnitude of the problem and determined to end post-war fudging, is pressing to put an end to ivory tower attitudes and to replace them with a new utilitarian education system that functions smoothly in response to the needs of industry. As a matter of course now politicians denigrate 'an educational system which has scant concern for the outside world' (Young, 1985c, p. 9) and which must 'contribute more effectively to the improvement of the performance of economy'. The arguments of Wiener and Barnett, and several lesser luminaries, consonant with the times, have been seized with alacrity by those who would impose on education the burden of reviving the British economy from the depths.

Coda

We have sketched in this chapter elements of the 'English disease' thesis as a means of highlighting its role for those who would introduce major changes into education. It would be appropriate to stop at this stage were it not for the fact that the thesis has established such a powerful hold on politicians and even educationalists. The diagnosis being accepted, it is difficult for those encountering policies premised on its validity to resist with conviction. Briefly then, we suggest reasons why the 'English disease' argument is unacceptable as an account of the decline of Britain.

• One difficulty with the thesis is the claim that successful industrialists were assimilated into an open aristocracy. The detailed review by Lawrence and Jeanne Stone (1984) concludes that this is a myth such that between 1540 and 1880 'only a small handful of very rich merchants succeeded in buying their way into the elite' (p. 402). This, of course, does not mean that aristocratic values could not permeate the manufacturing classes, but it does cast doubt on those who would emphasise the aristocracy's willingess to absorb the *nouveaux riches* and thereby wean them from out-and-out capitalism.

• The 'English disease' argument has it that, while aristocrats in the eighteenth century spearheaded agrarian capitalism, during the industrial period they hindered it. A problem here is to explain how aristocrats can be avid capitalists at one time while negative towards capitalism later on. Wiener (1981) does distinguish 'rentier' and 'productive' capitalism, but it is unclear why the former should be less authentically capitalist than the latter. What we can be sure of is that, from being capitalist pioneers, the aristocrats, *without changing their ways*, are said to have become burdens to capitalism without the 'English malaise' theorists telling us how and why.

• The thesis of 'English malaise' hinges on the notion that *industrial* capitalism is the key to continued success and that upper class distaste for this weakened the economy. The approach is willing to concede that public school products went into the City (without explaining why aristocratic products could happily engage in this commerce if the values to which they subscribed were disdainful of 'mere money-making'), but its fixation with the notion that successful capitalism must be production-based blinds it to the possibility that a sound capitalist economy can be engaged primarily in finance. The 'English disease' theorists are trapped in the dogma that manufacture provides the base to capitalist structures, yet there is no reason why a capitalist society cannot thrive when grounded in services.

• The thesis does not allow for the possibility that people may pursue their interests irrespective of their ideologies, though it seems to us reasonable to suppose that 'gentlemen' on the boards of corporations have not felt unduly constrained by a chivalric code. Indeed, comparative evidence suggests that American and English business leaders do not act in business decisions in any significantly different ways (cf. Jamieson, 1980).

• Similarly, the charge that the 'pseudo-aristocratic' ethos debilitated English elites does not take seriously the question that it was an ideology which served to convince themselves (and others?) of the appropriateness of their lifestyle *without* significantly affecting their economic interests. The doctrine of 'social duty', Leonore Davidoff argues, 'continued to be used to justify what could be looked at as an intensely selfish way of life based on leisure, sport, dining and entertainment, long after its country estate context had faded away' (1973, p. 39).

• The thesis, notably as delineated by Barnett, assumes that the market economy is the most appropriate way of conducting affairs. He contends that British culture has weakened the country's capacity to hold its own in the international economy, but a serious question is why should the domestic economy have to operate in a game that, as a requirement of entry, demands commitment to commerce?

• The 'English disease' thesis does not appreciate that the typical businessman is not, and never was, a 'gentleman'. As Eric Hobsbawm (1968) points out:

> the actual management of medium-sized firms (the sort of people who would in 1860–1890 certainly have been owner-managers) contains not ... much more than one in four who have been to a public school, including not more than one in twenty who have been to one of the top twenty or so public schools. (p. 156)

• Moreover, against the preoccupation of 'English malaise' writers with 'aristocratic' values, there is considerable evidence to suggest that Victorian industrialists – and a wider public – had great enthusiasm for *laissez-faire* principles and for the splendours of technological advance (Harrison, 1957). Recent surveys find a similar commitment to technological innovation in Britain (Daniel, 1986).

• The thesis does not seriously examine alternative accounts of decline, notably economic, thereby becoming monocausal and simplistic.

• More generally, but perhaps most importantly, the thesis is developed in an excessively impressionistic way, drawing at once on literary productions, parliamentary speeches, statements of art critics and television advertisements. This can give it a superficial plausibility, yet it is striking that nowhere is it demonstrated that a given attitude resulted in a particular decision.

Further, the argument constructs stereotypical types abstracted from context, such that what is depicted is an unworldly romantic who is countered, implicitly, with the equally abstracted enterprising, technology-oriented entrepreneur. Were real people actually like that? Did 'gentlemanly' codes really – consistently and motivated by principle – affect business decisions? Perhaps they did, though the 'English disease' theorists provide little evidence of it.

• Finally, the delineation of education as an unworldly ivory tower is a gross over-simplification, since there is ample evidence of extensive industry-academe collaboration from early in the nineteenth century (Sanderson, 1972).

6

Education for what Jobs?

' "We go upon the practical mode of teaching, Nickleby; the regular education system. C-l-e-a-n, verb active, to make bright, to scour. W-i-n, win, d-e-r, der, winder, a casement. When the boy knows this out of book, he goes and does it. It's the same principle as the use of the globes. Where's the second boy?"

"Please, sir, he's weeding the garden", replied a small voice.

"To be sure", said Squeers, by no means disconcerted.

"So he is, b-o-t, bot, t-i-n, tin, bottin, n-e-y, ney, bottiney, noun substantive, a knowledge of plants. When he has learned that bottiney means a knowledge of plants, he goes and knows 'em. That's our system, Nickleby: what do you think of it?" ' (Charles Dickens, *Nicholas Nickleby*)

Introduction

The two previous chapters have demonstrated that education is set to undergo decisive changes in the 1980s. The direction in which this change is heading is also clear: schools, colleges and universities are *en route* to being more closely involved with the 'real world' that graduates will be better equipped to play a full part in the wider society. A new mood, backed by funding strategies and organisational rearrangements, is evident in the education system: course design gives greater credence to the 'needs of industry', 'work experience' has taken on an urgency in curriculum development, and local businesses are invited into classrooms where their views on course form and content are solicited so that the school's products can better suit the requirements of employers.

We have seen too government determination to push education towards this end with integrated policies of expenditure reductions, increased central direction and an emphasis on instrumental goals for schools and colleges (Lawton, 1984). Cuts, control and training are dominant themes of British education in the present period, refrains that have been amplified by claims that education has contributed to our economic and social malaise by its promotion of the 'anti-industrial' culture which we described in Chapter 5.

At the storm centre of these developments is the issue of Information Technology (Cherrington, 1987). From the premise that quantum leaps in computer communications have decisively altered economic conditions and prospects, it has followed that all around must rapidly adjust. Education, perhaps more than any other sphere, must move especially fast to come to terms with this pre-eminently 'real world' phenomenon. Its history of cloistered elitism and disdain for the technological bodes ill, but education must respond, not only because I.T. is of such import that everything and everyone will be influenced, willing or not, but also because education has the prime responsibility to society as a whole of delivering the skilled and competent personnel required to manage the 'Information Society' into which we are tumbling.

Government plans to restructure and thereby revitalise an ailing economy hinged on I.T. being efficiently and effectively introduced wherever it may save money, increase productivity and stimulate market advantage. Once this is achieved, so runs the argument, the additonal growth will ensure that there are jobs for the unemployed. This strategy demands that technically proficient people are made available to ease and speed the adoption of advanced technology and it is here that education is called upon to make an essential contribution. As a recent Minister of Education has it, 'The ability of the education system to match the needs of the information society for highly educated people has now become the main determinant of a country's employment prospects' (Williams, 1985, pp. 74–5).

Although economic recovery will be led by the computer scientists and electronic engineers, it is argued that in the 'information economy' no-one will be able to stand aside from computerisation. A recurrent theme in educational and political circles is that 'computer literacy' will be an essential qualification for work – and life itself – in the 'post-industrial' society (ITAP, 1986, p. 12, passim). For this reason Kenneth Baker instructs that 'All children as they leave school should have skills in electronic keyboard techniques so that they can operate the electronic gadgetry of this revolution since it is going to have such a dominating effect upon their lives' (Baker, 1983, p. 5). Without keyboard skills, without facility in computer techniques, school-leavers will find themselves unemployable in an era in which automation will have made unskilled, and even semi-skilled, jobs disappear. This vocational imperative, the argument that 'computer illiteracy' will ensure permanent unemployment for huge numbers, has been an especially powerful mobiliser of teachers and lecturers. With unemployment high, particularly amongst the young (under twenty-four-year-olds accounted for 37 per cent of the total workless in 1986), and a widespread feeling that it will remain so in the foreseeable future, teachers feel anxious that their charges will be less employable than they might be should they fail to help them acquire requisite skills.

Educationalists have responded to the call and have set about developing programmes that will provide really useful skills which will appeal to employers. Schools and colleges have bought quantities of micros and software packages (the average British school now has a dozen micros at secondary level), many have participated in initiatives that aim to give pupils direct experience of the working environment, the further education sector has leapt aboard Manpower Services Commission schemes that have been designed to instill proficiencies relevant to employment, higher education institutes have created a variety of degrees in I.T. and cognate disciplines, and the Council for National Academic Awards has instructed all subject areas that it validates to incorporate I.T. into their teaching (CNAA, 1982). It is safe to say that in 1989 there is scarcely a school in the country without its micro and quota of teachers that has undergone a course in computer awareness. Already the changes have been formalised, the Associated Examining Board, for instance, announcing new forms of assessment for school-leavers which measure 'basic skills of use to employers', prominent among which is a 'computer awareness test . . . to enable young people to see the computer in its contemporary context, to develop a positive attitude towards using computers and to be able to use the computer' (Hodges, 1985).

Of course education has not acted entirely of its own volition. Government, convinced of the urgency of having a population that is 'computer literate', and apprehensive of Britain's declining competitiveness, has pressured assiduously on a number of fronts to ensure that schools and colleges enter the 'Information Age'. If one sought for a symbol of its priorities, one could choose the creation of a Minister of Information Technology, Kenneth Baker, in the early 1980s, and his elevation soon after to Minister of Education. In the transition Mr Baker has not changed his tune: throughout he has hymned the praises of the computer revolution and urged national responsiveness that pays special attention to education. A roll-call of government initiatives suggests the importance it places on I.T.: the Microelectronics Education Programme (1980–86), Micros in Schools (1981–84), the Information Technology Initiative launched in 1982, Information Technology Education Centres, and City Technology Colleges. These are the most conspicuous elements of government endeavours to promote I.T. in the curriculum, but it should be noted that less obvious, though still pertinent, have been 'steers' of funds away from arts, humanities and social sciences towards technological disciplines, the establishment in 1983 of the Technical and Vocational Education Initiative aimed at harmonising school and work which puts technical competences to the fore, the designation in Youth Training Schemes of 'computer literacy' as a 'core skill', and other Manpower Services Commission schemes that account for a quarter of further education provision in the UK and carry with them a skill-oriented emphasis. Since all of these developments have entailed financial support, it is not surprising that educationalists, starved of funds in most areas, have been enthusiastic to participate.

Because the 'needs of industry' have been the subject of so much of the debate it is to be expected that captains of industry have been given time and opportunity to offer their diagnoses of education's failings and their recommendations for reform. As depression has continued unabated industry's requirements have come to be regarded as synonymous with those of the commonweal. 1986, for instance, was announced as *Industry Year*, and heralded by no less than three ministers of state as an opportunity to make tighter the 'closer links' between schools and employers that 'have been our constant aim' since 'we need a new and enhanced relevance in the work of our schools to prepare young people for adult and working life' (DES, March 1986, Foreword). Predictably, industrialists have not been slow to perceive a 'technological revolution which necessitates a high level of technical education if Britain is not to lose out to her competitors' (Goldsmith, 1984, p. 34) and to pronounce on the necessity of education to 'train people in science and technology for real-life situations' (Durham, 1984, p. 18).

In addition, it is noticeable that there is frequently a shift from the narrow concern to train children and students how to use a particular computer package to a much wider set of requirements. A curious slippage takes place whereby calls for 'computer literacy' translate into complaints that there is insufficient attention given to 'technology' of all sorts in education institutions. Then, by an easy extension, this moves on to identification of deficiencies as regards 'numeracy' amongst school-leavers. It continues to complain about an array of dispositions that range from lack of awareness of 'industry', to incapacities of 'communication' and 'elucidation', and attitudinal shortcomings as regards 'enterprise'. Behind calls for 'computer literacy' trail all manner of assertions and insistences about education, all of which, taken singly, are contentious and challengeable. Nonetheless, because of the novelty and presence of I.T., because 'the speed at which technology changes . . . mean[s] that education, training and re-training throughout life will become more important' (Baker, 1982, p. 11), because 'It is essential that the youngsters of today should be taught the skills of tomorrow' (p.·12), because of all this, a whole series of demands can be imposed upon education in the name of adjustment to the 'information technology revolution'. Because I.T.'s *hereness* is so often the starting point for those who want to rearrange education in profound ways, it is appropriate that we question the rationales presented for 'computer literacy' initiatives. In no area is it more pressing than to query the alleged connection between employment and training in I.T.

Computer training and jobs

(i) Blaming the victim

'Everywhere countries are clamouring for new-technology skills', 'The British skills shortage is particularly severe' (Williams, 1985, p. 139). These statements are the conventional wisdom in Britain today, and any educationalist reading these pages will hear echoes of other conversations in the words of the Oxfordshire headteacher who rationalises the inclusion of microcomputers in his school on grounds that 'In ten years time even lathes will be operated by computers – therefore they [pupils] need to know keyboard skills and how computerisation works' (Starsmore, 1987, p. 10). In a few moments we consider the question of the relation between advanced technology and skills, but here it must be stated forcefully that the argument that education has a vocational spin-off – 'there are jobs out there going begging for those with appropriate skills!' – has the unfortunate, though politically useful, effect of blaming the unemployed for their unemployment. Talk of 'skills shortages', and such talk is pervasive whenever the issue of I.T. is raised, unavoidably focuses upon the supply side of labour and necessarily posits that the fundamental problem is the deficiency of that supply – that is, potential employees lack the requisite skills to perform the jobs that are available.

During the 1930s depression Orwell noticed that the middle classes often talked about 'lazy idle loafers on the dole' who 'could all find work if they wanted to' (Orwell, 1937, p. 76). Today there remains something of this sentiment – 'social security scroungers' and 'on yer bike' are updates of older themes and Jeffrey Archer's recent complaint that the young unemployed were 'quite unwilling to put in a day's work' (Archer, 1985) would have been familiar to Jeffrey Farnol. But more common is to concentrate on the lack of qualities possessed by those in search of work that makes them, alas, unemployable. If only, goes the line, if only these people had received training in advanced technology, then they would readily find employment in the 'sunrise' industries that are, tragically, being held back from success because of shortages of skilled staff.

Against this, it cannot be said too often that the problem of unemployment is not with the labour supply but with the lack of demand for labour; that the problem lies not with the unfortunates who seek employment, but with the lack of openings in the job market. Bluntly, unemployment is structural because of a slump in the advanced capitalist economies such that in Britain the number of vacancies, officially put at around 150 000 – leaving aside the important variables of location, age, gender and remuneration – is massively outweighed by the official (under)estimates of over three million workless. The unemployed can scarcely be blamed for their plight since 'it is the lack of vocations rather than the lack of training which is the source of difficulty' (Barker, 1983, p. 4). Nonetheless, the talk, heard from employers, politicians and teachers, about education in I.T. being an investment in a job helps shift the blame for unemployment away from structural issues back to the personal, to the 'what-do-you-expect-studying-divinity?' kind of argument. This is a classic instance of 'blaming the victim'.

In effect it says to the sixteen-year-olds of Sunderland and Swansea that their difficulties stem not from the closure of shipyards, factories and coalmines, but from within, from their failure to apply themselves at school and in technical college to appropriating the skills 'of use to industry'. If they find themselves useless today, then it is not the fault of industry which is desperate for 'computer literate' personnel. Unemployment is their personal responsibility, so let them dwell on that rather than ponder why recession should have decimated their locality. It should not be surprising that these people frequently retreat into themselves, lose their self-confidence, feel impotent and despondent, begin to conceive of themselves as personal failures (cf. Coffield *et al.*, 1986, pp. 56–85). Orwell expressed amazement when he discovered that many of the unemployed whom he encountered were ashamed of being unemployed. Why should we remain amazed 50 years on when the insistent message from on high is that plenty of work is available for those who achieve qualifications in I.T.?

The computers-as-passport-to-work story can raise false hopes amongst those most concerned to get a job. For instance, when Lord Young spoke recently to the Society of Education Officers he was reported as saying that 'Too many [school-leavers] were emerging from eleven years of compulsory education without a single qualification that employers would accept' (*The Guardian*, 26 January 1985). This has to be interpreted as the sort of advice that pupils should take up I.T. courses if they hope to find work. But does anyone seriously think that, even if all the young emerged with I.T. skills, there are three million vacancies in computer science and electronic engineering? Can it really be mooted that the recession is caused by a mischannelling of talents in the schools? Fantastic, yet this is the logic of those occupied with Youth Training Schemes which claim that proper training will lead to employability.

There are figures readily available which give the lie to claims that I.T. skills are the answer to youth unemployment. In 1980 the Electronic Computers Sector Working Party of the National Economic Development Council found a shortage of 25 000 people with computer-related skills (of whom about 16 000 were programmers and analysts) (NEDC, 1980); four years on the Information

Technology Skills Shortage Committee at the Department of Trade and Industry reported a shortfall of 1500 I.T. graduates (chiefly computing, physics, and electronic engineering) that could rise to 5000 by 1988 (I.T. Skills Shortage Committee, 1984); and in 1985 a House of Lords Select Committee concluded that by 1990 Britain might be short of up to 10 000 personnel qualified in computer technology (House of Lords, 1985). At the uppermost level, one estimate claims that 'the shortfall of people with information technology and engineering skills is probably between 60 000 and 80 000' (Williams, 1985, p. 141). These are undoubtedly serious shortages which may cause some anxiety in the boardrooms of Hewlett Packard and GEC, but even the highest estimate would find work for only 2.5 per cent of the present officially unemployed and little more than one per cent of the truly unemployed.

Of course, it could be argued that this represents but a cadre of I.T. specialists which must be created so that an expanding economy can generate employment for the mass of the workless. Shirley Williams seizes on this 'ricochet effect' to suggest that each 'highly skilled' person generates 'several' jobs at a lower level (Williams, 1985, p. 141). Since she does not quantify her assertion, we can only guess at the number this may represent, but if we assume that each I.T. expert generates four jobs we can suggest that a sustained injection of I.T. into the curriculum might remove 10 per cent from the dole. This is a significant, if small, dent in the total, but two points ought to be borne in mind. First, there is no reason to suppose that these spin-off jobs require I.T. skills just because their creators need them. Indeed, a recent survey of employers found precisely this: while there was a high demand for a few thousand systems analysts and computer managers, there was no evidence of I.T. skill shortages at the lower levels. Employers agreed that many of the lower ranks would be using I.T. in their work, but were confident that they could provide any necessary training on site, not least because the 'few at the top of the pyramid [would] make I.T. user-friendly and idiot-proof for those on the shop-floor' (Donaldson *et al.*, 1987, p. 78). Second, when one compares the absolute number of shortages with total numbers of people graduating from schools and colleges every year, then any necessary adjustment in education programmes and priorities is minor. With some 350 000 students currently in full-time higher education, over four million pupils in the secondary schools, and some 800 000 school-leavers per year, it would require minimal adaptation to fill all I.T. vacancies several times over (Waddilove, 1985; cf. Gordon and Pearson, 1984). This being so, why the demand that all children should undergo 'computer literacy' programmes when there are so few openings in the world of work for those with I.T. skills? The question would be merely rhetorical were it not the case that job prospects for the young are so bleak (1.25 million people under the age of twenty-four were unemployed in 1986) and when there is so much evidence that the unemployed are blamed and blame themselves for their demise (see, *inter alia*, Economist Intelligence Unit, 1982; Jahoda, 1982; Golding and Middleton, 1982).

(ii) Technical skills and jobs

We have suggested already that widespread I.T. skills are unnecessary to fill present vacancies on the job market, but in spite of this time and again one encounters assertions that 'the information society demands highly qualified people' (Williams, 1985, p. 74). This is repeated *ad nauseam* in the media and, not unexpectedly, it has become a maxim of those who argue that I.T. instruction is essential for all. Since it is I.T. which is ushering in the 'Information Society', it must follow that mastery over I.T. is a requisite of employment in the dawning age.

We might start examining the validity of this reasoning by heeding the views of the Chancellor of the Exchequer. Mr Nigel Lawson's opinion is that we are amid the throes of a restructuring of the economy which, though it is undeniably uncomfortable for many, will eventually result in the transition from an order in which employment in manufacture (factories) is the norm to a service economy where work typically answers people's needs for additional services. Some social theorists, most notably Daniel Bell, have been

enthused by this prospect, envisaging 'post-industrial' society being populated by social workers, lawyers, psychiatrists,
teachers, researchers and similar sorts of professionals
ministering to all and sundry. Were this future to be realised
there would indeed be a strong case for radical changes in
education to raise the skill levels of the work-force.

However, a Chancellor's time-scale cannot be so generous
as that of an academic, so while Bell may peer into the
twenty-first century, Mr Lawson must ask of now 'where will
the new jobs be?' (Lawson, 1983). Certainly he looks to
services to ease unemployment since agriculture is statisti-
cally hardly significant and industrial automation rules out
hopes of manufacture taking on more workers, but to Mr
Lawson the service work likely to grow is not that located in
the professions, but that found in the lower reaches formerly
occupied by servants:

> We must not be seduced by the wonders of high-tech into
> overlooking the fact that many of the jobs of the future will be in
> labour intensive service industries which are not so much
> low-tech as no-tech. (Lawson, 1984)

Mrs Thatcher puts these words more idiomatically:

> We must . . . expect a lot more of our jobs will come from the
> service industries – from the McDonalds and Wimpeys, which
> employ a lot of people, from the kind of Disneyland they are
> starting in Corby . . . (Thatcher, 1983)

Lawson's conviction that 'new jobs [will be] created at the
lower end of the wage scale' with 'no-tech' (Lawson, 1984)
surely makes a nonsense of 'computer literacy' classes. With
estimates running at nine unskilled jobs becoming available
for every computer programmer opening (Levin and
Rumberger, 1983, p. 19), Theodore Roszak pointedly
observes:

> Clever educational software . . . will make no greater contribu-
> tion to the students' employability than will rudimentary courses
> in outmoded forms of programming. In the job market students
> will face when they leave school, the choice high tech careers
> will require many years of more professional and specialized

education. Even so, those careers will be for the high-achieving few. For the many, the five most available jobs in the information economy will be employment as janitors, nurse's aids, sales clerks, cashiers, and waiters. (Roszak, 1986, p. 55)

What expertise in Basic is required of waiters, floor cleaners, doormen and tea-makers?

If these new jobs have little to do with I.T. it is still the case that the majority of established occupations will remain and require replacement in due course. Since I.T. is a heartland technology that will find application almost everywhere, then the next generation of factory operatives and office workers must be made technologically competent. *Ipso facto*, 'computer literacy' initiatives are still necessary if today's youth is to occupy the posts that are set to be changed as I.T. is adopted: tomorrow's typist must be able to function on a word processor, the tool-maker must be adept with computer numerical control technologies. Thus it is that the claim that work in an 'information-rich' environment will demand new and higher-grade skills can survive the criticism that most service jobs becoming available will require no technical dexterity.

However, what this assertion begs is a questioning of the relation between technological innovation and skill requirements. Underpinning 'I.T. initiatives' in education is the presumption that high tech leads to high skill demands from employees which, while it has a superficial appeal – work with computers appears recondite and pre-eminently professional – can by no means be taken for granted. Indeed, the evidence available suggests that, in the round, the process of technological innovation this century has been one which has brought about a reduction in the performance skills of the bulk of workers (Thompson, 1983). It is at the least arguable that what Craig Littler (1982, p. 52) has called a 'dynamic of deskilling' has guided the adoption of technology in the workplace, leading to the simplification and routinisation of operations required of employees. The epitome of this process whereby advanced technology has led to reduced skills is the assembly line, that characteristic feature of modern industry, in which machinery and the division of labour have resulted in operatives having next to no skill.

This is *not* to contend that all work has become deskilled due to technology, but it is to suggest that innovation has been largely guided by the search for simplification of workers' roles and, integrally connected, for increasing output, and that these goals are likely to diminish rather than to enhance skill requirements. Indeed, while we accept that there has been a relative and absolute increase in professional work (rising from something like 4 per cent to about 15 per cent of the workforce since 1910), what appears striking about the expansion of law, architecture, education, accountancy, management and the like is that these occupations have not called for technological dexterity. Quite the contrary, their distance from technological operation has been a defining characteristic of their professional roles. Today the introduction of I.T. into the lower realms of such professions may presage the onset of deskilling in hitherto immune areas (Cooley, 1981).

While considering the issue of the relation between technology and skill it is salutary to be reminded of 'one of the commoner ideological features of industrial society, whereby social processes are disguised by formal acts of reclassification and relabelling' (Kumar, 1978, p. 262). On the basis of such changes of classification, and no more, there has been this century a massive decrease in 'unskilled' workers and a corresponding increase in the 'semi-skilled': the 'unskilled' farmhand who tended sheep, cows and poultry, looked after buildings and tools, and husbanded crops through the seasons, has been replaced by the 'semi-skilled' truck driver who negotiates nothing more difficult than the motorway network and the factory worker whose role is to perform three or four actions the livelong day. Reminding ourselves of the way in which statistics can disguise real changes in skill, we may note too that 'skill' is a much used but rarely defined term, though it is one that undoubtedly is shaped by social values. Thus, for instance, it appears that gender plays a part in defining jobs as 'skilled' (almost everywhere women appear in an occupation it suffers an apparent reduction in skill). Power is also a significant force in characterising particular jobs as skilled, as witness the ability of some trade unionists to perpetuate the title of skilled worker to their jobs long after technology had made this a nonsense (printers are the classic case, but it is arguable whether electricians occupy a similar position). Advertising and self-assignment may also achieve the designation 'skilled', for example look at the depiction of police constables and ordinary soldiers as 'professionals' over the past decade. It is surely significant that these latter press for their promotion to the category 'skilled' by associating themselves with advanced technologies of one sort or another.

Recognising these factors which influence the meaning of skill leads one to beware the ready conclusion that nowadays the workforce requires more than yesteryear. Against arguments that assert modern occupations require greater skill than those of the past one might cite the research of R. M. Blackburn and Michael Mann which, examining more than three-quarters of the male manual workers in Peterborough, found that 87 per cent of these men required less technical skill in their jobs than they would have required in driving to work, and 'most of them expend more mental effort and resourcefulness in getting to work than in doing their jobs' (Blackburn and Mann, 1979, pp. 121, 180). It is hardly possible to blame the men of Peterborough for not trying to extend themselves because challengingly skilled jobs were simply unavailable: since 85 per cent of them had the capability to do 95 per cent of all the jobs on offer any individual choice or initiative was restricted to different kinds of 'Mickey Mouse' work.

In addition, very large proportions of white-collar work which are assumed to be more professional and skilled than manual labour, are composed of clerical employment that is as routine and mundane as most shop floor work. We do not claim that manual and non-manual employees see the world in the same way, but with as much as 35 per cent of all white-collar work made up of clerical labour it is worth reflecting on Harry Braverman's complaint that it is but a 'reflex response' to 'accord a higher grade of skill training, prestige and class position to any form of office work' which is overdue for challenge (Braverman, 1974, p. 435). The tedium and routine of filing invoices, typing standard letters, checking a limited range of orders, taking dictation and answering the telephone in the 'factory office' are perceived as skilled by convention alone.

This striking *lack* of skills in the workforce originates not in the inabilities of the people, but in the fact that modern industy requires little of its operatives, and advanced technologies, in their conception, design and application, are a major cause of this. Historians have argued that, commencing in the early years of this century when large scale production led to the breakdown of personal supervision, employers began to initiate new strategies to ensure control of workers who are regarded as an input that must be carefully 'managed' in order to achieve maximum efficiency for the corporation (Noble, 1977, pp. 257-83). Employees will persist in working at their own pace rather than that set by management, they will ask for *more* at most inconvenient times, and these traits will always present them as a problem. One way of alleviating this has been to organise the skills required of production so that there are several individual contributions each of which can be undertaken by the relatively untutored person. Complementing this, and increasingly more common, has been the practice of putting the skills required into advanced technologies which reduce the intellectual contribution and technical adroitness of employees to a minimum.

Against assertions to the contrary, we would argue that I.T., as it is being constituted, stands in the same tradition of technological control and deskilling. With Harley Shaiken we would identify

a pervasive engineering ideology that views human participation in production as inherently 'unscientific' [which] . . . serves to propel technological development toward the elimination of human input. Engineers tend to perceive a fully automated process as the ultimate solution to factors, human and otherwise, outside direct control. (Shaiken, 1984, pp. 58–9)

This is the only way in which one can appreciate the language of Russell Heddon, president of Cross and Trecker

Corporation, when he observes that computer controlled machine tools are 'taking more of the skill off the shop floor and putting it into the computer' (Heddon, 1981, p. 63; cf. Noble, 1984), or the evidence gathered by Barry Wilkinson (1983) on the introduction of microelectronic technologies into West Midlands engineering factories which suggests that the 'ideal worker is essentially mediocre, working steadily at an average pace, accepting meekly the dictates of the technology' (Blackburn and Mann, 1979, p. 187).

In more recent years technological innovation has begun to penetrate the white collar sector in a big way (Crompton and Jones, 1984, pp. 42–77) after decades of relative neglect. In banks, building societies, estate agencies, travel companies, insurance brokers and offices in general, machinery now being installed incorporates most of the skilled work (it computes interest rates, recalls accounts, sorts files, spells, recalls addresses, counts notes, plots routes, calculates costs etc). To be sure, to the novitiate these areas, boasting an array of impressive-looking computer technology, appear the province of high-powered experts who move across the terminals with astonishing facility. But the truth is that these are roles that have been achieved with few hours or days training, often the 'skill' required involving little more than knowledge of how to log on and read the system's instructions. As regards clerks the 'skill fiction' (Crompton and Jones, 1984, p. 74) persists and they are invariably classed by social investigators as 'skilled non-manual', but in fact the bulk of such work is entirely rule-bound, requiring no discretion or autonomy in carrying out job tasks. The short history of computing itself has also experienced, with the application of modern management's precepts, routinisation and deskilling by procedures such as increased division of labour, standardised languages, structured programming, user-friendly packages and the increasingly extensive recourse to data dictionaries (Kraft, 1977): the great part of the work is divided between programmers and operators who frequently 'complain of boredom, lack of interest, and the loss of self-esteem' (Greenbaum, 1979, p. 163). *Plus ça change . . .*

Something else follows from the point that technological

developments may demand less, rather than more, skill from workers. This concerns the value of teaching 'computer literacy' in schools and colleges when so much I.T. is already easy to use and is constantly being made more 'user-friendly'. We have suggested that this is happening in the world of work (to the detriment of much of the employee's skill), but a moment's reflection may lead one to see the same process operating on a much wider scale. A great deal of I.T. is already transparent, is so easy to use that people have difficulty in conceiving it as part of the 'computer revolution': think of kitchen gadgets, automobile controls, 'intelligent' photocopiers, computerised library catalogues, viewdata networks, teletext systems or television games. In contrast to this increased simplification there is much concern in 'IT awareness' courses for instruction in computer use, in elementary programming, in developing spread-sheets and so on. This latter is a popular view of what the 'microelectronics revolution' involves, but it is quite erroneous. To envisage I.T. in the narrow sense of manipulating a microcomputer or even accessing a mainframe to perform some statistical test is something akin to mistaking the spark plugs for the motor car or to believe that to drive capably requires knowledge of the working of the internal combustion engine. In truth, the technologies that we 'just use', that we take for granted since they are so elementary to handle, are much more what the Information Society will be about than mastery of any programming language. Indeed, it is a truism of I.T. that the more advanced the technology the more simple to use and unobtrusive it will be to the user.

Increasingly I.T. is becoming like the telephone, radio and electricity: technologies we use without hesitation because we have a task to perform which they help us achieve. People want to speak to a friend, so they pick up the phone and dial – without concern for the mechanics of telephony; they want to hear a programme, so they switch on the radio – without regard for broadcast frequencies; they want to read in the evening, so they switch on the light – without awareness of how electricity is generated or transmitted. The majority of people are neither telephone literate nor radio literate nor electricity literate, but they are in no ways incapacitated because of this. What is so different about computerisation, why do we feel a need for 'computer literacy'? Since typically it takes but a few minutes to learn how to operate I.T. such as word processors and on-line information services, and since it requires no training to speak of to use computerised technologies in washing machines, cars and banking terminals, why should we be urged to receive formal instruction when, in the course of time and depending on choice and circumstance, we can take aboard the requisite skills?

(iii) Overeducation

These observations surely must lead one to query the recent enthusiasm for training people in I.T. so they will be up to the high skills required by future employment. It also raises the intriguing question of whether the current workforce is not actually *overeducated* for the work that it does. Much evidence is indicative of this, demonstrating that for work of all kinds education has virtually no direct pay-off, that the bulk of work has few highly developed skills that are not taught on the job (Berg, 1970; Dore, 1976). Without doubt recent decades have seen an inflation of formal qualifications demanded by employers – we are now living most certainly in what has been called a 'credential society' (Collins, 1979). This is evident all around: shop assistants are asked for GCSEs nowadays, bank clerks need A-level passes, and primary school teachers require degrees since the 'profession' is deemed to be 'all graduate'. In itself, it may be worthwhile that the citizenry is better educated than its predecessors, but what is missing is evidence that these improved qualifications are prerequisites of, or even related to, the work that people are actually called upon to do. Illustratively, Crompton and Jones report from their research that 'Despite the fact that the majority of jobs we examined required very little in the way of skill and qualifications, all three organisations formally required new recruits to be at least 'O' level standard . . . In reality, many jobs at all levels . . . were successfully carried out by people with no or only minimal qualifications' (Crompton and Jones, 1984, p. 75).

Let us not be misunderstood. We are not deploring educational progress, but what we are criticising is the assertion that increased educational certification is indicative of a rise in the skill requirements of jobs. The catalogue of complaints from employers of 'unrealistic expectations' of work held by school-leavers and reports from newly-employed graduates of routine and undemanding labour are indicative of precisely this mis-match between work as it is now and the quality of recruits.

Nevertheless, even if the work does not need it, access to the job in the first place does call for additional educational certificates, and it is here that demands for 'computer literacy' become pertinent. It may be that employers, responding to the present concern for 'I.T. skills', will begin to require of their workforce evidence of achievement at school in computer communications, thereby confirming the relevance of 'computer literacy' programmes and ensuring their retention in the syllabus. This is certainly not unprecedented: many readers will recall that Latin was, as recently as the 1970s, a requisite of much university entry, irrespective of the course of study proposed.

(iv)   Education for enterprise

Government is aware that technical training in I.T. will not guarantee employment for the mass of the workless. It does not say this too loud or too often, since to do so would challenge much of the legitimacy of policies which depend on unemployment being explained by way of deficiencies of education rather than economic and political factors. If enough people can be convinced that depression has been brought about by inability to produce internationally competitive products and services because the workforce has been inadequately educated, then it follows that adjustment in schools and colleges is the uncontentious technique that will set things right. This is the official version, but government knows things are more complex and acts accordingly. Thus, inserted within 'computer awareness' courses and training-oriented policies, there is frequent reference to 'attitudinal' qualities that are deemed essential if the work-less are to hope for employment. In the speech to which we have referred Lord Young coupled school-leavers' lack of qualifications acceptable to employers with shortcomings of motivation and personal qualities that make young people attractive ('too often they [school-leavers] were de-motivated and lacked the personal qualities required' (*The Guardian*, 26 January 1985)). Increasingly this argument – job-seekers need technical expertise plus – has been evident in the Manpower Services Commission schemes which play a prominent part in mediating education and work/ worklessness for 16 to 18-year-olds. Moreover, recently the 'plus' side has been promoted over the technical, so much so that 'character' appears to be coming a defining feature of employment possibilities (see Chapter 4).

It appears that education has failed the nation not only in that it has trained far too few technologists, but also in that it has not managed to nourish an 'enterprise culture' which is, we are told, essential to make technology succeed in the marketplace. This being so, the Thatcher government has determined that the young are not only technically incompe-tent, but also that they are deficient in 'enterprise'. The intention now is that the young will 'have the attitudes *and* skills necessary to enable them to play a full role in the creation of wealth' (Whyte, 1986, p. 9). 'Computer literacy' will provide the techniques, but in addition 'substantial shifts in attitudes' (Ibid) are required. Therefore, a key feature of Youth Training Schemes and of the amended curriculum in secondary and further education is 'enterprise training'. Senior Cabinet Minister Lord Young declares that 'Young people who act in a self-reliant and entrepreneurial manner will be the workforce of tomorrow' (Young, 1987); his director of the Manpower Services Commission echoes that since 'British industry needs more enterprising, risk taking and adventurous people if we are to compete against our trading rivals' (Holland, 1987, p. 13) then 'enterprise train-ing' is to be a 'high priority' (ibid).

'Enterprising', and the adjective often presented as its synonym 'entrepreneurial', a Youth Training Scheme handbook tells us, 'begins with having positive and alert atti-tudes. It goes on to embrace personal qualities such as confidence, initiative, and determination' (YTS, 1987, p. 14). Elsewhere George Whyte contrasts an 'enterprising' with an (presumably unemployed) unenterprising one thus:

An enterprising person is someone who:

Creates opportunities	rather than	waiting for someone else to do so
Wants to generate wealth and resources	rather than	being dependent on others
Has the confidence to use his or her initiative	rather than	being powerless to use his or her initiative
Takes advantage of chance	rather than	being confused and depressed by chance

(Whyte, 1986)

When one considers 'enterprise training' in light of these conceptions, then it seems very far removed from the technical emphasis of 'computer literacy'. It could be that one replies cynically that these personality traits are useful as a means of excusing unemployment even where the workless are technically skilled: 'sorry, lad, you're marvel-lous on the PC, but you've not got the attitude we're looking for'. There is certainly a message in 'enterprise training' for the unemployed: it is to 'smile while you're taking it and go find a job yourself'. There is surely something in these points, but 'enterprise training' is more related to I.T. than at first might appear.

This relation tells us something about I.T. which is easily overlooked. We refer to the fact that I.T. is a rapidly changing technology, so much that its speed of innovation is without precedent. This means that 'computer literacy' programmes with a technical emphasis are constantly out-of-date, teaching skills that are outmoded before their pupils even enter the labour market. There is some irony, for instance, that in Britain some 84 per cent of micros in secondary schools are BBCs made by Acorn, a company which discontinued production of the machines it made available to schools in 1986 and which has told its customers that spares will no longer be available after 1991 (Berliner, 1987). Our point is not to underscore the shortcomings of 'computer literacy' classes when technology is changing at such a fierce pace, but to draw attention to rapid technological change's consequences for employment. Today and in the future the 'new worker' must be taught not only to anticipate operating with computerised technologies for which training is required, but also to expect that retraining and personal adaptation will be a constant in the I.T. future. YTS put the matter clearly:

> The upshot is that 'change becomes the norm' and individual workers will need to become more flexible – in their personal lives as well as at work. Indeed, the workforce as a whole needs to be able to adapt, to initiate, and to be confident that it can cope with change. And that means enterprise training because one of the chief characteristics of the 'enterprising' is that they don't fear change as a threat – they welcome it as an opportunity. (YTS, 1987, p. 15)

In sum, what 'enterprise training' is most importantly about is educating the young to be 'flexible'; it is concerned with socialising school-leavers at once to believe that unemployment is a result of personality defects ('I.T. illiterates *and* moaners are unemployable') at the same time as to accept that their work experiences will be punctuated by regular periods of retraining and readjustment to technological change. As a Treasury *Economic Progress Report* has it: 'A flexible labour market is essential because the demand for different types of labour is constantly changing as technology advances' (January–February 1986, no. 182, p. 1). Therefore a key element of 'I.T. training' will be inculcation of appropriate attitudes and expectations for work – and worklessness – in the 'information society'. Behind technical instruction, much of which is irrelevant and will be redundant by the time pupils get out of school, is a battery of attitudinal learning that could assist considerably in accommodating the unemployed to their situation and making more malleable those in work.

Employers' needs and 'computer literacy'

Excessive talk about 'skill shortages' in industry has justified a re-emphasis in education on technical training. The incessant message is that employers are desperately searching for the technologically competent, all to no avail since the schools and colleges have signally failed to produce adequate numbers (cf. 'Higher Education output in engineering', 1987). Higher education apparently produces insufficient engineers while awash with graduates in arts and humanities; the schools release thousands upon thousands of youngsters well-versed in 'life studies', but lacking in numeracy. . . Most are unappealing as investments to employers in industry. Now education has been called to account, and there is no-one to whom education should be more accountable in this day and age than an employer. Employers' needs ring out, the bells being tolled by politicians and administrators calling together teachers in the nirvana of *Training for Jobs* (1984). I.T. is at the font of this new church.

Education has responded with alacrity to this service, but before doing so it might have examined employers' needs more closely.

(i)   Personal transferable skills

What do employers want out of the education system? A quick retort at the present moment is that employers' needs are well known: education should be vocationally-oriented with a technological bent. This is indeed the spontaneous reply of many, but only a little examination leads one to realise that, beyond buzz words such as 'relevant' and 'industry-oriented', employers are often neither clear about what they do look for in recruits nor do they require, for the most part, technical expertise.

There are undoubtedly vacancies in industry which do require technical expertise and employers understandably look to education to fill such posts. However, these represent a small proportion of even graduate recruits (chiefly they are engineers of one sort or another posts for whom constitute about 12 per cent of vacancies). At the 16–18-year-old level technical attainment in education is more or less irrelevant to employers since adequate training will be given on the job, complemented perhaps by day release to further education college. This sort of arrangement is often the case even with technical personnel recruited at graduate level: for instance, Finniston reported that engineering graduates were equipped with fundamentals of the discipline at university, but employers were called upon to supplement this with practical training (Finniston, 1980, pp. 84–91). A good many undergraduate courses such as accountancy and law have a vocational dimension, but require much further study and certification before a chosen profession and they do not, of course, call for I.T. skills of any significance.

However, a greater number of graduate recruits entering industry require nothing vocational in their studies since they are hired as management trainees and as part of a general intake destined to fill junior and middle management positions. It should be stressed that currently almost half of all jobs are open to graduates of any discipline (CSU, May 1987). Moreover, for all that there is an affinity between undergraduate study and area of employment, there are fluid boundaries: for instance, while the bulk of civil engineers practice, nearly 30 per cent do not work as engineers, and while economics graduates gravitate towards employment with financial dimensions, as much as half do not (CRAC/CBI, 1987). Employers of graduates are in the main not looking for specific technical expertise, but for a range of abilities that have come to be called 'personal transferable skills' such as analytical ability, communicative competence and working in groups. Christopher Ball elaborates:

> The abilities most valued in industrial, commercial and professional life as well as in public and social administration are the transferable intellectual and personal skills. These include the ability to analyze complex issues, to identify the core of a

problem and the means of solving it, to synthesise and integrate disparate elements, to clarify values, to make effective use of numerical and other information, to work co-operatively and constructively with others, and, above all perhaps, to communicate clearly both orally and in writing. (Ball, 1986)

If it is these sort of 'skills' that graduate employers need from their recruits, then it is noteworthy that they do not restrict the call for 'personal transferable skills' to management trainees. Even in the schools it appears that employers look for qualities other than technical in their recruits. Invariably these revolve around terms like 'able', 'motivated' and 'good character', qualities which have not declined in importance to employers in spite of an inrush of I.T. As a representative of a retailing company employing 62 500 said:

we need the same skills now, even though we've got the computers there, as we did 10 or 15 years ago. I wonder why there is this emphasis to teach kids about computers? How many of them, when they leave school, are actually going to get hands-on experience? We're looking for people who treat customers as human beings . . . mix well with their colleagues . . . communicate well with customers. (quoted in Donaldson *et al*, 1987, p. 63)

Throughout education, employers search above all for recruits whose inter-personal abilities appear sound: note well the conclusion of a recent Manpower Services Commission-sponsored 'Skills for the Future' survey:

Far greater emphasis was placed on the need for general abilities and qualities, along with personal attributes such as appearance, enthusiasm, commitment and ambition than on *specific skills*. Indeed, one wonders if the language of 'skills' and 'skill shortages' which so often pervades discussion linking education and employment is either useful or appropriate . . . The emphasis in employers' selection criteria was overwhelmingly on the need for personal attributes in a new recruit: flexibility, initiative, reliability, honesty, interest, enthusiasm, ambition, leadership, commitment, ability to communicate and work in a team, were all stressed highly . . . When employers did ask for 'skills' they almost exclusively mentioned . . . the more general abilities such as critical thinking . . . and communication. (Donaldson *et al*, p. 63, 74)

At this stage in our argument it is interesting to return to Finniston's report on the engineering profession. While it did regret the two-tier system that divided higher education in engineering (theory) from the world of work (practical), Finniston did not urge that university courses should become more technical. What was most required was an integration of the programme of study in college and workshop and measures to achieve in engineers the personal attributes employers felt essential. In this regard what is particularly striking is Finniston's note that 'Qualities which employers claim to seek from graduates are almost invariably expressed in terms of personal attributes such as "motivation", "ability to work in a team", "ability to communicate", etc, in addition to technical knowledge' (Finniston, 1980, p. 85). The report iterated that 'Employers frequently described deficiencies of their engineering staff in terms of personal qualities rather than specific engineering skills . . . Frequent remarks were made about the lack of engineers with the personal attributes essential for management . . .' (p. 194). In short, even in the highly vocational and technical sphere of engineering, employers require skills that are much more than technical expertise.

Thus we may see that even at the technical end of the educational spectrum 'personal transferable skills' are of considerable importance; as we shift away from the minority of posts in industry that are specifically technical, we discover that what employers require above all from the education system are analytical, critical and communicative competences. Technology has little or no relevance to the development of such skills. This being so, key questions must surely be: why is there such emphasis on 'computer literacy' in the name of enhanced employability and why are there 'steers' towards scientific and technical courses, when it appears that the most sought-after skills such as problem solving, flexibility, co-operation, and communication can be developed in the most clearly non-vocational disciplines imaginable? (cf. Slee, 1986).

(ii)   Personality and place

It is a recurrent, if usually unstated, assumption of 'computer literacy' programmes that knowledge of advanced technology gives one access to power. It follows that, without 'I.T. awareness', the ignorant will not only be unemployed, but also that they will be subordinate to the technically expert. While this idea has a long history in social thought, it has to be said that the claim that technical knowledge rules and will rule in the future is intellectually discreditable chiefly because it confuses indispensibility with power. As Max Weber observed many years ago, 'If "indispensibility" were decisive, then where slave labour prevailed and where freemen usually abhor work as a dishonor, the "indispensible" slaves ought to have held the positions of power' (in Gerth and Mills, 1967, p. 232). Education in the technicalities of I.T. will not give technologists power because they do not have it in the first place.

Employers' prioritisation of 'personal transferable skills' indicates as much, but we may extend the point by taking another look at graduate recruitment practices. The major point that has to be made is that employers overwhelmingly select on the basis of personality and place: they have a notion of the sort of 'character' they are seeking to employ (well-rounded, adaptable, articulate, motivated) and a clear hierarchy of institutions from which they will choose (Oxbridge, old universities, red bricks, polytechnics in descending order). Research reveals that the majority of employers do not have a straight-forward list of technical vacancies which they must fill (in which case expansion and retraction within colleges would solve their difficulties) and that for the most part course contents were irrelevant to their needs. What recruiters looked for above all else were candidates educated in a traditional discipline (it did not matter much what, provided that it was intellectually – and socially – approved), at an established institution, with strong personal attributes (Hunter, 1981, pp. 19–22). Even academic achievement at degree level was not especially significant, A-level grades weighing more heavily as indicators of intellectual capability (Roizen and Jepson, 1985). As Robert

Miller dryly commented, research findings on graduate recruiters' criteria should tell the 'bright secondary student that the road to a good job is to work hard only long enough to secure high A levels (with maths) for entry into the best possible university, upon arriving, to work part-time, taking up golf, rugby and bridge and, after graduation, to apply far and wide' (Miller, 1986).

It might be thought that if employers' selection relies so much on personality, then education itself, even formal qualifications, are irrelevant. Quite the contrary: personal attributes and personal transferable skills (which are easily confused and conflated) are the decisive qualities looked for by employers at every level of the education system, but a key function of each level is to sort and select recruits for a particular type of occupation. The point is simple if paradoxical: credentials are absolutely essential in the allocation of school-leavers and graduates to jobs since they signify a level of ability and attainment to the prospective employer; at the same time, certification in specific subjects is largely irrelevant to recruiters, so long as the qualifications are socially approved (physics rather than sociology, economics higher than art . . .), because employers have to the forefront of their minds the search for personal qualities in those whom they employ.

Selection of recruits undermines any presumption that technical proficiency is a requisite of high achievement in our society. Of course, given current shortages, graduates in computer science and electronic engineering are assured of employment in the future, but the suggestion that I.T. skills will help them scale the heights of industry is a nonsense. The evidence to which we have referred indicates quite the opposite, revealing that if one does aim to go high in modern Britain one ought not to be a 'doer' (one may finish in charge of a research laboratory, rarely in the boardroom), but rather a 'leader' with all the 'personal transferable skills' – and 'leadership qualities' – that implies. The qualifications for these are in detail variable, but there are a few decisive prerequisties: be well born, marry well, be assured of a sizeable inheritance, go to a prestigious private school, avoid vocational courses like the plague, attend Oxford or Cambridge, and read PPE, Greats, or possibly English Literature (see, *inter alia*, Scott, 1982, Chapters 6–7; Giddens and Stanworth, 1978). The evidence is overwhelming that the resources of power lie with inherited advantage and privileged (usually non-technical) education.

'Computer literacy' and mythology

The dubiousness of the claim that it is deficiencies of I.T. skills that have made people unemployable, the evidence that computer skills are unnecessary for the bulk of those in work, the fact that employers look for personal attributes rather than technical expertise in most of their recruits, the reality that power positions are occupied by the privileged and non-technically qualified, all of these factors make the vogue for 'computer literacy' questionable in the extreme. Nonetheless, Computer Studies has raced up the scale of most popular O-levels in recent years, rising from 3000 entrants in 1976 to over 62 000 in 1985, driven by the claim that it is a passport to work (Robertson *et al.*, 1987, p. 10). We cannot see the relevance to employers of these immersions in Basic, potted histories of computer technology, binary notation, and the obligatory (and we suspect inept) 'social and economic impact' element (Ruthven, 1984). There are enthusiasts for I.T. within education who share our scepticism about Computer Studies, but for very different reasons. These critics resent the monopoly of computer equipment by mathematics departments, its location in exclusionary 'computer rooms' and its association with number crunching. They favour 'computer awareness' across the curriculum rather than the 'vertical' mode that an emphasis on Computer Studies imposes on grounds that *everyone* requires familiarisation with I.T. because it will impact on everyone's work and life and not just those who study it in maths. Advocates of 'computer awareness' would have I.T. introduced in English, Geography, History, Social Studies, Music, across the entire range of educational provision.

Our objection to 'computer awareness' revolves around its vagueness. On the one hand, as teachers ourselves we favour means of supporting and improving the educational process, hence we approve automation of library facilities, we are excited by the potential of data bases such as Domesday that give ready access to historical, geographical and sociological materials, and word processors undeniably simplify typing. The problem is that if this sort of thing passes for 'computer awareness' then there is much fuss about nothing. Most of the technologies are transparent as far as users are concerned and there is neither a need for special initiatives to get them introduced nor can they, in themselves, be presented as having inherent educational qualities.

On the other hand, 'computer awareness' generally returns to offer the same sort of thing as most 'computer literacy' courses, only at a more basic level: how to load a floppy disc, how to produce some rudimentary programme, how to play with a spreadsheet, how to use a printer and so on. With that emphasis, we are back with our questions about the vocational relevance of this 'computer literacy'. We will not reiterate our objections, but we conclude this chapter with a further criticism. These introductory courses, whatever their variability, are all practical, each stressing hands-on training as an essential aspect of understanding I.T. Since at the end of such a course, however simple, pupils will be able to *do* something with a computer it will appear that they have at least moved some way towards grasping the nature of the 'information technology revolution'.

Against this, it is our contention that such a practical introduction to computers of one sort or another, but chiefly micros, actually represses and mystifies what the 'information revolution' is much more significantly about. How can such courses begin to understand the military dimensions of command, control, communications and intelligence technologies that set the pace in development of I.T., secure enormous quantities of research and development funds, capture a lion's share of the computer expertise available in and out of the universities, and dominate discussion of the Strategic Defense Initiative (see Chapter 8)? How can they comprehend the corporate information networks that wire together national economies and raise the most profound questions about an emerging new international division of labour, transnational data flows and violations of national sovereignty? How do they commence consideration of the relentless increase in surveillance at the behest of government departments and corporate interests which is all around, yet hidden from public view, in welfare organisations, credit agencies, telephone companies and corporate data bases? When teachers introduce their pupils to the wonders of an Acorn, an Apple or an Apricot in the name of 'computer literacy' that will gain them employment in the 'information age', then they appear supremely realistic. The technology is *there* and its capabilities are easily witnessed; let the students master the micro and they will have a grasp of, and leverage over, the 'information technology revolution'. In this chapter we have tried to show that educationalists too often are mistaken about the needs of industry and the employment potential of 'computer literacy'. We also believe that 'computer literacy' courses are profoundly ignorant of the true substance of the 'information revolution'. In purporting to reveal the character of I.T. with catchy introductions to microcomputers, 'computer literacy' courses all the more effectively mythologise the meaning of I.T.

7

The New Disciplines

'For capital, the reassertion of authority is the precondition
for everything else.' (John Holloway, 1987, p. 163)

So far we have concentrated, in this part of the book, on the
relationship of the education system to the world of industry
and business. We have focused on the changing nature of
this relationship in the context of a broad shift from a Fordist
to a neo-Fordist regime of capital accumulation. In this
chapter our concern is with the implications of this transformation for the prevailing power relations in society. The
emergence of neo-Fordism, we shall argue, is closely associated with changes in the form and modality of social control.
Of course, the control dimensions of education are related
to the economy since the latter depends upon an adequate
machinery of social discipline and control as its precondition. However, this does not mean that relations of power
are simply subordinate to, and functional for, economic
needs: we recognise that the relationship is complex and
difficult and, indeed, a contentious matter in social theory to
which we cannot do justice here. Our aim is, more modestly,
to explore changes in the nature of education as a system of
discipline and control, and to signal moves towards synchro-
nisation of these changes consequent upon the transition to
neo-Fordism. What we offer in this chapter is a series of
questions, explorations and agendas, centred around the
relation between education, social control and the economic
system.

Neo-Fordism and social control

In his classic account of Fordism, Benjamin Coriat argues that this regime of accumulation entailed an innovative economic sequence centred around mass production, changes in the relationship of classes, and new forms of social regulation. Fordism, he maintains, was built around a combination of factory discipline and consumer and welfare dependence orchestrated by the Keynesian state apparatus (Coriat, 1979, Chapter 1). The emerging regime of neo-Fordism in the 1980s should be seen in terms of a new articulation of economic sequence, class alignments and social control. The new mode of accumulation, as we have argued in Chapter 4, is centred around flexible (decentralised, fragmented, disseminated) forms of production, and the new class relations are those between core and peripheral or aleatory workers. But what about new forms of regulation and management?

At one level, it is a matter of reasserting control in the face of insubordination and de-subordination contingent upon the decline of the Fordist/Keynesian consensus. At the heart of this collapse, as John Holloway argues, 'is the failure of an established pattern of domination', one that 'can be resolved only through the establishment of new patterns of domination . . . through the restoration of authority and through a far-from-smooth search for new patterns of domination' (Holloway, 1987, p. 146). The initial stage in this reassertion of discipline is what Holloway refers to as the transitional, or 'macho', period of confrontational tactics, aimed at destroying the vestiges of Fordism/Keynesianism. It is expressed very much as the imposition of centralised control from above with even economic policy being subordinated to the 'politics of hegemony' (Jessop *et al*, 1987, pp. 113–15).

Education has been one key area in and through which there have been efforts to reassert social and moral discipline, and many of the Thatcher government's strategies have exemplified the macho posture. One element of this approach has been to break the power base of teaching staff and their unions. Teachers have been held responsible for generating the 'English disease' and for failing to stimulate scientific and technological education. This was the argument of Callaghan's Ruskin College speech and it has been the message of critiques from the Black Papers of the 1970s to the Adam Smith Institute's polemics now. Teachers, through their political bias or, at best, their liberal unworldliness, are responsible for Britain's failure to develop its scientific and technological base and to compete effectively in world markets. The solution must be the establishment of centralised control and direction (the Education Reform Bill of November 1987), an improvement in 'teacher quality', and the better management of the teacher force (*Better Schools*, 1985, Chapter 5). Alongside this attack on teachers, there has also been an undermining of local authority controls over education and an assertion of government power. Thus, the Department of Education and Science (DES) has become increasingly *dirigiste* and centralist (Lawton, 1984). This process of centralisation, and its associated interventionism, is most manifest in the growth of the Manpower Services Commission (MSC), which has functioned to by-pass and erode local government and local education authorities (Fullick, 1986). At the level of schools and further education, and also in the sphere of higher education, centralised direction, inspection and control aim to erase local autonomy in favour of centralised power.

Discipline has been targeted, of course, pre-eminently at the clientele of schools and colleges, at the young people destined to become the workforce of tomorrow. In the context of the crisis of Fordism and high unemployment 'the young workless [have been seen as] some sort of delayed high explosive device attached to the hull of the ship of state' (Mungham, 1982, p. 34). Young people as a whole have been seen as a disruptive and destabilising force, and moral panics around mugging, hooliganism and urban violence have intensified demands for discipline and control. In face of 'threatening youth' (Davies, 1986) it has been necessary to teach young people their proper place in the order of things, to reduce unrealistic expectations, and to subjugate them to the 'real' world. The White Paper on *Better Schools* (1985, p. 57) is clear that 'discourtesy, disorder and disruption' must be replaced by 'high standards of conduct within the school and beyond', by 'good behaviour and self-discipline'.

Education for flexibility: towards a new consensus

Neo-Fordism is not, however, just about clearing away the debris of a now anachronistic disciplinary structure. It is also about 'integrating the responsible worker' and 'moving towards the construction of a new consensus' (Holloway, 1987, p. 161). The objective is to elaborate a new commitment and involvement from the worker, new forms of integration, a new conformism and complicity. Traditional forms of organisation and union are to be replaced by a new individualism, and out of this reconstructed and remoralised sense of self new forms of organisation are to be made. Quality circles, for example, which aim at 'getting employees truly involved in their work and committed to their company' (Dale and Lees, 1986, p. 3) are paradigmatic of the new consensual strategy.

Fundamental to the shaping of this new individualism and to the moralisation of the neo-Fordist workforce has been the promulgation, by a broad church of educational and para-educational agitators, of a new and instrumental philosophy of education. This evolving orthodoxy, associated particularly with initiatives in further education by the Further Education Unit (FEU) and the MSC, but reinforced by cognate initiatives from a range of industrial and educational organisations, has been centred around a reconceptualisation of the relationship between education and training. It can be characterised in terms of the teaching of competences and skills rather than traditional subjects; experiential, project-based and problem-solving pedagogy rather than didactic academic methods; individualised learning contracts in which students assume responsibility for their own development; an orientation to the world of business and industry; an emphasis on technological and computer literacy; a focus on personal and social as well as technical and vocational education; new forms of profiling

and assessment which are criterion rather than norm refer-
enced – the objective is education for flexibility, education
for flexible production.

An important document that brings together the various
elements of this new pedagogy was produced in 1982 by
none less than the Rubber and Plastics Processing Industry
Training Board. Recognising that the education system has
failed to 'produce the range of skills, abilities and knowledge
required to sustain and expand the productive power and
prosperity of the nation', it argues for a new vocationalism,
but one that 'is not simply preparation for work, but the
acquisition of competences of a general character that will
be called upon by the young person in a broad spectrum of
situations arising in both his working and personal life'
(RPPITB, 1982, pp. 9, 17). Here we have the now familiar
invocation of skills, competences, personal learning agendas
and learning contracts, work experience, relevance, profiling and so forth. But there is also a clear insight into the
significance of these various elements: the objective is to
create a person who is 'a competent adult, in a variety of
situations in working and private life' (Ibid, p. 29). 'A fully
developed person', we are told,

> a mature adult, is one who is able and prepared to accept
> responsibility for himself and his actions and has developed a
> range of competencies to support that position . . . The long
> path of learning that starts in the pre-school period and leads
> through school and out into adult life is directed towards the
> goal of acquiring a range of competencies at a level that enables
> the possessor to cope with situations and pressures he will
> encounter and to establish a measure of genuine autonomy.
> Knowledge alone is not sufficient to develop competency. Skills,
> attitudes and experience are also necessary. (Ibid, p. 29)

Similar principles of flexible education are also to be
found in the various pronouncements of the 'Education for
Capability' movement. The message is the same: competence, coping, creativity, co-operation. There is the same
insistence that training should equip the student for both
work and life: 'The challenge is to discover a more reward-
ing education in which thinking and doing and making are

206 The Industrialisation of Education

fused into a new concept of living and learning' (Patrick Nuttgens, in Burgess, 1986, p. 32). There is the same emphasis on 'discovery methods', project work and independent learning. According to Tyrell Burgess (1986, p. 66), there 'is a continuum of learning, whose logic is the same, from the new-born babe to the research worker on the frontiers of knowledge. Each is engaged in the formulation of problems, in solving them and in testing the solutions'. The new pedagogy is concerned with 'method', process, competence. It is predicated, according to Burgess, on both a new theory of learning and a new theory of knowledge.

The FEU/MSC pedagogy that has developed around the New Training Initiative (TVEI, CPVE, YTS) undoubtedly contains the most powerful articulation of this 'education for flexibility' philosophy. It is a position that has been elaborated over a period of time, and it reflects certain conflicts between the FEU and MSC, but it is reasonably crystallised in such FEU publications as *A Basis for Choice* (FEU, 1982a), *Supporting YTS* (FEU, 1985a) and *Supporting TVEI* (FEU, 1985b). Recognising the need 'to provide a flexible, adaptable workforce able to cope with change', the FEU puts an emphasis on the development of competence and 'personal effectiveness', not just for work but also for the 'world outside employment'. To this end, 'trainees should acquire an insight into a learning strategy, which will enable them to find out what skills and knowledge they need to add to their existing stock' (FEU, 1985a, pp. 1, 26). It emphasises 'the development of initiative, motivation, enterprise, problem-solving skills and other personal qualities', and 'encourages active partnership in learning and the promotion of self-reliance in the learner, thus fostering personal development' as the only way to cope with 'a world of increasing complexity' (FEU, 1985b, pp. 13, 21–22).

We need not overstate the consistency and cohesiveness of these various positions for it to be clear that we are witnessing the emergence of a new strategic philosophy of education/training, one that is dedicated to producing an adaptable, flexible, integrated, self-controlling workforce for the embryonic regime of neo-Fordism. However, what does seem increasingly and, initially at least, paradoxically clear is that the new instrumentalism is in fact rooted in progressive educational traditions. Thus both pedagogies share, for example, a common focus on child-centred approaches, experiential learning and relevance, the continuum between work and life, and the use of negotiated, criterion-referenced forms of assessment. As Andy Green (1986, p. 113) observes, 'the training paradigm has evolved precisely by drawing on key progressive themes and elaborating them in new ways'.

Another writer usefully outlines four different categories of progressivism:

- *Child-Centred Progressives*, 'who conceive progress in terms of each child being more fully enabled by education to develop individual interests and potentialities authentically and without constraints'.

- *Radical Progressives*, who judge education 'by the extent to which it succeeds in promoting a basic reconstruction of society'.

- *Liberal Progressives*, concerned with 'the fuller integration of ever larger proportions of children into liberal knowledge'.

- *Instrumental Progressives*, 'whose central concern is to make education increasingly more efficient in serving what they see as the economic, political, or cultural needs of their own society'. (Partington, 1987, p. 5)

Instrumental progressivism is what particularly concerns us in this chapter.

What appears paradoxical is the discrepancy between progressivist ideals, on the one hand, and the functionalist and technocratic objectives of the new instrumentalism, on the other. Is the problem one of the misuse of what are fundamentally sound, liberatory and progressive techniques and principles? We would argue that it is nothing so simple. We cannot counterpose a 'pure' and emancipatory progressivism against its profanation and subordination to relations of power. Instrumental progressivism is clearly about control, but it is about a particular expression and modality of control, and this is the significant issue. As Philip Cohen has argued, this approach constitutes 'a modern version of self-improvement', an 'attempt to construct a ... mobile form of self-discipline, adapted to changing technologies of production and consumption' (Cohen, 1984, p. 105). The form and function of discipline are being redefined in more 'subjective' terms:

> The shift is from a system of external controls and negative sanctions, towards a more invisible process of regulation aimed at eliciting a voluntary reform of working-class structures of feeling and motivation around a system of personal controls. (Ibid, p. 114)

Cohen sees the emergence, through this process, of a new 'flexible' individualism, 'capable of adapting itself to the changing demands of market forces, while sustaining the illusion of its autonomy from them ...' (Ibid, p. 137). Instrumental progressivism is also a form of control and 'subjectivisation' that stresses 'realistic' self-assessment and self-appraisal. In Stewart Ranson's words, it emphasises 'place above horizons' (Ranson, 1985b, p. 71), the recognition of one's designated and proper station in life.

We should recognise that this particular form of (self-) discipline is not specific to what has been called the new vocationalism or instrumental progressivism. This reform of feelings, motivations and aspirations is, in fact, also characteristic of earlier and apparently more humane forms of progressivism (Sharp and Green, 1975). According to Andy Hargreaves (1977, p. 614), even in the 1960s and early 1970s, progressivism was shaped by 'the call for a new economic man characterised by adaptability and the need for the installation of an "internal supervisor" in those engaged in the shifting relations of dominance and subordination in industry'.

A fundamental insight into the common basis of both radical and instrumental progressivism is provided by Basil Bernstein in an article 'On the Classification and Framing of Educational Knowledge' (Bernstein, 1975). In this essay, which asks how forms of experience and identity are maintained and changed by the formal transmission of educational knowledge, Bernstein distinguishes what he calls 'collection' and 'integrated' codes:

> Any classification of educational knowledge which involves strong classification gives rise to what is here called a collection code. Any organisation of educational knowledge which involves a marked attempt to reduce the strength of classification is here called an integrated code. (Bernstein, 1975, p. 90)

Collection codes are characterised by well insulated subject hierarchies within educational knowledge, and under this system 'social order arises out of the hierarchical nature of the authority relationships, out of the systematic ordering of the differentiated knowledge in time and space, out of an explicit, usually predictable, examining procedure' (Ibid, p. 106). In the case of the integrated code, there is a shift to a curriculum in which the contents stand in open relation to each other and classification is reduced, and the consequence, according to Bernstein, of this disturbance in classification of knowledge, is 'a disturbance of existing authority structures' (ibid, p. 101).

What is especially important in Bernstein's argument is his recognition that progressivism, which exemplifies the integrated code, reflects a changing relationship between knowledge and power. His concern is with the implications for social control and social order of a significant transformation in the status of knowledge. As such, the direction of his inquiry is very much cognate with Lyotard's examination of the postmodern condition of knowledge (see Chapter 4). 'The growing differentiation of knowledge at the higher levels of thought, together with the integration of previously discrete areas', make necessary, in Bernstein's view, 'a form of socialisation appropriate to these changes in the structure of knowledge' (Bernstein, 1975, p. 110). Changes in workplace knowledge and skill requirements – the displacement of context-tied expertise in favour of general principles from which a range of diverse operations can be derived – also have important implications for the socialisation process: 'In crude terms, it could be said that the nineteenth century required submissive and inflexible man, whereas the late twentieth century requires conforming but flexible man' (ibid, p. 110). There is, then, in Bernstein's account, an acute awareness of the interrelationship between knowledge structures and systems on the one hand, and power structures and principles of control on the other.

In terms of the transmission of educational knowledge, the present shift from collection to integrated codes 'involves a change in what counts as having knowledge, in what counts as a valid transmission of knowledge, [and] in what counts as a valid realization of knowledge' (ibid, p. 104). This change of code, Bernstein continues, 'involves fundamental changes in the classification of knowledge and so changes in the structure and distribution of power and in principles of control' (ibid, p. 106). With the integrated code, there is a concern with the general principles, the deep structures of knowledge, upon ways of knowing (rather than states of knowledge). In contrast to the didactic theory of learning associated with the collection code, the learning process characteristic of the integrated code is more group or self-regulated and is 'likely to exhibit considerable flexibility'. Thus different concepts of what counts as knowledge have implications for the organisational framework of knowledge acquisition and for the forms of power and control that underpin this process. For example, in the case of assessment, the integrated code tends to emphasise the dispositional attributes of the student, to 'encourage more of the pupil/student to be made public; more of his thoughts, feelings and values'. The consequence, Bernstein argues, is that 'more of the pupil is available for control . . . socialisation could be more intensive and perhaps more penetrating' (ibid, p. 109).

The therapeutic state

Bernstein's analysis provides important insights into the nature and significance of what we have called instrumental progressivism. It also allows us to relate current pedagogical and curricular changes to broader social processes. What Bernstein makes clear is that strategies of instrumentalism have not been created *ex nihilo* by MSC bureaucrats, but rather that they come out of a more global and epochal mutation in the structures of power and control. In its account of the shift from the collection code to the integrated code, Bernstein's work in fact converges with many of the broader concerns of historians and sociologists of social control.

The development of social control is a process that occurs in the *longue durée* of historical time, the long-term history of institutional and discursive forms. It is a process that does not readily synchronise with the succession of regimes of accumulation. In his discussion of deviancy control systems, Stanley Cohen describes their development in terms of 'master patterns', arguing that there have been two transformations in the history of Western industrial societies. The first took place between the end of the eighteenth and the beginning of the twentieth century. The second, 'which is supposed to be happening now, is thought by some to represent a questioning, even a radical reversal of that earlier transformation, by others to merely signify a continuation and intensification of its patterns' (Cohen, 1985, p. 13). A fundamental issue, then, concerns the continuity or discontinuity between contemporary transformations in the nature of social control and earlier forms of regulation. A second, and equally difficult, problem concerns the relationship between the periodicity of control structures and that of forms of accumulation; particularly, it raises the question of the relationship between changes in the forms of social control and the emergence of neo-Fordism as a new pattern of accumulation.

For Morris Janowitz (1975, p. 84), the historical development of social control is associated with 'the reduction of coercion' and with 'a commitment to procedures of redefining societal goals in order to enhance the role of rationality'. Steven Spitzer (1979, pp. 188–90) also emphasises this growing rationalisation, and associates it with a more abstract and depersonalised form of social regulation. Control becomes less dependent upon direct coercion, and increasingly impersonal, automatic, routine and banal in its operation. It also becomes ever more intensive and extensive – Cohen (1979) refers to this process as 'thinning the mesh and widening the net'. 'Rational' control becomes invasive and pervasive, proactive as well as reactive. It increasingly colonises the everyday world; it penetrates the lifeworld; it disciplines the social body.

As social control becomes increasingly 'rational', impersonal and continuous, it can, we would argue, be characterised in terms of one fundamental principle: surveillance and information gathering. According to Anthony Giddens (1985, p. 2),

> information storage is central to the role of 'authoritative resources' in the structuring of social systems spanning larger ranges of space and time than tribal cultures. Surveillance – control of information and superintendence of the activities of some groups by others – is in turn the key to the expansion of such resources.

Direct and coercive supervision is increasingly replaced by surveillance and the accumulation of coded information. In similar vein, Edward Shils (1967, pp. 329, 341) refers to the 'cognitive passion' of control agencies, and notes that 'the cognitive appetite is an anomic one – it is incapable of satiation'. What we have seen, continues Shils, is 'an invasion of personal privacy of an extreme character' reinforced by the 'belief that it is perfectly proper to gather knowledge about the individual's past, his inner life, and his idiosyncracies' (Ibid, pp. 331, 333). Individual privacy is increasingly eroded by cognitive intrusion and intrusive perception, and this penetrative seeing and knowing is increasingly reinforced by technologies of observation and recording.

The question of the relationship between surveillance, knowledge and control has been most fully developed in the work of Michel Foucault. Foucault argues that power and knowledge imply each other, 'that there is no power relation without the correlative constitution of a field of knowledge, nor any knowledge that does not presuppose at the same time power relations' (Foucault, 1979, p. 27).

Axiomatic to the accumulation of knowledge about a subject population is its visibility. Foucault insists that

> The exercise of discipline presupposes a mechanism that coerces by means of observation; an apparatus in which the techniques that make it possible to see induce effects of power, and in which, conversely, the means of coercion make those on whom they are applied clearly visible. (Ibid, pp. 170–71)

The paradigmatic case of seeing/knowledge/power is, for Foucault, Jeremy Bentham's Panopticon. This instrumental structure, for example a prison or asylum, allows inmates located around the internal circumference of a wheel-like building to be continuously observed from a central inspection tower. The inmates are seen, but they cannot see. Nor can the communicate with one another; they remain in 'a sequestered and observed solitude' (p. 201). Within the Panopticon the punished/ill individual is observed in two ways: 'surveillance, of course, but also knowledge of each inmate, of his behaviour, his deeper states of mind . . .' (p. 249).

For Foucault, the Panopticon is not a historical curiosity, but rather an 'indefinitely generalisable mechanism' (p. 205), a monument of modern power relations. What Foucault emphasises is a distinctively modern power and control system, one which hinges on universal visibility, upon an extensive and intensive process of surveillance and knowledge gathering. What is distinctive about its operation is that it dispenses with coercion in favour of self-policing. The Panopticon 'induces in the inmate a state of conscious and permanent visibility that assures the automatic functioning of power' (p. 201):

> He who is subjected to a field of visibility, and who knows it, assumes responsibility for the constraints of power; he makes them play spontaneously upon himself; he inscribes in himself the power relation in which he simultaneously plays both roles; he becomes the very principle of his own subjection. (pp. 202–3)

In so far as the inmates are continuously observed they internalise the relations of power and regulate themselves.

The operation of power, moreover, is automatic and impersonal. We are, says Foucault, 'in the panoptic machine, invested by its effects of power, which we bring to ourselves since we are part of its mechanism' (p. 217).

The Panopticon is a prefigurative element in the formation of what Foucault calls a disciplinary society. What Foucault helps us to understand are the mechanisms through which individuals are rendered compliant within 'the disciplinary culture of the therapeutic state' (O'Neill, 1986, p. 43). This disciplinary or therapeutic culture is characterised by surveillance and cognitive intrusion, and the consequence of this absolute visibility is to 'automatize' and 'disindividualise' the functioning of power. Christopher Lasch (1980) has written of the increasingly expansive and intensive activities of the 'therapeutic state', of the invasion of individual privacy by its 'tutelary apparatus'. Such areas of life as physical and mental health, childcare, moral behaviour and even sexuality are subjected to surveillance and administrative documentation. Lasch (1985, p. 47) describes 'the shift from an authoritative to a thereapeutic mode of social control – a shift that has transformed not only industry but also politics, the school and the family'. 'Observation', he notes, 'initially conceived as a means to more effective forms of supervision and control, has become a means of control in its own right' (ibid, p. 48). The education system constitutes an important element of this shift towards therapeutic discipline. Like other elements of the 'tutelary complex', it 'both reflects and contributes to the shift from authoritative sanctions to manipulation and surveillance – the redefinition of political authority in therapeutic terms . . .' (ibid, p. 49).

Cybernetics and social control

Changes in the education system, we are arguing, constitute just one aspect of a broader transformation in patterns of social control. It will be obvious from our account so far that periodising this process of transformation is extremely difficult. Are contemporary forms of social control continuous with the 'disciplinary society' Foucault sees emerging early in the nineteenth century? Or is there a significant shift in the master pattern of control in the late twentieth century? These are highly problematical issues and are the subject of much debate. Our own view tends to emphasise the continuity of disciplinary patterns. What might appear to be innovative and progressive developments towards self-regulation are, we maintain, fundamental to the panoptic model. The theme of the Panopticon – 'at once surveillance and observation, security and knowledge, individualization and totalization, isolation and transparency' (Foucault, 1979, p. 249) – remains the paradigm for social control.

However, there has been one highly significant disciplinary innovation in the late twentieth century in the developent of the computer and other information technologies. These technologies have not changed the master pattern of control, though the computer is today the fundamental technology of seeing and knowing, surveillance and information storage. What the computer has achieved is the extension and intensification of panoptic control; it has rendered social control more pervasive, more invasive, more total, but also more routine, mundane and inescapable. Following Foucault's line of argument, Mark Poster (1984, pp. 115, 103) suggests that the new information technologies

> extend the reach of normalizing surveillance . . . In the electronic age, spatial limitations are bypassed as restraints on the controlling hierarchies . . . As a consequence Panoptic monitoring extends not simply to massed groups but to the isolated individual. The normalized individual is not only the one at work, in an asylum, in jail, in school, in the military, as Foucault observes, but also the individual in his or her home, at play, in all the mundane activities of everyday life. (Cf. Webster and Robins, 1986, Part 3)

On the basis of the new technologies, surveillance becomes continuous and encompassing, 'a diffuse panoptic vision' (Marx, 1985, p. 26).

Cybernetics, through its escalation of this panoptic vision, becomes fundamental to the process of social control. We can speak of 'a *cybernetic society*, in which the moral principle of democratic societies – individual autonomy – becomes more and more anachronistic and is replaced by *technical imperatives* handed down from the administrative-economic spheres' (Wolin, 1984–5, p. 27, original emphasis; see also Goodwin and Humphreys, 1982). With Bentham's architectural Panopticon cognitive and scopic intrusion ensure power without coercion: 'Thanks to the techniques of surveillance, the "physics" of power, the hold over the body, operate according to the laws of optics and mechanics . . . without recourse, in principle at least, to excess, force or violence' (Foucault, 1979, p. 177). To these laws, the electronic Panopticon adds those of cybernetics, of information processing and handling, and in so doing it intensifies the mechanisms of social control. This generalised panopticism operates through individual, and ultimately social, interiorisation of surveillance. As Marike Finlay (1987, p. 177) argues, disciplinary constraint 'functions by means of the internalization of procedures of discourse within the consciousness of the "controlled" subjects'. At one level, this entails a vulnerable sense of visibility, such that these subjects come to 'watch themselves', to exercise power over their own selves. It also entails the introjection of procedures and behaviours – ways of acting, of speaking, of thinking – appropriate to a disciplinary institution. That institution defines the parameters and the conceptual framework through which the subject experiences and thinks the world. In the case of the electronic Panopticon,

> there is an internalization of such discursive procedures as means/end logic, a problem-solving conception of knowledge, and certain patterns of information and ordering. Once internalized, all of these procedures have a surveillance capacity over the subject's social interaction. (Ibid, p. 177–8)

The subject's relationship to both internal and external realities (and possibilities) becomes fixed around certain rationalist principles, and alternative perceptions and relationships become foreclosed.

The computer, according to Sherry Turkle (1984, p. 3), 'changes people's awareness of themselves, of one another,

of their relationship with the world . . . it affects the way that
we think, especially the way we think about ourselves'; it
'holds up a new mirror in which mind is reflected as
machine'. Turkle is, of course, building upon the conceptual
foundations of cybernetic theory which, for some considerable time now, have interpreted social, psychological and
biological processes in terms of the processing of information. The language of servomechanisms, self-regulation,
feedback loops and control loops, it was claimed, applied to
all – mechanical, natural, social, human – processes. Furthermore, the recognition that people and computing
machines had fundamentally common features meant that
'the analogy between them becomes more compelling'
(Neisser, 1966, pp. 74–5).

Recognising that people are increasingly coming to see
themselves as information processing machines, Theodore
Roszak suggests that this may reflect 'a haunting sense of
human inadequacy and existential failure' (Roszak, 1986,
p. 44). Referring to what he calls the 'data processing model
of the mind', Roszak suggests that this conception '– even if
it is no better than a caricature – easily carries over into a
prescription for character and value. When we grant anyone
the power to teach us *how* to think, we may also be granting
them the chance to teach us *what* to think, where to begin
thinking, where to stop' (ibid, p. 217).

This cybernetic model is not, then, simply a neutral,
technical, phenomenon. It entails a particular concept of
mind, of reason, of knowledge and skill, and it forecloses
alternative conceptions. It privileges mechanistic over holistic thinking; cognition over intuition; calculative over deli-
berative rationality (Dreyfus and Dreyfus, 1986). It also
reinforces the dissociation of reason from the emotional life
(see MacMurray, 1935). Thus, according to Christopher
Lasch (1984, p. 27), the cybernetic image of the machine-
like self 'satisfies the wish to believe that thought can divorce
itself from emotion'; it is predicated on the faith that thought
can 'overcome the emotional and bodily limitations that
have encumbered humanity in the past'. Underpinning this
image, Lasch argues, 'is the fantasy of total control, absolute
transcendence of the limits imposed on mankind by its lowly

origins'. In accepting this cybernetic discourse, and internalising its procedures, we imprison ourselves within its horizons.

Instrumental progressivism

Our discussion of instrumental progressivisim has sought to locate this pedagogical strategy in the context of broader patterns of social control. The real significance of recent developments in schools and colleges can only be grasped adequately, we would argue, from this disciplinary perspective. We want now to return to an examination of the new instrumentalism, the FEU/MSC pedagogy particularly, and to consider it specifically in terms of control. YTS, TVEI, CPVE have been very much shaped by strategies of social control (Fowler, 1985; 1986). Rather than just meeting 'the needs of industry', these initiatives constitute 'a massive state intervention in socialization', 'a new "science" of youth in which notions of work preparation and "life" management are united, an attempt to technologise previous cultural patterns that are regarded as either inadequate or no longer produced "naturally"' (Stronach, 1984, pp. 59–60). As such, this constitutes a strategy which requires situating in the context of other control measures aimed at youth.

We want to look at two aspects of the new pedagogy in particular: first profiling and assessment; and then the question of skills and competences. Profiling is at the core of panoptic discipline. It is central to that process whereby 'ever widening aspects of student life and identity [are] brought within scrutiny [and] the possibility is created for ever stronger forms of social control and the "pedagogic colonisation of everyday life"' (Atkinson *et al*, 1986, p. 163). Profiles and records of assessment have become a constitutive feature of all the educational and training schemes and profiling has been advocated by a wide range of organisations (for example, MSC, FEU, Royal Society of Arts, City and Guilds, and the National Union of Teachers). Whilst there are clearly significant divergences in the profiling schemes that have been introduced or proposed, we want to focus here on what they have in common. Profiles are a fundamental aspect of student-centred, 'progressive', teaching methods, and have the objectives of both recognising and documenting achievement as well as increasing motivation by stressing 'positive qualities such as enthusiasm, enterprise, adaptability, persistence, punctuality, willingness and capacity to accept responsibility, ability to participate constructively in group activity and ability to work independently' (DES/Welsh Office, 1984, p. 4), as well as academic achievement.

The principles upon which profiling is based are characterised by Patricia Broadfoot as threefold: a formative principle, which emphasises diagnosis of strengths and weaknesses and 'mastery and achievement rather than norm-referencing and failure'; a concern for 'open and collaborative relations between teachers and pupils'; and a summative function, which provides 'information about skills, aptitudes and capabilities which will be useful for pupils, their teachers and their families, and for potential consumers of such records' (Broadfoot, 1986, pp. 5–6).

What is seen by many as the emancipatory aspect of profiling, with its emphasis on guidance, counselling and negotiation, has its roots in progressivism. But so too do the control dimensions. As Bernstein argues, with reference to the integrated code, assessment becomes more intrusive and penetrating, taking into account the attitude and dispositions of the student. Profiling is concerned not just with cognitive and academic achievements, but also with social and behavioural qualities, with the evaluation of personality (Morrison, 1983).

The belief that profiling will motivate students also has strong control dimensions. In the words of Tyrell Burgess and Elizabeth Adams (1986, p. 78), 'the emphasis on a factual account of what students have achieved and experienced and an acceptance of accounts by students themselves of what they have done suggests a new place for students in the management of their own education'. A Schools Council research programme found teachers to believe that students who were involved in their own assessment would 'feel that their behaviour would affect their own future' and that 'the realization that qualities such as courtesy and discipline or behaviour were being formally recorded would encourage better behaviour' (Balogh, 1982, p. 40). What we see here is that process of self-regulation characteristic of Bernstein's integrated code; that internalisation of patterns of thinking and behaving which is characteristic of panoptic discipline.

Profiles are about power and control. This is not a question of their misuse, with the possibility that they might be used more rigorously and sagaciously, as some accounts suggest. In our view, profiling is inherently a mechanism of surveillance and discipline, one that functions both intrusively and unobtrusively. According to Andy Hargreaves (1986, pp. 217–18), such penetrating scrutiny has been characteristic of all forms of progressivism:

> In theory, no place was private; there was no hiding place from the teacher's relentless, if benevolent, pursuit . . . If the conversion of developing persons into easily processable cases is one surveillance-related danger inherent in personal recording, another is the development of a principle of observation and monitoring whose sophistication and comprehensiveness is virtually unsurpassed in the history of schooling.

What are the possibilities when such systems become fully computerised? Do computers not promise to bring the potential of profile surveillance to fruition?

The second aspect of instrumental progressivism that we want to look at in this section is the new conception of trainee skills and competences which has been central to all recent FEU/MSC initiatives (Pratley, 1985). This doctrine of skills has been elaborated and expounded by a number of different organisations, and there are a number of disagreements and differences of emphasis in the various positions. It has also evolved over the past ten years in response to the changing economic and political context. Again, however, we are less interested here in doctrinal variants than with the broader meaning of the enterprise as a whole. This, we would argue, is about control. The language of competence, transferability, personal effectiveness, and so on, is a manifestation of the new technics of disciplinary power. In Basil

Bernstein's terms, this is centred around that shift in what counts as having knowledge and skill which underpins the transition from 'submissive and inflexible man' to 'conforming but flexible man'. It is also about, in Marike Finlay's terms, panoptic, self-regulation through the assumption and internalisation of particular discursive procedures and constraints on knowledge.

Initially, in the late 1970s, the developing new pedagogy focused upon what were called Social and Life Skills (SLS). Social skills were those needed when dealing with other people, both at work and in private life; life skills are those 'we need to go about our daily lives' and consist of coping skills, job finding skills and leisure skills. The focus here is on coping and surviving in a world of high unemployment and adapting to a future of enforced leisure. SLS is predicated upon a deficit model of the student and stands in the tradition of compensatory education (Atkinson *et al.*, 1982). It assumes that young people are responsible for their own state of unemployment: unemployment is a consequence of personal deficiences, such as illiteracy, innumeracy, lack of punctuality or communication skills, and these must be rectified (Davies, 1979). The skills taught were extremely content (or product) based: 'job-hunting skills, self-marketing skills, knowledge of how to get information on retraining opportunities, government grants and schemes, and further and higher education options' (Hopson and Scally, 1981, p. 9). It is a matter of interview techniques, handling money, using spare time properly, talking to the boss, and various other accomplishments (Blythe *et al.*, 1979).

Retrospectively, we may see SLS very much as a strategy for the transitional (Holloway's 'macho') phase of restructuring. In its tendency to 'blame the victim', to focus on survival and coping, and to reintroduce 'realism', it was a provisional, containing strategy. In the 1980s, however, we begin to see the emergence of a new stage concerned with remoralisation and reintegration. Drawing upon traditions of progressivism, this new approach emphasises the positive qualities of trainees, their (albeit differential) integration into the world of work, and their self-regulation and social responsibilities. As the nature of the new regime of accumulation became more clear, so the rhetoric of training shifted to a concern with flexibility, basic skills, process skills, transferable skills. 'The future', it was realised, 'may demand a radically different approach to enable people to cope with non-routine tasks as well as with rapid change in job content. "Training for versatility", "training for flexibility", are alternative phrases which have been used to describe what is required' (Duncan and Kelly, 1983, p. 6).

Overall, the new doctrine of skills contains complexities and nuances that are scholastic in their complexity. It is the consequence of a herculean labour of social research which reflects the complicity of a great deal of such research in the project of social engineering. With its imprimatur of 'scientific' and 'objective' methodology, such research is, according to Edward Shils (1967, p. 330), 'the highest and purest manifestation of the expansion of the cognitive interest in human beings'. An example of such work is that undertaken at the Occupational Research Unit of the University of Wales Institute of Science and Technology. Their premise is that 'there is an urgent and growing need for people at work to be far more adaptable than at present' (Downs, 1982, p. 9) and, on this basis, it is argued that training must increasingly focus on skill transfer, skill ownership and 'learning to learn'. This entails, pre-eminently, a shift in emphasis from what has to be learned (product) to how it is learned (process): 'The teaching of process skills, such as identification of error, awareness of standards, questioning and fault diagnosis, require very different methods from those traditionally used by the teacher or trainer' (Downs and Perry, 1984, p. 26). Trainees must be encouraged to 'learn to improve their ways of learning' and to 'see learning as their own responsibility' (Downs and Perry, 1986, pp. 42–3). What we see here is a thoroughgoing systematisation of progressive methods (the integrated code).

A second contribution from social research has been that of the Institute of Manpower Studies (IMS) which has been influential in shaping MSC policy. In their report to the National Economic Development Office and the MSC (NEDC/MSC), the IMS makes clear its emphasis on flexibility, self-reliance and occupational competence. In a number of reports (notably, Hayes *et al.*, 1982; Townsend, 1982; Hayes *et al.*, 1983) the IMS developed a dense conceptual grid which elaborated on the notion of 'abstract and open-ended process skills' and sought to relate them to particular occupational groupings or 'occupational training families' (Hayes *et al.*, 1981). 'What is new' in the IMS work, we are told, 'is the link between occupational training families and the way in which competence at work is developed. It is a combination of identifying transferable skills and of enabling young people to transfer such skills because they "own" them' (Hayes and Fonda, 1982). What is being developed in the IMS research is a form of instrumental progressivism in which self-regulation is adapted to a context in which, because of specific economic and technological factors, job specific vocational preparation is no longer an adequate socialising force. Within this perspective young people 'own' their skills, and as they move about in search of work, they take these skills with them and sell them in the labour market.

Though not taken up in their entirety, these arguments have converged with those of the FEU to shape significantly MSC thinking. In its report on *Basic Skills* (FEU, 1982b), the FEU takes up the ideas of skill ownership and training families too, arguing that vocational preparation should 'provide young people with a range of skills that have utility across vocational areas . . . competence over a core of skills common to many occupations will improve their adaptability' (ibid, p. 3). The basic skills necessary to a trainee include core, transferable skills alongside vocational area skills and specific occupational skills. In its account of *Core Skills in YTS* (MSC, 1984) – which has a somewhat different emphasis to that of the FEU – the MSC emphasises the importance of core skills for achieving competence, for transferability, for progression to further education, and for coping with the world outside employment. Developing core skills (number, communication, problem solving, practical skills) has 'as much to do with how trainees are learning as it has to do with what specific knowledge they are acquiring'. Its objective is competence: 'Competence is not the same

thing as having acquired skills; it is being able to apply them
in the right way and at the right time . . . [it is] the ability to
perform in a real situation' (MSC, 1984, pp. 6–7).

It is only in the process of development that the 'progressive', as opposed to simply repressive, aspects of the new
instrumentalism have become clearer and more theoretically
grounded. The concept of competence – defined as the
possession and development of skills, knowledge and
appropriate attitudes and experience – has been central to
this process. Extremely important in this context is the
FEU's short but concise booklet, *Towards a Competence-
Based System* (FEU, 1984). The FEU argues for a 'wider
definition of competence than that associated with working
life', one that also includes 'life roles' (ibid, p. 3). This
extension of competence from occupational skills to 'life
skills' aims to break down the polarisation of the education
system 'between academic and vocational learning, between
high and low-level teaching, between "real" work-based and
"abstract" classroom assignments, and so on' (p. 5). Here
we have realised Stronach's (1984) 'science of youth' in
which 'life management' coalesces with vocational preparation.

A second important FEU document is *Ability Learning*
(Smith, 1984), which makes a contribution to the theoretical
justification of FEU/MSC positions. Smith aims to mobilise
a 'scientific theory' – Piaget's theory of cognitive development – to 'clarify' the nature of general, transferable skills.
'There is', he argues, 'an evident similarity between a basic
skills curriculum projected in [FEU research] and Piaget's
account of general, transferable abilities in the adolescent/
adult' (Ibid, p. vi). Smith associates transferable ability with
formal operational thinking, and argues that 'general, cognitive abilities . . . can be transferred from one context to
another [and] have an acceptable, psychological basis' (ibid,
p. 87; see also Kuhn, 1986).

We shall say more of Piaget in a moment, but for the
present it is enough to note the vigour with which instrumental progressivism is being buttressed. We end this
section by asking whether the MSC, FEU and IMS have
made some fundamental educational breakthrough, or

whether this is not a case of the emperor's new clothes. Veering towards the latter, we would tend to agree with Philip Cohen that transferable skilling in fact amounts to a deskilling of the many. This because skill has come to be

> defined in terms of certain abstract universals – as a set of instrumental properties common to the functional co-ordination of isolated operations of mind/body machine. Training in these so called transferable skills is essentially training for abstract labour, i.e. labour considered in its generic commodity form as an interchangeable unit/factor of production. The main function of this reclassification, in fact, is to increase elasticities of subsitution between different occupational categories, and thus indirectly to undermine the residual forms of control exercised by skilled manual workers over conditions of entry and training in their trades. (Cohen, 1984, p. 113)

This new doctrine of skills and competence – which is currently moving into the world of higher education (NAB, 1986b) – is about reconstituting skills and knowledge on a new basis in order to reconstruct and control structures. As such, it is but one phase in a long history of such initiatives and strategies of social control.

Computer literacy

Computers and computer literacy are central to the MSC's instrumental progressivism (see Vincent and Vincent, 1985). The computer is the totem of the post-industrial 'revolution' in education and computer literacy is the passport to its rewards. What is more astonishing even than the number of tracts about computer literacy is their conformity and pre-dictability. Each chants a familiar litany about a new kind of learning that is individualised, student-centred, active, experiential and so on.

We want to focus here on computer literacy only in the context of social control. In order to do this we shall begin by exploring the concepts of learning, knowledge and the mind which inform this messianic doctrine. The fundamental premise is that of cybernetics: the axiomatic belief that the human mind functions like, or as, a computational machine. According to Stonier and Conlin (1985, p. 194), 'the human mind is an exquisite information processing device'. Asserting that 'the computer-brain analogy seems to becoming culturally acceptable', two other proponents of computer literacy suggest that 'the ways by which good organisations of knowledge in a computer are developed suggest guidelines and insights into how learning environments might lead to the development of good organisations of knowledge in a child's brain' (O'Shea and Self, 1983, p. 246, 5). 'Computer science', they assert, 'is not just about computer machinery. It is also about ways of describing processes – understanding, thinking, reasoning, recognizing, learning. Education could well do with more precise descriptions of these activities' (p. 268). Computer science, according to Marvin Minsky (1977, p. 245), has 'given us a wholly new collection of concepts for thinking about Thinking itself', one that will allow us 'to compose theories of Learning, and of Education, based on adequate descriptions of mental processes'.

This approach privileges rational procedures, goal-directed behaviour and cognitive structures. It emphasises that problem-solving skills entail solving problems through 'algorithmic thinking', which according to one writer 'is the third stage in problem solving that began to succeed the intuitive and prescriptive stages even before the computer era, with such precursors as scientific management' (Paisley, 1985, p. 23). This also tends to lead to an emphasis on process (rather than product) learning. According to Kenneth Ruthven (1984, p. 144) the development of computer skills is very much 'conceptualised within a process-oriented model for the curriculum which emphasises the development of information handling and problem-solving skills'. The concept of knowledge that is mobilised is instrumental in the extreme and is concerned with control. It is about the use of powerful electronic tools to manipulate and control the world. Thomas Dwyer (1980, p. 88) refers to this as 'liberating control', which means control over both the environment and over oneself:

Control over the environment would include control of social, physical and economic factors. More important, education should teach internal control. After three decades of work with progressive education, Dewey could still write, 'the ideal aim of education should be self-control'.

The major exponent of this cognitive instrumentalism, the deity of the computer literati, is Seymour Papert, whose book, *Mindstorms* (1980), is a constant point of reference. Papert expresses a concern in his work with the 'theoretical consideration of education, computational models and the human psyche' (Papert, 1979, p. 73). It constitutes undoubtedly the most coherent and successful version of the cognitivist position with its assimilation of human psychic processes to that of the computer. Papert envisages children as miniature programmers, arguing that 'in teaching the computer how to think, children embark on an exploration about how they themselves think' (Papert, 1980, p. 19). The emphasis is on process skills and learning how to learn. Papert stresses 'the power of ideas and the power of the mind' and their importance for gaining a 'sense of mastery' (p. 119, 5). Fundamental to his conceptual framework is the developmental psychology of Piaget which places particular emphasis on the cognitive dimensions of infant and child maturation. It was from Piaget that Papert took over the idea of 'child as epistemologist', of 'children as the active builders of their own intellectual structures' (p. 19). Subsequently, his project was to 'uncover a more revolutionary Piaget, one whose epistemological ideas might expand known bounds of the human mind', and to do this by placing Piaget's psychology within the framework of artificial intelligence theory (p. 157).

What should be clear by now is the affinity between Papert's position (and, indeed, the doctrine of computer literacy in general) and the instrumental progressivism we discussed earlier in this chapter. Papert, who refers to himself as 'an educational utopian', locates his work within progressive traditions. There is, he suggests, a form of educational computing, characterised by drill and practice, which reinforces traditional and reactionary educational structures. Within such structures, the teacher is 'an authority figure who prescribes the exercises and judges their performance', while the child learns 'how to accept authority in a way prescribed by school and society': 'Replacing the human teacher by a machine changes nothing, except perhaps that it makes the process more effective by giving it a mechanical image that is in fact more resonant with what is really going on' (Papert, 1979, p. 76). Such an approach creates a situation in which the student is passive, programmed by the computer rather than programming it.

This is the kind of teaching situation that Bernstein refers to as the collection code. Against it, Papert counterposes a cognitivist progressivism that we can characterise in terms of the integrated code. In this approach the child programmes the computer, 'the child himself is in control, and the results of the child's programming are limited only by his imagination' (Ibid, p. 81). According to Papert, 'the authoritarian model is broken': 'The teacher becomes a partner with the child in a joint enterprise of understanding something that is truly unknown because the situations created by each child are totally new' (p. 83). There is also, we are told, a change in the child's relation to knowledge, which now becomes a source of power, the capacity to 'make things work'. Interaction with the computer 'can put the learner into contact with his most private self, it can also nurture in him an image of himself as an independent intellectual agent' (p. 86). Papert explicitly situates his work in the context of progressivism, in the tradition of Dewey, Neill and Montessori, arguing that their views were fundamentally correct but 'failed for lack of a technological basis' (p. 85).

Bernstein's observations on progressive education should make us suspicious of any attempt, such as Papert's, to counterpose egalitarian and collaborative progressivism against authoritarian and dominative didacticism. Relations of power do not just dissolve away. Because of this the question we should raise is that of the particular form which relations of power and control assume. Into what decisive structures and procedures are Papert's students socialised?

As a number of critics have pointed out, Papert has an excessively rationalistic understanding of human development and identity (Dreyfus and Dreyfus, 1986; Roszak,

1986; Davy, 1984). This cognitivist emphasis is characteristic of instrumental progressivism (cf. Smith, 1984). As Valerie Walkerdine (1984, p. 164) has observed, the panoptic discipline that underpins progressivism is based on 'a transformation from regulation by overt coercion to regulation by covert normalization, based on apparatuses and techniques for the classification and therefore regulation of the normal'. What has come increasingly to distinguish this process of covert regulation is an emphasis on rationality. Thus, Piaget asserted the normality of a progression in child development from emotion to reason, and he 'suggested that the best course for mankind was to channel children's development away from the dominance of the emotions towards the rationality which alone would be the guarantor of progress' (Ibid, p. 176). Development was seen in terms of the acquisition of knowledge, and the normalised child was seen as spontaneously and naturally rational. Drawing on Foucault, Walkerdine suggests that rationality came to be regarded as an intrinsic feature of development, one that could be observed, normalised and regulated. The current obsession with skills, competences, process learning, and so on, is a further stage in the normalising 'scientific' discourse of cognitive development. Its achievement is a conception of the student or trainee as an information processing machine. An MSC advertisement from 1986 shows a photograph of a trainee with various parts of her body labelled: her head, 'memory of over 2048 megabytes (larger than a £170m. computer)' her eyes, 'unequalled visual response mechanism'; her ears, 'highly sophisticated listening device'; and so on.

What this account suppresses is the intuitive, emotional, aesthetic side of human experience, in favour of an exclusive preoccupation with cognition. Even in terms of cognition, it privileges analytical thinking over holistic forms of understanding (Dreyfus, 1980). This faith in logic, rationalism, quantification, models, finds its most developed expression in cybernetics and artificial intelligence theory (cf. Searle, 1984). As Douglas Noble (1986, p. 20) has demonstrated, cybernetics has been an important shaping force in the development of instrumental progressivism: cybernetic and information theory 'came to be absorbed – through the work of Jerome Bruner and others – into an "intellectual" reform of American education, culminating in educators' recent fascination with the cognitive: problem-solving, thinking skills, and the microcomputer'. There is also an affinity with cybernetics in the work of Piaget. John Broughton refers to his work as 'cybernetic bio-psychology' and suggests that what Piaget 'strives to capture in his theory, that pragmatic quality of human beings that can be comprehended within a cybernetic worldview, is purposive-rational and goal-directed action' (Broughton, 1981, pp. 269–70).

This cognitivist position is perhaps the most refined form of instrumental and technocratic rationality. Broughton (1985, p. 105) refers to it as 'systems positivism' and suggests that its significance is in 'socializing individuals in the cognitive mode appropriate to functioning within bureaucratic organizations . . . socialization into deference to a particular, functionally defined form of authority'. Computer literacy, in its more 'progressive' forms, claims to liberate students, to endow them with control over their environment and their selves. Papert (1980, p. 155) acknowledges that the computer makes people afraid of 'losing respect for their intuitions, sense of values, powers of judgement. They worry about instrumental reason becoming a model for good thinking'. For him, however, these are not 'fears about computers themselves but rather . . . fears about how culture will assimilate the computer presence'. His is a use/abuse model: the computer is a neutral force in society, which may either be used beneficially or, alternatively, misused. Our own view is that the problem is a great deal more profound. The computer, we believe, is deeply implicated in transformations in our self-image and in relations of power and control. This is not some unfortunate by-product, a temporary problem of misuse, but is, rather, an intrinsic and constitutive aspect, one that is central to evolving forms of 'progressive' social control.

Part III
Beyond Technocracy?

8

The Military Project

'For the existing crisis is advancing towards a point where,
either we will be confronted with a natural or social catas-
trophe or, before or after this, human beings will react in one
way or another to try to establish new forms of social life
making sense to them. We cannot do this for them, or in their
place; any more than we can say how it could be done. What
we can do is to destroy the myths which, more than money or
weapons, constitute the most formidable obstacles in the way
of the reconstruction of human society.' (Cornelius Castoriadis,
1984/85, p. 35)

In this chapter and the next we want to conclude our
discussion by looking at how, in the late twentieth century,
the politics of technology have become bound up with the
politics of education. Though many readers might expect
some 'positive' alternatives, we do not forward a list of
policies to counter the perspectives we criticise. Such a
policy agenda would, no doubt, be worthy and well-
meaning, but in the end it would, we are sure, be tokenistic
and hollow. How could we, as two individuals, really have
all the answers? We do not know the way to the yellow brick
road. We can, however, contribute by alerting travellers to
obstacles in the way of reconstruction that are profound and
formidable, and which, most certainly, will not be overcome
by the superficial technical fix dreamed up by I.T. utopians
and futurologists.

The problems are more intractable. As John Broughton
(1985, p. 115) argues, 'the computer exemplifies a particular

vision of civilization, past as well as future'. To question it means beginning to query the whole project of modern science and technology (cf. Jonas, 1984). 'To question the computer in a rigorous way also means', according to Douglas Sloan (1984, p. 541), 'to begin to ask critical questions about the whole of modern education as it has increasingly taken form even before and up to the advent of the computer'. In what follows, we confront major barriers to meaningful social change: the myths that surround and underpin, first the technological system, and then the sphere of education.

The politics of technology

For post-industrialists and futurists technology is neutral, technique appears 'as value-free, referred to efficiency as its only touchstone of value' (Castoriadis, 1984, p. 242). Thus, to take a single example, one advocate of computer literacy asserts that 'the purposes for which the power and versatility of the computer are used are human choices; they are not the inevitable consequences of the machines themselves' (Gerver, 1984, p. 106). Computers in themselves are asocial; they are not 'in themselves responsible for the power that often exploits them' (ibid, p. 30). Hence computers can be both potentially liberatory and potentially menacing – though the former is more probable – and the issue is one of their use or misuse rather than some intrinsic tendency. If the abuse of technological potential can be obviated, then it is a force for human betterment and progress. 'The machine', Daniel Boorstin (1978, pp. 90–1) contends, 'is the great witness to man's power ... The power of the machine is man's power to remake his world, to master it to his own ends'. It is this unswerving faith in technological advancement and deliverance that characterises the Republic of Technology.

We think that our society has been seduced by 'a collective fantasy of technological power', such that 'whatever the question, technology has typically been the ever-ready ... answer' (Noble, 1984, pp. xi–xii). Technology has become second nature, a given and unquestionable part of the order of things. Such is the standing of technology that 'there is an appearance of arrogance when one attempts a moral examination of the technological enterprise' (Borgmann, 1984, p. 174). Technology contains the 'promise of liberation and enrichment, and to refuse the promise would be to choose confinement, misery, and poverty . . . technology has the tendency to disappear from the occasion of decision by insinuating itself as the basis of the occasion' (ibid, p. 103). Technology has become both means and ends, the instrument of progress but also its fulfilment. As Langdon Winner (1986, p. 39) observes, 'in our times people are often willing to make drastic changes in the way they live to accommodate technological innovation while at the same time resisting similar kinds of changes justified on political grounds'. Technology has become the myth of our times.

Cornelius Castoriadis has contributed enormously to our understanding of this technological myth. According to Castoriadis (1982, p. 8) 'the alleged neutrality and supposed instrumentality of technique, and even scientific knowledge, are illusions . . . it forms part of the contemporary constitution of society, that is to say, it forms part of the dominant social imaginary (*imaginaire social*) of our epoch'. The social imaginary of any society expresses itself through those ideas, values and attitudes, those definitions of reality and of being, that appear incontestable: it is that society's 'singular way of living . . . [the] source of what is each time given as indisputable and indisputed sense, support of the articulations and distinctions of what matters and of what does not' (Castoriadis, quoted in Thompson, 1982, p. 664). Modern society is fixated by the idea of progress, growth and development without end, and by the power of instrumental reason to achieve this dream. The 'hidden motor' of this technological development is, according to Castoriadis (1984/85, p. 31), the idea of 'total mastery', 'the fantasy of total control, of our will or desire mastering all objects and all circumstance'. The fundamental myth of our time is that of control, omnipotence, domination, and its power lies in the fact that it appears to be a purely neutral phenomenon, an expression of reason and rationality that is incontestable.

This, argues Castoriadis, is the myth which, more even than money or weapons, constitutes the most formidable obstacle in the way of any reconstruction of human society (cf. Pepper, 1984, chapters 1–2).

The culture of technology is a culture of control, of normalised and routinised control. 'The delusion that underlies the present system', argues Christopher Lasch (1987, p. 88), 'the delusion that we can make ourselves lords of the universe . . . is the heart and soul of modern technology'. What it represents, according to Arnold Gehlen (1980, p. 30), is a separation of the intellectual from the moral impulses of Enlightenment rationality, a separation in which the latter 'are now reduced to the unhappy role of seeking in vain to hold back the advance of the efficient, the functional, the technologically possible'. As Leo Marx (1987, p. 71) reminds us, 'The initial Enlightenment belief in progress perceived science and technology to be in the service of liberation from political oppression. Over time that conception was transformed . . . by the now familiar view that innovations in science-based technologies are in themselves a sufficient and reliable basis for progress'.

The roots of this imperative of technological control lie deep. For Christopher Lasch (1985) they may originate in an unconscious, and pathological, attempt to restore illusions of infantile omnipotence. For many feminist writers on science and technology too, this compulsion to control is rooted in neurotic masculine development. Their argument is that rationalistic control is intrinsic to an androcentric conception of the technological project (Harding, 1986). What is undoubted is that in our society technique has become central to both our relationship to the external world and also to our self-image. 'This is what is happening today', writes Arnold Gehlen (1980, p. 11), 'when for instance we look at cybernetics, to the theory of techniques of regulation, for clues to the working of our own brains and nervous systems'. At the heart of technique, of instrumental rationality, is the drive to control both external and internal worlds.

The tendency towards control and domination is not, then, external to the technological project. It is not the abuse or misuse of a fundamentally neutral, and even benign, technological system. Rather, it is a constitutive and integral factor. Undoubtedly the clearest and most distilled expression of this will to power is to be found in military technologies. Its most refined expression comes in the form of nuclear weapons. These, argues Joel Kovel (1983, p. 131), are 'not just an aberration but the logical result of an entire attitude toward the world'. Military technologies are the most perfected expressions of the compulsion to command and control. Yet, within social theory, the military is treated as an exceptional and atypical variant of the technological project: 'neither the expanded role of surveillance, nor the altered nature of military power with the development of the means of waging war have been made central formulations of social theory' (Giddens, 1985, p. 294). 'The impact of war in the twentieth century', Giddens continues, 'upon generalized patterns of change has been so profound that it is little short of absurd to seek to interpret such patterns without systematic reference to it' (p. 244). We want to argue that military developments are central, rather than marginal, to the technological project. As Edward Thompson (1980, p. 23) argues of nuclear weaponry, it 'does not occupy a vast societal space, and official secrecy encourages low visibility; but it stamps its priorities on the society as a whole'. As the purest expressions of 'rational' command and control, military technologies are axial to our understanding of broader relations of control and coercion.

Needs of industry, needs of war

Modern warfare is about information and communications technologies:

> Modern military operations are not to do with weapons. They are to do with information, command, control . . . Information does things. It fires weapons. It tells them where to go. The signals network is the key thing . . . It's not about the muscle, the strong arm of the warrior. It is his nervous system that

matters. Signals and communications.   (John Erikson, quoted in *The Guardian*, 11 November 1982, p. 4)

Preparation for electronic and nuclear warfare has absorbed stupendous sums of public money, diverted research and development resources away from civilian priorities and, in the process, significantly influenced our education system. It has also powerfully shaped the constitution and development of I.T. and has nurtured the growth of a culture of control and surveillance.

Let us begin by looking at the economic implications of information technologies. Their growth has been very much determined by the 'needs of industry', but alongside projected economic regeneration and renaissance have been military expansion and the needs of the industries of war. As the House of Commons Defence Committee (1982b, p. vi) has observed, procurement by the armed forces 'represents by any standards an enormous programme of direct purchase of goods and equipment from industry. Clearly it has a major impact on British industry and equipment.' A recent calculation estimates that over 12 per cent of UK manufacturing is dependent upon defence sales. In itself a striking figure, this pales in comparison with the 37 per cent of British engineering industry reliant on military markets (Kaldor *et al.*, 1986, p. 33). Though engineering is not synonymous with I.T., it is in this sphere that these new technologies are concentrated and, moreover, they are increasingly becoming its dominant component. Illustrative of this is the fact that just two sub-sectors of engineering – aerospace and electronics – absorb over half the total defence procurement allowance (ibid, p. 35), and it is in these areas, themselves converging, that most advanced forms of I.T. are to be found. What should be emphasised is that, from the development of the transitor through to more recent artificial intelligence projects, it has been the demands of military and space agencies that have nurtured the growth of computer communications technologies (Schiller, 1984, Chapter 2). According to one knowledgeable source, about 35 per cent of the massive costs of military equipment is now devoted to electronics (Westinghouse, 1982b, p. 5).

Not surprisingly, then, when we look at the major I.T. corporations in Britain we discover that they rank high in the list of Ministry of Defence contractors. Precise figures are not revealed, but in the highest category of orders we find such concerns as British Aerospace, GEC, Ferranti, Plessey, Racal and Thorn–EMI (*Statement of Defence Estimates*, 1985). It is generally acknowledged that an average of 20 per cent of the sales of electronics corporations goes to the military (Southwood, 1985, p. 23), though it is known that in several cases the dependency is very much higher and that the strategic value of contracts at the cutting edge of technological change can make this factor considerably more important.

Such military hegemony must, necessarily, have an over-riding influence on the direction of research, development and exploitation of the new technologies and, thereby, on the shape of technological and economic development more broadly. The military-industrial lobby imposes a dynamic of corporate and military self-interest which distorts and per-verts economic and social priorities through procedures, moreover, which are closed to public scrutiny (Kaldor, 1981).

It can be argued, for example, that high expenditures on defence tend to undermine economic competitiveness. The reason for this lies in the channelling of research and development (R&D) funds away from the civil sector into military applications which have minimal commercial use (cf. Maddock, 1983). Thus, in Britain, 70 per cent of government R&D expenditure is taken up by the Ministry of Defence (*Annual Review of Government Funded R&D*, 1985). Moreover, electronics is the most R&D intensive sector in the British economy, absorbing fully 30 per cent of all R&D funding, but it has 45 per cent of this coming from government, chiefly the Ministry of Defence, and around two-thirds of the sector's R&D commitment is defence-related (Kaldor *et al.*, 1986, pp. 38–9). While these dispro-portionate resources have driven technological develop-ments in militaristic directions, it is also the case that military contractors have found it difficult to transfer their expertise and products to civilian products and markets. The upshot is that the vigour of the economy is considerably depleted and drained by the military incubus (Gummett, 1986).

To question the direction of R&D expenditures is not just to ponder implications for economic competitiveness and vitality, it also confronts the common belief that technologies are pre- or para-social phenomena that 'society' can choose to put to either good or bad use. Is it not the case, however, that if funds are channelled in particular directions, they will result in the constitution of technologies that reflect the values of those who chose one R&D road rather than another? Is it not clear that, since the 'feeding of the world's military machine is . . . the predominant occupation of the global research and development enterprise' (Norman, 1981, p. 72), the technologies that are merging, and will emerge in the future, reflect the values and priorities of the military-industrial lobby? Thus, to take but one prominent example, the capacities of the new super computers for the Strategic Defense Initiative (SDI) are shaped by the military's requirements for machines that will allow simulation and real-time control of highly complex systems. Such a development has no clear civilian applications (Tucker, 1985). In such ways the particular needs and priorities of the military are privileged, whilst other applications are discarded, displaced and devalued.

Military priorities are, then, at the heart of the 'information revolution' and, like other social and economic resources, education is being harnessed to them. Appropriately skilled and qualified personnel are needed to develop, maintain and operate sophisticated weapon systems. This means that the military creams off a large number of students considered to be crucial for its technological operations. For instance, a recent report notes that some 10 per cent of British scientists and engineers are employed in the Scientific Civil Service, and that of this group almost all classical physicists and electronics engineers, along with a large concentration of computer scientists, are located in the Ministry of Defence (Council for Science and Society, 1986, p. 47). Large corporations with a stake in military research also absorb significant numbers of qualified graduates from scientific and technological fields. It has been suggested that, taking account into Ministry of Defence employment and its funding of R&D in private industry, 'rather over thirty per cent of all Britain's highly qualified scientists and engineers are employed in the defence sector' (Kaldor *et al.*, 1986, p. 39). Moreover, it is argued that the 'brightest and the best' graduates tend to be drawn into military R&D (Council for Science and Society, 1986, p. 47), lured by the prospect of working on what Smiths Industries (1986) describes as 'Projects so advanced they stand on the verge of the future'. Joseph Weizenbaum poignantly describes the trajectory of 'desirable' graduates:

> Students coming to study at the artificial intelligence (AI) laboratories of M.I.T. . . . or Stanford . . . or the other such laboratories in the United States, should decide what they want to do with their talents without being befuddled by euphemisms. They should be clear that, upon graduation, most of the companies they will work for, and especially those that will recruit them most energetically, are the most deeply engaged in feverish activity to find still faster, more reliable ways to kill even more people . . . Whatever euphemisms are used to describe students' AI laboratory projects, the probability is overwhelming that the end use of their research will serve this or similar military objectives. (Weizenbaum, 1983, p. 61)

Military priorities are not only evident in recruitment from the graduate pool. Through its funding of R&D work in universities, the military's reach penetrates much deeper into the academic world (Nelkin, 1972). Defence spending is small in relative terms: in Britain the Ministry of Defence puts about £11 million research money directly into universities each year; in the United States military funding of research in higher education accounts for around 16 per cent of the total research budget (Dickson, 1984, p. 109). However, at a time of reduced funding all round, the attraction of military finance must increase. Moreover, military investment is very much concentrated in I.T. research, the crucial dimension of modern battle systems. SDI is an obvious example, with about 5 per cent of its budget likely to go to university research (Hartung *et al.*, 1985) and already delivering $200 million per year to universities (Zuckerman, 1987a, p. 40). This spending is likely to significantly divert and distort academic goals (Zegveld and Enzing, 1987, pp. 140–63).

Whilst SDI's targeted focus on advanced electronic systems, space science, ultra-high-speed computing, and so on is, according to one physicist, 'quite out of proportion to the scientific community's interest in such projects' (Kistiakowsky, 1986, p. 11), Pentagon allocations will ensure that such work is promoted to a leading position. Moreover, SDI will advance such specialisation in the next generation of research students that they 'will have to choose between working in a weapons programme or not using their training' (ibid, p. 12).

Military research can also have profound implications for academic freedom and the unrestricted communication of intellectual work. In the view of David Dickson (1984, p. 111), military support 'is the root of a new Faustian bargain being offered to universities: more funding for basic science provided they are prepared to accept more controls on the findings of their scientists'. Thus, in the United States, the deputy director of the Central Intelligence Agency recently expressed his worries that 'indiscriminate publication' of research results in scholarly journals 'could affect the national security in a harmful way'; academics in the field of computing, he contended, should refer sensitive research to government so it could be vetted prior to publication, as is the case already in the field of cryptography (Inman, 1982; cf. Ferguson, 1983). The same advice is evident in *Business Week* (1 December 1986, p. 34) which reports that the American government 'intends to apply new controls over the contents of computer data bases to stem the flow of scientific, technical, and economic information to the Soviet bloc'. In like manner, Under Secretary of Defense, Donald Hicks, is quoted as saying that he is 'not particularly interested in seeing department money going to someplace where an individual is outspoken in his rejection of department aims'; he is, it seems, 'principally upset by computer scientists who depend in part on Department of Defense support, but voice skepticism about the feasibility of creating the software demanded by a comprehensive missile defense' (*Science*, 25 April 1986, p. 444). The message here is unmistakable: if academic researchers want funding, then they must become advocates of entire military strategies.

The bleeding edge

If information technologies are the cutting edge of 'progress', then military information technologies are its bleeding edge. War, and preparation for war, have been the most fundamental stimulus to the development of the new technologies. As one commentator bluntly states, 'electronics is what war is all about' (Hanson, 1982, p. 283). We might well ask whether war is what electronics is all about.

Computer communications technologies are essential to the entire repertoire of modern military equipment: strategic and tactical nuclear missiles; airborne warning and control systems (AWACS); ground-to-air-missiles; electronic measures, counter-measures and counter-counter-measures; battlefield communication systems; surveillance satellites; and so on (Barnaby, 1986). The Exocet missiles, for example, which were so devastating during the Falklands War, were 'smart' weapons which according to their manufacturers Aerospatiale, contained such sophisticated electronics that the user could 'fire and forget'; their speed, range, accuracy and skimming capacities made them practically 'invulnerable' to enemy defences. The June 1982 confrontation between Israel and Syria in Lebanon's Bekaa valley also exemplified state-of-the-art battle systems. Through the use of airborne warning and control aircraft circling Lebanon, the Israelis were able to use sophisticated radar, computer, communications and electronic warfare devices to orchestrate attack and defence systems (Hoag, 1986) and to massively damage the Syrian air-fighting force.

Supporting and integrating electronic weapon systems are increasingly indispensable command, control, communications and information (C3I) networks. These are crucial to maintain what have been referred to as peacetime and wartime 'information regimes' (Bracken, 1983). In non-war conditions they are used to manage routine military affairs and logistics, to facilitate long and short range communications, and to observe and analyse the actions of enemies and potential enemies. In war conditions they are all the more essential. With speed of detection and response at a premium in modern warfare because of the rapidity with which any attack may be executed, armed forces are spending billions of dollars to improve the detection and communications stages of their defence networks. Only the most advanced computers could offer any hope of achieving this, and accordingly computer systems are massive investments. Such is the urgency for speed of response that defence interests are now seeking ways to computerise the decision-making processes of military encounters, for example by developing 'launch on warning' programmes with help from expert systems and perhaps even totally automated systems (McCrone, 1985). 'There is no technological reason', writes Frank Barnaby (1986, p. 2), 'why warfare should not become completely automated, fought with machines and computerized missiles with no direct human intervention'.

As such a route is followed, the military becomes absolutely and utterly reliant on information systems to conduct its affairs: without such communications, control and surveillance structures the military would be disabled even before engaging in battle. Precisely such reliance has led military planners to conceive a strategy of 'decapitation': if one side aims to be victorious in a nuclear confrontation, then it is useless trying to attack missile silos or ground troops since they are so large and dispersed that a retaliatory strike would be inevitable. Instead, it must pre-emptively destroy the enemy's C3I systems, hoping to eliminate disconnected forces in the ensuing turmoil (Bracken, 1983, pp. 232–7; Ford, 1985, pp. 122–46).

Innovation in military capacity is now 'largely due to developments in microelectronics' (Barnaby, 1982, p. 243), and such developments are, therefore, increasingly central to the arms race. Nations now compete to gain advantage over advanced computer communications technologies: one side produces electronic systems to guide aircraft, ground and naval forces; another develops electronic measures to jam these systems; the former retaliates with counter-measures; the latter with counter-counter-measures; and so it goes. With the development of the Strategic Defense Initiative (SDI), and the complementary Strategic Computing Initiative (SCI), this whole process reaches a totalising conclusion. The promise of 'machine intelligence' technology is that it will co-ordinate battle, defence and control systems for both terrestrial and space wars.

These developments cannot be dismissed as the 'misapplication' of otherwise neutral or benevolent technological progress. We would argue that they are, in their essence, the ultimate expressions of an entirely rationalistic and technocratic attitude towards the world. Their rationality embodies that of the nuclear state (Kovel, 1983).

Military surveillance

The modern state, Joel Kovel (1982/83, p. 157) argues, operates through surveillance: 'The technocrat peers out of his tower, sends killer-satellites into orbit, arms his CIA, monitors the Other, and waits to get before he is gotten'. The state today is, he maintains, 'characterised by the emergence of the technology of surveillance . . . Computerized electronic surveillance has ushered in a whole new phase of domination' (Kovel, 1983, pp. 76–7). Surveillance and intelligence procedures become increasingly central to the state, and it is in military command and control activities that this has found its purest expression.

As we have said, information is crucial to military and control agencies. There is an insatiable hunger for data, information, knowledge and intelligence about any factors affecting 'national' interests. The consequence has been the construction of a massive system of interlinked technologies to routinely and continuously monitor and inspect events and activities – military and civilian – around the globe (Richelson and Ball, 1986). Thus, the United States National Security Agency (NSA), which employs some 70 000 persons and consumes a $10 billion per annum budget,

monitors Soviet and allied communications signals throughout the world. It achieves this through an extensive grid of
listening and watching posts, and through 'what are believed
to be the largest and most advanced computers now available to any bureaucracy on earth' (Burnham, 1983, p. 121;
cf. Bamford, 1983). Likewise, *Computer Weekly* (19 February 1987) reports of Britain's GCHQ intelligence gathering
centre that 'Few organisations can boast the awe-inspiring
power of its linked IBM and Amdahl mainframes and its
Cray and CDC super computers'.

Alongside computers, satellites have become a lynchpin
of surveillance activities. According to two recent commentators, it is getting to the point where the military 'would be
struck deaf, dumb and blind should their satellites be
destroyed' (Jasani and Lee, 1984, p. 4). Illustrative of the
importance of these C3I systems are the accounts of the
reasons for and consequences of the destruction of Korean
Airlines flight 007 after it trespassed into Soviet airspace late
in 1983. Several writers argue that the flight was intended to
enter Soviet territory to get the Russians to activate new
defence systems and to open lines of communication between Moscow and their Far East nuclear command stations
so that orbiting American satellites could spy on them
(Mann, 1984; Johnson, 1986). Even those who argue that
the plane's trespass was due to navigational error do not
dissent from the fact that the United States enjoyed an
intelligence bonanza when the Soviet C3I system was alerted
(Hersch, 1986).

Necessarily these systems are hidden from public view,
secrecy being essential to ensure security from the enemy
(see, for example, Campbell, 1987). Thus is constructed an
anonymous and unexaminable, national and worldwide,
web of surveillance and transmission of messages between
defence agencies. As William E. Burrows (1986, p. 22)
recently observed:

> the system that does all of this watching and listening is so
> pervasively secret – so black – that no individual . . . knows all of
> its hidden parts, the products they collect, or the real extent of
> the widely dispersed and deeply buried budget that keeps the
> entire operation functioning.

The security services assume themselves to be continually under attack from enemies and malcontents. Constantly wary of the spy, they come easily to be pervaded by suspicion and fear of disclosure, characteristics which reinforce their impenetrability, distance them from public accountability, and serve to corrode democratic values and open government (cf. Knightley, 1986).

Computer communications systems have become increasingly central to nuclear defence strategies. Nuclear weapons reached 'maturation' during the 1960s and have not themselves changed dramatically (except in numbers and warheads) during the intervening period. What has developed, however, is the 'vertical integration' of warning and intelligence systems with weapon systems, and the 'horizontal integration' of dispersed military command points into a single centralised command structure. Such strategic developments depend, of course, upon the contruction and articulation of complex electronic surveillance and C3I networks into 'surely ... the most technologically elaborate organization ever constructed by man' (Bracken, 1983, p. 214). With the SDI programme and concept nuclear surveillance strategies, already accelerating for over two decades, have reached a point of massive, and perhaps decisive, escalation (Stares, 1985). SDI is perhaps the ultimate C3I system, intended to gather, process and act upon information pertaining to potentially thousands upon thousands of missile launches, tens of thousands of warheads, and possibly hundreds of thousands of decoy missiles. It relies on the incessant and untiring observation of Warsaw Pact territories for the slightest sign of mobilisation. SDI surveillance and computer networks must perform all these functions almost instantenously and with complete reliability without benefit of testing in real conditions (Office of Technology Assessment, 1986). The information-gathering and processing requirements placed on this surveillance and intelligence system are mind-boggling and perhaps infeasible (Lin, 1985; Parnas, 1985; Zuckerman, 1987b). In it the panoptic project finds its most pure expression.

The surveillance machine is not only directed against external enemies, however. Increasingly, and particularly in the context of a nuclear society, it becomes directed against an enemy within (Campbell, 1984). In its pursuit of internal 'subversives', Britain's secret security service, MI5, has at its Mayfair headquarters a Joint Computer Bureau with the capacity to hold twenty million records, with files on some half a million people, and a network of 200 terminals accessing the mainframe (Campbell and Connor, 1986, p. 274). Leaks and occasional exposés have revealed that surveillance is exercised on trade unionists, CND activists, educationalists and media personnel, as well as on what might be thought to be more obvious candidates (Leigh, 1980; Massiter, 1985). In addition, MI5 works in close association with the Special Branch of the police force, thereby extending its information gathering network nation-wide (Davies and Black, 1984, p. 19). The security services also have access on request to a vast array of data banks, including the Police National Computer, Inland Revenue records, British Telecom files, and data held by the Depart-ment of Health and Social Security.

In the name of security, state surveillance has become a pandemic, and even normative, feature of modern society. In the process, it has extended from intelligence activities to routine policing activities. This has been encouraged parti-cularly by the expanding police use of computer facilities which has promoted new forms of proactive and pre-emptive policing. As it becomes possible to maintain 'a broad data base that can be inexpensively screened, it becomes prudent to consider everyone a possible suspect initially' (Marx and Reichman, 1984, p. 442; cf. Laudon, 1986).

Such developments can be seen, in Foucauldian terms, as part of 'an irreversible continuing historical process of more intensive and extensive social control' (Marx and Reichman, p. 444). As the former Commissioner of the Metropolitan Police, Sir Kenneth Newman, has expressed it, 'it would be better if we stopped talking about crime prevention and lifted the whole thing to a higher level of generality repre-sented by the words "social control"' (quoted in BSSRS Technology of Political Control Group, 1985, pp. 19–20). However, what is particularly significant is that these sur-veillance and control strategies are modelled on the military paradigm. In their computerisation strategies, 'the police are moving to a more military style of operation' (Ibid, p. 59). Thus the policing strategy of 'targeting and surveillance', which undertakes surveillance activities in order to 'target' individuals, groups, locations or areas of special interest, is military in origin. It was developed by Sir Kenneth Newman out of his experiences as Chief Constable of the Royal Ulster Constabulary in the late 1970s, where the British army had 'set up, under the direction of the leading counter-insurgency theorist Frank Kitson, just such a system for the collection and analysis of masses of intelligence information' (ibid, pp. 104–5). Rather than being some extraordinary and exceptional state of affairs, the military paradigm of surveillance technologies interlinked with command and control systems that are insistently hidden from the public eye, has become a generalised model for control and policing strategies.

Towards a military regime of accumulation?

Why have we made so much of these military aspects of I.T.? Why put so much emphasis on military command, control and surveillance networks or nuclear weapons systems? Are these not just extreme and atypical (mis)applications of the new technologies? Why not leave this exotic specialism to defence experts and investigative journalists? Why not look on the bright side?

Well aware that we will be seen as spectres at the banquet, we still insist on the absolute centrality of the military paradigm within the current process of economic and social (and educational) restructuring that is now taking place. One good reason for such insistence is the almost complete repression of this issue in post-industrial and futurological literature and also in 'computer literacy' courses. For most celebrants of the wonderful 'information revolution', war and weaponry simply seem to be another world, another universe. When they are, very occasionally, referred to, then military I.T. is actually seen as providing a panacea for war and strife. Tom Stonier's book, *The Wealth of Informa-*

tion (1983), provides an exemplary illustration of this logic. According to Stonier, the information society will be 'a world of peace and plenty unprecedented in recorded human history' (ibid, p. 189). 'War', he avers, 'is an institution on the demise':

> That ancient institution, first appearing in force with the rise of the ancient civilisations, no longer fulfils social needs and is disappearing in the post-industrial era, as slavery disappeared in the industrial era. The primary social need for war, the need to expand to match growing populations, is being met more effectively through technological ingenuity and relative population stability. (p. 202)

For Stonier, authoritarianism and conflict will be undermined by the general availability of communications and information resources. In his view, 'no dictator can long survive for any length of time in communicative society as the flows of information can no longer be controlled from the centre ... The reduction of the threat of war in the post-industrial society, coupled with the increasing tendency towards consensus democracy, is a result of our extending communications networks' (pp. 203–4).

Christopher Evans' book, *The Mighty Micro* (1979), expresses a similar faith in technology. He too believes that 'the Computer Revolution may ... put an end to war' (p. 209). 'As our social, political and economic problems grow', he continues, 'we shall turn to the computers for advice, prediction and strategic planning'. We shall do all this because 'the computer's predictions, unlike those of a human, are objective and realistic, free from emotional biases and optimistic hunches': 'Today, when ... statistics are fed into the computer's unemotional, apolitical interior, what comes out is as true and objective an appraisal as can be made from the facts. Furthermore, whenever the data involves confrontation between nuclear powers, the unequivocal message that spills out – to both sides – is: You will lose!' (pp. 210–12). This same trust in computers and 'Ultra-Intelligent machines' to forestall nuclear annihilation informs Ronald Reagan's conviction that SDI can render nuclear weapons impotent and obsolete (see Reagan, 1983). The new technologies vindicate the faith of our epoch in scientific and technological mastery as the basis for expanding wealth and social and political harmony.

One reason, then, to emphasise the military aspects of I.T. is to counter this complacent and deluding technological utopianism. But we are not just correcting oversights and omissions. We also want to make a stronger, theoretical, case for putting the military project centre stage. As Anthony Giddens has very powerfully argued, its significance for the control of authoritative resources (for power over people), especially of the means of violence, has made the military fundamental to the social, economic and political genesis of the nation state. As we have demonstrated with regard to I.T., and as Giddens elaborates on the wider plane of industrialisation as a whole, technological, administrative and organisational structures have been profoundly shaped by the needs of war and defence. Integrally related to these developments, surveillance and control frameworks directed against external enemies of the nation state have developed in tandem with the monitoring of internal populations, and with all has been erected a gigantic panoply of information and communications technologies dedicated to prepare for, and if necessary wage, war.

There is no need to invoke conspiracy theories and Big Brother imagery to explain these surveillance and control activities. Indeed, as Nicholas Abercrombie and his colleagues (1986) observe, much of 'the growth of the state apparatus may derive from those very pressures that originally produced individual citizenship' (pp. 151–2) since the recognition of the rights of individuals necessarily resulted in 'Individuation [which] . . . leads to greater surveillance and control of large populations' (p. 155).

What cannot be ignored, however, is the fact that military imperatives have played a major role in the growth of the state and the systems of surveillance that are its requisites. As Giddens (1985, p. 181) argues, 'surveillance as the mobilising of administrative power – through the storage and control of information – is the primary means of the concentration of authoritative resources involved in the formation of the nation state'. The logistics of administration and control in the nation state are interwoven and indissociable. The profoundly important and difficult consequence of this is that 'tendencies toward totalitarian power are as distinctive a feature of our epoch as is industrialised war'; totalitarianism is 'a tendential property of the modern state', developing out of the 'consolidated political power generated by a merging of developed techniques of surveillance and the technology of industrialised war' (p. 310, 295). Giddens' most important political insight is that 'there is no type of nation state in the contemporary world which is completely immune from the potentiality of being subject to totalitarian rule' (p. 302).

How much more profound this awareness of totalitarian tendencies is than the futuristic blind faith in the logic of technological progress and the spread of democracy. Even a cursory glance at the world that surrounds us must demonstrate that, rather than trusting in benign technological advance, we need to struggle against authoritarian and oppressive tendencies found in already constituted technologies.

At root, our argument is that we should be vigilant and aware of the ambivalence of technological rationality and, ultimately, of what passes for reason itself. As Castoriadis (1984/85, pp. 34–5) emphasises, we cannot reject reason, but we cannot also 'freely separate "reason qua reason" from its actual historical realisation. We would be mad to think . . . that reason could be considered as an "instrument" which could be assigned to better us. A culture is not a menu from which we can choose what we like and ignore all the rest'. We would advise readers to pay attention to the Dialectic of Enlightenment. Military and control technologies ought not to be considered as a specific and exceptional matter: they are at the centre of the project of technological rationalisation. If we want to sustain – and perhaps even survive – the technological project then we must confront, rather than repress, this its dark side. The military system of technology has not been some vast historical accident. It has been a fundamental and intrinsic aspect of scientific, technological and industrial development.

There are signs that the military sector may be even more at the heart of the emerging neo-Fordist regime of accumulation. Whilst most accounts of the present restructuring process have tended to overlook or de-emphasise this sector, increasing military and defence expenditure point to its centrality. Martin Carnoy and Manuel Castells (1984, pp. 499–500) describe the emergence of 'a neoconservative model of capitalist growth' which prioritises 'military security, not economic development and greater equality between and within nations'. 'This rapid military expansion', they argue, 'accompanied by cuts in social welfare spending, suggests that a transition from a welfare to a warfare state is under way'. The current process of restructuring also entails a restructuring of the world military order. As John Lovering (1987, pp. 144–5) suggests, we may be witnessing the emergence of a new 'Atlantic Arms Economy' and the possibility of a military regime of accumulation:

> The military, political and corporate networks which structure the Atlantic Arms Economy can be seen as an embryonic transnational mode of regulation, while the transnational economic relationships with which they are associated form an international military regime of accumulation.

A neo-Fordist regime of accumulation may well be characterised by both decentralised, flexible civilian production and a reformed military-industrial apparatus. In both aspects, the new information and communication technologies will undoubtedly play a key part (Schiller, 1984, Chapter 2).

Giddens argues that totalitarianism is a tendential property of the modern state. He does not argue that all states are equal in this respect. Nor does he suggest that any nation state will necessarily succumb to this temptation. However, with the rapid growth of electronic warfare and C3I technologies, the totalitarian tendency becomes increasingly more actual than potential. In this global military structure we have perhaps the ultimate consummation of the rationalised and technocratic ordering of society. Here authoritative and administrative control cohere in pursuit of total mastery. Technocracy is political domination shaped by technical and instrumental reasoning, 'a streamlined kind of domination, much the most powerful – materially – the world has ever seen, but the same pustule for all that' (Kovel, 1983, p. 9). Within a technocratic order

> the logic of the machine settles into the spirit of the master. There it dresses itself up as 'value-free' technical reasoning. And the hidden meaning of this is domination – precisely because it is hidden and disguised as value free. Thus it dominates – and denies that it dominates – all in the same gesture. The more it denies, the more it dominates; and the more it dominates, the more it denies. Give it enough time, and it will come up with 'limited nuclear war'. (Ibid, pp. 9–10)

Within the technocratic project, even to its military-nuclear culmination, 'the technical world view itself becomes the very embodiment of neutrality and objectivity . . . the technical world view becomes mythical thought' (Larson, 1972, p. 24). Ultimate goals go unquestioned; technological control and mastery become an absolute value. In this 'Pentagon of power', writes Lewis Mumford (1964, pp. 5–6),

> there is no visible presence who issues commands: unlike Job's God, the new deities cannot be confronted, still less defied . . . The ultimate aim of this technics is to displace life, or rather to transfer the attributes of life to the machine and the mechanical collective, allowing only so much of the organism to remain as may be controlled and manipulated.

In its military culmination, this displacement of life becomes literal as well as metaphorical.

What we are emphasising here is the centrality of the military project. Questions about the social value of technological systems cannot, and will not, be addressed until we are prepared to confront, in real seriousness, the significance of military science and technology. Military technologies, we maintain, are characteristic of the fantasy of total control that has long inhabited the technological domain. They exemplify 'a system that deliberately eliminates the whole human personality, ignores the historic process, overplays the role of the abstract intelligence, and makes control over physical nature, ultimately control over man himself, the chief purpose of existence' (Mumford, 1964, p. 6).

'Reason' and 'rationality' are not natural forces, but rather historical creations of humanity, and creations, moreover, that have become increasingly destructive. What we should acknowledge is the indissociability of their creative and destructive aspects. Only if we are prepared to confront the authoritarian elements in the technological enterprise can we move beyond that naive technological utopianism which characterises post-industrial and futurological pundits. Our survival may depend on our ability to confront the rationalist myths that underpin the technological system and its military-nuclear culmination. So absolutely and insidiously is this system incorporated into Western thinking that we must doubt the possibility of any significant radical contestation. Is it actually possible, in the late twentieth century, to move beyond technocracy?

9

The Technocratic Condition, or Schools Cannot Teach what Society does not know

'Rouze up, O Young Men of the New Age! set your foreheads against the ignorant Hirelings! For we have Hirelings in the Camp, the Court & the University, who would, if they could, for ever depress Mental & prolong Corporeal War.' (William Blake, *Milton* (1804–8))

The argument of this book is that the root problem of the education system has nothing to do with an 'anti-enterprise culture' and unworldly liberalism. In rejecting this myth (Daniel, 1986), however, we do not believe that present difficulties are simply a matter of a misguided and discriminatory vocationalism, as many critics of the new instrumental progressivism have suggested. The problem is more profound and troublesome. What must be confronted is this, the technocratic imagination which has come to dominate and deform education (and, indeed, society as a whole) and which finds its apogee in the current obsession with computer literacy:

The technological conception of education took over the schools quite some time ago. Moving in the devices cannot be seen as an innovation; rather, it brings a technical vision to completion. Computers would not have a place in schools had schools not already become possessed by the technical imagination. (Sardello, 1984, p. 633)

256

Over a long period, the technocratic condition, born out of the Loom of Locke, has come increasingly to dominate our schools, colleges and universities (see, for example, McCulloch *et al*, 1985). The real problem that we face, and one that even now threatens our very survival, is in truth what might be called the technocratic disease. 'The practice of education', writes John Broughton (1985, p. 115), 'would appear to be engaged in a willing symbolic subordination of itself to the practice of technology'. The new pedagogy is about education for technocracy; about the increasing subordination of education to this ideology. In this chapter, we conclude our discussion with some final comments and observations on this logic of technocracy and its implications for education.

Information technocracy

The new information technologies and artificial intelligence projects that are presently stimulating computer literacy campaigns have been profoundly affected by military objectives and values (see Athanasiou, 1987). Douglas Noble (1986) has described how the apparatus of instrumental progressivism – teaching machines, educational systems, programmed instruction, criterion-referenced instruction, task analysis, and so on – owes a great deal to the military. 'A plausible case can be made', he argues, 'for the claim that the thrust of educational policy in the last four decades emerged, concretely and historically, within a human capital economic ideology grounded in military technology' (ibid, p. 4). Concepts of society, of education, and of the human mind, Noble affirms, have 'relied for their models on military developments in information theory, cybernetics, computing, psychology, training, operations research and weapons systems' (ibid, p. 5). What he notes as particularly important is a new ontology shaped by cybernetics which 'offered the language of "feedback" to translate the purposive behaviors of organisms, including human beings, into automatic servomechanisms'; 'a person is regarded as a "human component" within the "personnel subsystem" of complex "man/machine systems" (i.e. weapon systems)' (ibid, pp. 9, 13). The military development of information theory, cybernetics and cognitive psychology has given support to a 'vision of a planned, technocratic, "post-industrial" society' (ibid, 1986a, p. 9).

This cybernetic conception of mind, society and nature is at the heart of instrumental progressivism and its control strategies, as we argued in Chapter 7. Douglas Noble emphasises that this ontology became absorbed into apparently progressive and reformist philosophies of education back in the 1950s and 1960s, 'culminating in educators' recent fascination with the cognitive: problem-solving, thinking skills, and the microcomputer' (ibid, p. 20). Especially important in this process of assimilation was the educationalist and psychologist, Jerome Bruner, whose work was crucial to the development of a philosophy of mind as information processor and of education as the cultivation of skills, intellectual processes and cognitive resources. Bruner's work had an important 'influence on the marriage of education and technology in postwar America, transforming the "process" of education into the cultivation of cognitive resources for a post-industrial society' (ibid, p. 28). 'There is', maintains Noble, 'an important connection between the idea of a technocratic, "post-industrial" society and the development of the new "cognitive paradigm" ... The information society and the human information processor are woven of the same cloth' (ibid, p. 25).

The work of Seymour Papert which, as we have already noted, has been so influential for the new pedagogies of the 1980s, is descended from the 'cognitive revolution' of Bruner. For all its ostensible progressivism and radicalism – an issue to which we shall return in a moment – Papert's work can be seen to be imbued with technocratic values. In *Mindstorms*, Papert argues that computer instruction should operate through the creation of 'microworlds', 'each with its own set of assumptions and constraints': 'Children get to know what it is like to explore the properties of a chosen microworld undisturbed by extraneous questions. In doing so they learn to transfer habits of exploration from their personal lives to the formal domain of scientific theory'

(Papert, 1980, p. 117). The computer microworld is offered as a contained and manageable framework within which the child can explore the power of ideas and the power of mind. However, such a conception, with its stress on control and 'competent instrumentality', and its 'alienation from the fullness of human experience', is deeply rooted in the technocratic project (Davy, 1984). Moreover, this technocratic vision is an echo of military systems discourse with its 'view of the world as a complex technological system' (Edwards, 1987, p. 8). Military systems discourse operates in terms of a world of formalised rules, one that supposedly can be captured through mathematical logic and algorithmic analysis. It is a world of ontological closure, what Papert and his followers would call a microworld. Edwards argues that

> though computers and systems discourse more generally are not inherently militaristic, there is something systematic and computerlike about the forms of postwar American technological militarism . . . This confluence of forms partially explains the military penchant for computers. There is a suitability of the one discourse to the other, a kind of cultural 'fit', that makes fascination more likely, and that draws the two together. (Ibid, pp. 9–10)

Computer discourse on cybernetic systems and control parallels military discourse and its focus on planning, simulation and statistical analysis.

The control of information and knowledge resources has always been at the heart of technocracy (Larson, 1972), in its militaristic and other incarnations. This is seen, however, by the advocates of technocratic rationalisation as a purely and narrowly technical matter, the consequences of which can only be benign and liberating. According to Herbert Simon, a leading devotee of 'machine intelligence', 'to believe that knowledge is to be preferred to ignorance is to believe that the human species is capable of progress and, on balance, has progressed over the centuries' (Simon, 1977, p. 1190). The 'information revolution' is an advanced stage of human evolutionary progress, one marking the qualitative leap from a world of comparative ignorance to one of intellectual abundance, wherein the promise of Enlightenment rationality can be fulfilled. 'Information smacks of safe neutrality; it is the simple, helpful heaping up of unassailable facts', writes Theodore Roszak. 'In that innocent guise', he continues, 'it is the perfect starting point for a technocratic agenda that wants as little exposure for its objectives as possible. After all, what can anyone say against information?' (Roszak, 1986, p. 19).

Within the sphere of education, this faith in knowledge as the key to progress has manifested itself in the idea of the 'cognitive revolution'. Information processing, cognitive skills and competences, these are regarded as the necessary qualities of human capital in the post-industrial era. Educational activities, boosted by the power of computers, can supposedly expand the creative and intellectual capabilities of young people out of all proportion. Moreover, within this dream knowledge and education will become increasingly democratised. Old and obstructive monopolies will crumble as learning becomes decentralised and accessible. Thus Seymour Papert declares that his 'image of learning suggests a critique of what a school is all about and even raises the question if such demarcated institutions as schools make any sense' (Papert, 1979, p. 85). Interaction with the computer, he maintains, 'can put the learner into contact with his most private self, it can also nurture in him an image of himself as an independent intellectual agent' (ibid, p. 86). Papert appeals to Ivan Illich's well-known conception of a de-schooled society:

> The presence of the computer is what will make a deschooled society possible and even necessary, because if my vision of the way computers will be used is realized, it will come into conflict with the rational structure of schools on every level, from the epistemological to the social. (Ibid, p. 85)

Families, he contends, will come to see the private computer as a viable alternative to the school system; they will undermine the old vested interests and the hierarchical system of knowledge that now characterises society. Others are in full agreement. According to one advocate of computer literacy, 'the very existence of powerful learning tools outside schools will gradually help to undermine the identification of learning with formal instruction' (Chandler, 1984, p. 86). Again invoking Illich, this author argues that the computer 'could find a convivial role as a major means of supporting a society in which learning was not regarded as something separable from living' (ibid, p. 79). The same emphasis on 'flexible strategies for learning' is put forward by J. J. Wellington, who maintains that 'the equation of education with schooling will become increasingly less tenable' (Wellington, 1985, p. 253). Information and its technologies are seen as the basis for an educational renaissance, for a new, decentralised, post-industrial epoch in which learning returns to the home and power to the learner.

This of course appears humane and unassailable. After all, what can anyone say against education? In the guise of innocent and utopian progressivism, however, it is the perfect starting point for a technocratic agenda that wants as little exposure for its objectives as possible. In our view, this post-industrial philosophy of deschooling is far from being benign and progressive. We are suggesting that, behind a liberal smokescreen, we are now witnessing a new phase in the technocratic appropriation of education. The new pedagogy extends and deepens the grip of instrumental reason.

In an interesting essay on 'Knowledge as Power', Harold Silver argues that

> the most persistent dilemmas in educational debate in this century have been concerned with kinds of knowledge . . . [with] the question of access to knowledge, to the most appropriate knowledge, to one curriculum or another, to knowledge as in itself providing access to further education, to experience, to work. (Silver, 1980, p. 109)

Tensions have developed 'around the relationship between extended educational provision, the appropriate knowledges to make available, and the forms and structures in which to do so . . . how was knowledge to be distributed and who was to decide?' (ibid, p. 110). Emphasising that 'knowledge-as-power only has meaning within the historical circumstances in which it is acquired', Silver suggests that different forms of knowledge and culture have, in different historical conjunctures, been associated with different forms and expressions of power. Following this line of analysis, we may argue that, in the present period, we are seeing one further, and particularly significant, shift in the nature of social knowledge, and, consequently, in the form and structure of power.

Knowledge is becoming increasingly instrumental, organised and commodified. In this process the centrality of education institutions is being undermined and their functions transformed. Educational knowledge is now less associated with cultural transmission and reproduction. As Lyotard (1979, p. 14) observes, 'the old idea that the acquisition of knowledge is inseparable from the development (*Bildung*) of the mind, and even the personality, is becoming, and will increasingly become, obsolete'. In a world where 'knowledge is bleached into information', qualities of interpretation, judgement and understanding seem to become anachronistic (Carey, 1983, p. 48). Where education becomes subsumed into the rationalised world of the knowledge business and information markets, then the individual qualities and personal skills of the teacher start to become redundant and inappropriate. 'Skills that teachers used to need', suggests Michael Apple (1982, p. 113), 'that were deemed essential to the craft of working with children – such as curriculum deliberation and planning, designing teaching and curricular strategies for specific groups and individuals based on intimate knowledge of these people – are no longer necessary'. Planning and designing curricula is increasingly separated from execution and implementation. The former task is increasingly taken over by outside advisors and software houses, whilst the latter falls to the (Taylorised) teacher. According to Apple, 'as teachers lose control of the curricular and pedagogic skills to large publishing houses, these skills are replaced by techniques for better controlling children' (ibid, p. 114): the function of teachers becomes that of implementing school and classroom management strategies. In this process the qualitative and cultural aspects of education become subordinated to the quantitative and instrumental business of knowledge mobilisation.

Lyotard's analysis of the 'postmodern condition', to which we referred at the end of Chapter 4, is particularly helpful for understanding these broad transformations. As knowledge becomes systematically instrumentalised and technologised, so it overflows, as it were, the narrow channels of educational acculturation. 'The status of knowledge', attests Lyotard, 'as societies enter what is called the postindustrial age . . . ceases to be an end in itself, it loses its "use-value"' (Lyotard, 1979, pp. 11, 14). Once knowledge ceases to be an end in itself, for example such as oriented towards 'the realisation of an idea or human emancipation', then 'its transmission is no longer the exclusive responsibility of academics and students' (ibid, p. 83). With the increasing predominance of the performance principle and the delegitimation of liberal traditions and philosophies, the age of the professor is drawing to an end: the professor 'is no more competent than networks of memory banks for transmitting established knowledge, no more competent than interdisciplinary teams for dreaming up new moves and new games' (ibid, p. 88). In this context, liberal thinking and disinterested enquiry become outdated and meaningless: the function of education is, increasingly, to improve the system's performance, to supply appropriately trained personnel, to subordinate knowledge to the objectives of the dominant power structure.

Lyotard's account identifies the shift from Enlightenment ideals of emancipatory reason to a post-modern condition of technocratic rationalisation – a shift in which knowledge has become an integral aspect of the power system. This shift from critical to functional rationality is reflected in the changing role and responsibilities of educational institutions. At one level, this can be associated with the industrialisation and functionalisation of schools and colleges, where training increasingly becomes the paradigm for knowledge transmission. But it is also associated, we would argue, with the end of the era in which these institutions held a monopoly over this process of knowledge transmission. Thus 'the adjustment to the new [information] technology', according to two critics of the old system, 'is taking place outside schools and even outside universities', and, consequently, 'the function of schools as a means of initiation into interest groups beyond the immediate community is weakened; and . . . the status-legitimating role of schooling becomes irrelevant as people work for themselves or enter service industries which operate in small units and offer jobs which are problematically related to conventional social-class categories' (Meighan and Reid, 1982, p. 356). The performance principle may functionalise educational institutions, but it will also, in the longer term – if it proves instrumental for capital accumulation and competitiveness – displace responsibility for knowledge production and transmission outside the established institutions. For Papert and his epigones, this is a matter of the progressive liberation and release of education from the ossified grip of instructional bureaucracies. For others – more pertinent, we think – this process 'threatens to convert the entire society into a meritocracy and technocracy and to extirpate any residual sense of a common or collective life that extends beyond the moment or the morrow' (Carey, 1987, p. 198).

Iron cage, white heat

In this book we have been discussing the educational policies and strategies of the Thatcher governments. In seeking to understand their coherence in the context of recession, restructuring and the transition to a neo-Fordist regime of accumulation, we have perhaps suggested a greater degree of clarity, intentionality and unity in the Conservative position than is, in fact, the case. There is by no means a single, common position within the party. In the recent period, there has been a sequence of lobbying reports from different Tory interest groups (for example Scruton *et al.*, 1985; Hillgate Group, 1986; Baldry, 1986; Brown *et al.*, 1985, 1986; Seldon, 1986; Adam Smith Institute, 1985). These focus on a whole range of issues – standards and discipline, alleged Left-wing bias and indoctrination in schools, vouchers, the privatisation of education, parental choice, and so on – and they have, no doubt, been of significance in shaping the development of government policies. There is, then, debate within the Conservative Party on priorities and emphases. Nevertheless, this is all within a broad agreement that education should promote growth, competitiveness and progress. Those who in any way criticise the industrialisation of education and champion liberal values (for example Powell, 1986) are dismissed as redundant ideological dinosaurs. The force of his denials suggests that Education Secretary Kenneth Baker is sensitive to the criticisms that education is fast becoming 'little more than a utilitarian treadmill churning out unthinking technocrats . . . some kind of new barbarism' (Baker, 1987, p. 23).

The Conservative objective is to provide children with 'the knowledge training and character that will fit them for today's world'. This is a matter of 'basic educational skills' and such 'moral values' as honesty, hard work and responsibility (Conservative Party, 1987, p. 17). Education is imprisoned in what Weber called the iron cage of technical rationality. What then are the alternatives to this 'new realism'? Sadly, one hears in the social democratic and labourist positions only repetitive echoes. What is astonishing is the very uniformity that has made the whole notion of a Great Debate on education quite meaningless. To be sure, there is a good deal of sword-clashing at the level of rhetoric and polemic. We certainly do not want to deny that the oppositions' policies are more egalitarian and enlightened. But how real are the options? That, for us, is the real question to be asked. the real problem to be faced.

One central strand of the British social democratic position was developed by the former Social Democratic Party (SDP). This tradition traces its political and intellectual heritage to post-war Labour Party social democracy and, particularly, to the influential writings of Anthony Crosland. As such, the party's stance has always had a somewhat technocratic inflection, one that has very much converged with Daniel Bell's philosophy of a classless and meritocratic post-industrial society (Flude, 1983, p. 280). However, it has also moved, in some of its interpretations, towards a

Schumacherian philosophy, celebrating the importance of decentralisation, community and the small firms and self-employed of the so-called third sector (see Williams, 1985). This particular dialect of social democracy envisages a future neo-Fordist regime of accumulation very much in terms of flexible, localised economic and social structures. At its most interesting and radical it converges with some of the aspirations of Green politics. Where it diverges fundamentally, however, is in its unquestioning acceptance of new technologies, technological progress and the information society scenario.

The SDP's educational policy in consequence was very much shackled to the needs of science and technology and the needs of industry. 'The ability of the education system to match the needs of the information society for highly educated people has now become the main determinant of a country's employment prospects' asserts Shirley Williams (ibid, pp. 74–5). According to a policy document on *Education and Training*, the SDP 'believes that the skills and intelligence of our people can be increased and that we can and must transform ourselves into a technologically sophisticated, internationally competitive, highly skilled economy' (SDP, 1983, p. 1). The report goes on to argue that 'we need urgently a higher level of mathematical, scientific and technical competence among the community as a whole'; that 'we need to encourage a far more positive attitude to industry and the activities which lead to the creation of wealth'; that 'industry itself has a major responsibility for making possible both first-hand experience of the world of work for those still in education and periods of retraining and education for those in work' (ibid, pp. 3–4). And so on, and on. The SDP was pre-eminently concerned with competence, commitment, flexibility, responsibility. This very much reflects the influence, through the involvement of Tyrell Burgess in policy formation, of 'Education for Capability' philosophy. What we have, in fact, is a catalogue of the educational orthodoxies and dogmas of our time. Of course, there are significant differences in emphasis and detail, but it is difficult to see how the fundamental objectives and worldview depart from those of the Thatcher government. Both invoke a form of instrumental progressivism as the educational strategy appropriate to the coming 'post-industrial' era. Both do so because they adhere blindly to the rationalist ideology wherein 'progress' is indissociably linked to economic and technological 'efficiency' and the forward march of instrumental reason.

These perspectives are also adopted by the Labour Party, which shares a common ideological background with the social democrats. Labour too inhabits the iron cage of technocracy. It has, for a long time now, seen itself as 'the party of science' (Crossman, 1963). For the Labour Party it has been unquestionably the case that 'the Welfare State is grounded in science and without it would be impossible . . . science will bring its own dividends in the form of greater material and cultural prosperity' (Labour Party, 1961). The clearest statement of this technocratic politics was undoubtedly Harold Wilson's address to the 1963 party conference in which he discussed the question of 'Labour and the Scientific Revolution'. In a speech celebrating automation, technological progress, national planning and economic expansion, Wilson asserts that 'in all our plans for the future, we are re-defining and we are re-stating our Socialism in terms of the scientific revolution', and he looks to a future Britain 'that is going to be forged in the white heat of this revolution' (Wilson, 1963, p. 140).

In the context of the development of the new information and communications technologies in the 1980s, this technocratic emphasis has again asserted itself. The air is again full of the sound of modernisation, efficiency, growth, planning, and so on (see Labour Party, 1985; Smith and Park, 1987). Appealing to the politics of 'common sense', Neil Kinnock argues that

> Socialism is dedicated to progress. And progress means using the fruits of science and technology, of accumulation and production to enhance the living standards and the opportunities of all the people. (Kinnock, 1986, p. 192)

In 1985, Roy Hattersley made a major speech in which he argued that 'the progress of the second industrial revolution is irresistible . . . It is a great force for increased wealth which – if properly harnessed – can bring Britain the growth and prosperity which has eluded us for so long'. 'The Labour Party', he continued, 'is now the modern party of technology, industry and advance. It has the modern ideas and policies needed to take the out-dated and backward Britain we will inherit from the Tories into the 21st century . . . A Labour government will bring simple commonsense to the development of new technology' (Hattersley, 1985).

As Veronica Beechey has observed, underlying the 'modern' tone of this new rhetoric is an old-fashioned message which is very reminiscent of the Wilson–Callaghan era (Beechey, 1987, p. 28). What we have in effect, though the pitch is now a little more cautious, is White Heat II: there remains a deep technocratic commitment. Whilst we are told that 'Labour's approach could not be more different from that of the Conservatives' (Labour Party, 1985, p. 22), and that the 'Tories have become the latter-day Luddites' with 'no vision, always looking back to the 19th century rather than forward to the 21st century' (Hattersley, 1985), it is, in truth, difficult to see this as other than rather superficial product differentiation. Labour shares with the Conservatives fundamental objectives: recently its spokesperson for science and technology, Jeremy Bray, has even, it seems, spoken of establishing a bipartisan approach to high technology development with the Thatcher government (Large, 1987). The major criticism of the Conservatives is that their *laissez-faire* approach is inefficient, and that what is called for is a planned and orchestrated strategy (see Chapter 3).

Labour's education policies develop out of this technocratic emphasis. What is remarkable – and this, of course, applies also to the other main political parties – is the extent to which education issues are subordinated to technological and industrial policies. As David Selbourne has said, Labour's education policy has lost any moral dimension and any sense of the emancipatory purpose of learning (Selbourne, 1986). The 'common sense' justification for an instrumental and technocratic education system was made by James Callaghan in his Ruskin speech: education must be exposed to the White Heat. Subsequently, education policy has shrivelled to a narrow pragmatism and instrumentalism and broader appeals and purposes have melted away.

We are not dismissing the Labour Party's commitment to equality, justice and freedom. Let us take its integrity and sincerity as given. What we are concerned to emphasise is the framework within which policies are developed: the dominant social imaginary and its technicist and rationalist ways of seeing and being. Like the other parties, Labour bemoans the 'English disease' (Kinnock, 1986, pp. 133–4). It asserts the importance of 'changing attitudes' and 'entrenched resistance' in order to build up 'collective commitment to success' from people who 'can cope with changes in the environment, can redeploy their competence, can take greater responsibility for their own performance, can take initiatives, and are self reliant' (Sheerman, 1986, p. 20). A familiar enough rallying call! 'We live in the science society, the knowledge economy', said Neil Kinnock in the preface to a recent pamphlet, 'and it is investment in the abilities of our workers which will determine our future fortunes' (Labour Party, 1986, p. 1). 'As we move towards a knowledge-based economy', writes Labour's former spokesperson on education, 'it becomes ever clearer that our future will increasingly depend on our human capital – on the intelligence, information and creativity of our people' (Radice, 1986, p. 1). Tory politicians, Radice continues

> have failed to understand that modern industry requires not an updated version of the Victorian 'hewers of wood and drawers of water' but school leavers who have mastered a broad range of basic linguistic, communication, numerical, technical and scientific skills, and who are creative, adaptable and able to work with others . . . In an age of rapid change what is required is not pupils who are narrowly trained in techniques which rapidly become obsolete but independent-minded young men and women who have intelligence, imagination and skill to adjust to different jobs, different situations and different people. (Ibid, pp. 5–6)

Here again the wolf of technocracy is wrapped in the sheep's clothing of progressivism and individualism: flexible education for flexible accumulation.

Far from being innovative, the voices of Labour's education strategy speak in platitudes, in what have become conventional and reflex dogmas. The criticisms of Conservative policy seem to us disingenuous attacks on a straw person: Labour seems to be trying to arrogate unto itself a strategy which is in fact common to both parties. Certainly, there are notable differences and divergences. Labour's position invokes greater state involvement and planning of scientific and technological development, of industrial growth and of educational provision. As such, this particular blueprint for the new economic and social order of neo-Fordism is drawn into the 'gathering embrace of Japanisation' (Murray, 1985, p. 32). The ideological appeal of Japanese planning and social management is clear in Neil Kinnock's recent book (Kinnock, 1986), and it significantly influences his approach to education. But what kind of alternative does Labour really offer? The agenda for education is severely circumscribed by the imperatives of technological and industrial growth. The 'information society' appears as an inevitable destiny shaping the choices we can make. Politics becomes a narrowly technicist and instrumental matter. The future can only continue the technocratic route laid out today. That is the 'common sense' that Labour shares with all the major political groupings.

Appeals to other educational priorities, values and ideals are now seen as elitist, as self-indulgent, or as dysfunctional. Reminders of the emancipatory purposes of education are dismissed as anachronistic and irrelevant. It now seems quite frivolous and unrealistic to appeal even to liberal principles. *That* is the measure of the power of technocratic thought. We have, as Douglas Noble argues, 'become incapable of thinking of alternative visions, either for our children or for our own futures' (Noble, 1985, p. 20). The task we face, to paraphrase Noble, is to dismantle the dominant social imaginary, the technocratic ideology, whilst we are yet surrounded and infused by it.

Schools cannot teach what society does not know

> The project suggested here is unreasonable, and it would be a
> simple matter to demonstrate how far it is from realization. But
> then technocracy has staked out most of the claims to reason-
> ableness. To assert rationality under the reign of technocracy, a
> degree of unreasonableness is essential. (Kovel, 1982/83,
> p. 161)

Debates about education have, over a long period, centred
around the relative value of liberal and academic knowledge
on the one hand, and vocational, utilitarian and practical
instruction on the other. In the 'battle around knowledge'
(Silver, 1980, p. 117) there have been fundamental polarisa-
tions between those advocating the benefits and values of
each kind of knowledge and education. In reality, however,
neither position is inherently right or 'progressive'. Vocational education can be narrowly functional when it adapts
and relates only to the 'real world' – that is, the actually
existing industrial order. But there have also been more
radical proponents of practical education, concerned not
with improving the effectiveness of the present economic
and social system but, rather, with transforming it (Reeder,
1981). Similarly, liberal or academic knowledge may be
elitist and abstract, but it can also be associated with critical
reasoning, political awareness and cultural enrichment.

   This book does not attempt to make a simple defence of
liberal education against the new vocationalism. 'Mankind',
wrote John Dewey, 'likes to think in terms of extreme
opposites' (Dewey, 1963, p. 17). We acknowledge, with
Dewey, that reality is more complex. Liberal and practical
pedagogies are not opposites or alternatives, but should be
seen, rather, in terms of complementarity and a fundamental unity. This, as Dewey argues, is grounded in the
'intimate and necessary relation between the processes of
actual experience and education' (ibid, p. 20). Because
neither position is in itself sustainable, it can be suggested
that 'the contraries set up by liberal education on the one
hand and vocational training on the other ... are best
considered as ways of enabling us to think about education

in general' (Gregor, 1983, p. 159). In our view it has been the tension between two partial truths that has allowed the question of applied as opposed to pure knowledge and education to figure on the agenda for social and political debate. This was never an issue for resolution between one perspective or the other, but rather a matter of arriving at a more or less acceptable accommodation of the two principles. Was this to be a matter of the technocratic adaptation of knowledge to the 'needs of industry' and the status quo? Or was it possible to make knowledge 'relevant' in the context of a radical transformation of society? At its most significant level, this has been the issue raised by British cultural critics from Ruskin and Morris through to Raymond Williams: it has been about a fundamentally challenging critique of social values rather than a conservative defence of pure and liberal knowledge, as the exponents of the 'English disease' argument have alleged.

Nonetheless, those who emphasised the importance of liberal and critical reasoning were defenders of values under siege. They were defending qualities of knowledge, culture and education that were being continuously and constantly undermined by scientific and technological rationality. Moreover, what is becoming increasingly clear is that the balance of forces has become increasingly unequal; that technocratic reasoning has been becoming hegemonic. As Borgmann has argued, technology has become the major framework within which we relate to the world: 'technology is the rule today in constituting the inconspicuous pattern by which we normally orient ourselves' (Borgmann, 1984, p. 105). Rather than counterposing itself to moral and political life, technocratic consciousness has subsumed and incorporated them. Now technology and technique are offered as the very basis for social, political and moral choices. So powerful is the technocratic agenda that to question it seems arrogant, absurd and incredible. Technocratic rationality is fast becoming the exclusive way of experiencing and understanding the world. In the process its grip has become ever more totalising and dominative: 'Never did the critique of instrumental reason . . . have greater urgency. Never has the established form of rationality hung so disastrously over the earth. Never have emancipation and survival been so convergent' (Kovel, 1982/83, p. 161).

In the past the major battle around knowledge has centred upon the issue of who knows: who has the right and the means to gain access to knowledge. It has also been about what was known: about the content of knowledge. More recently, what has become important is *how* they know: the form of knowledge. What is becoming increasingly significant is the growing centrality of instrumental reason and the subjugation of other knowledges. The world of emotions, of feelings, of values and of the unconscious becomes increasingly repressed by the rationalist ideology (Harding, 1986, p. 245). Consequently, the question of the 'good life' becomes a matter of scientific and technological advance and the further application of instrumental reason. To question this centrality then seems to fly in the face of progress and reason itself.

Yet this is what is called for. We need to move beyond debates about liberal and vocational knowledge to the critique of the instrumental and technocratic reason which underpins comment on educational reform in the present period. This has nothing whatever to do with the defence of pure knowledge or the refusal to be involved in the 'real world'. Indeed, it is very much about active engagement with the external world. But as such it is about acknowledging and insisting that this relationship to the world is complex and many-sided: it is cognitive, but it is also emotional, moral, political, imaginative and aesthetic. Because we have disavowed these dimensions of expertise, we have become competent only in certain areas of instrumental reason, whilst 'at the same time we allow a scandalous incompetence in dealing with the fundamental recurring questions of human existence: How are we to live together? How can we live gracefully and with justice?' (Winner, 1986, p. 162).

These are big questions and they cannot be answered here. As we have already emphasised, we want, rather, to direct attention to the myths that constitute the dominant social imagery. However, what we can do by way of a conclusion is to indicate what seem to us some of the preconditions for beginning to address the central questions. Above all, it is necessary to appreciate that the future of education is a political and ethical matter. Education has, in our time, fast become 'a commodity both for the individual person and for society as a whole, to be assessed like any other commodity in terms of its profitability or usefulness' (Bailey, 1984, p. 177). In the context of developments in I.T. it is widely recognised that 'education offers significant commercial opportunities ... technological developments make the concept of education as a consumer product a real possibility' (ITAP, 1986, pp. 33–4). In the face of this growing commercialisation, it is vital that we think of education not in terms of consumer sovereignty, but 'in the framework of the extended rights of citizenship which have been the main benefit of political and social democracy' (Rustin, 1986, p. 17). This political emphasis is about over-coming the stance of acceptance, accommodation and adaptation involved in the commodification of education. 'Adaptation to change is inevitable', we are told, 'and we are all involved' (Department of Employment, 1985, p. 10). Against this message of capitulation to the inevitable, we must reassert the sense of agency. We need to recognise the human choices, interests and power that are disguised by technocratic reasoning. Within ourselves, we need to realise that 'Agency is about doing and learning that people, including oneself, have the right to action across a wide sphere. This is the opposite of helplessness and alienation' (Marshall, n.d., p. 2).

As a further precondition for emerging from the iron cage this sense of agency must become part of our relationship to the world. As Theodore Roszak argues, 'we are confronted by sprawling conceptions of information that work from the assumption that thinking is a form of information processing and that, therefore, *more* data will produce *better* under-standing' (Roszak, 1986, p. 165). 'It yields', he continues, to 'a world without shadows, secrets, or mysteries, where everything has become a naked quantity' (ibid, p. 187). What is needed is a more creative approach to the human mind, one that moves beyond a rationalist and cognitivist concern with logic and quantity towards validation of other dimensions of knowing, seeing and being. As James Carey observes, 'the growth in technology has not been matched by attempts to conserve other, slower methods of communication. If the skills of learning, understanding and interpretation are not conserved, we will be left with a high-speed system but with an exceedingly unstable world' (Carey, 1983, p. 48).

A deep concern with subjugated knowledges and with the arts of human communication was expressed 50 years ago by Virginia Woolf in *Three Guineas*. Virginia Woolf, too, was concerned about how education contributed to the barbarity of mechanised warfare. Since 'the old education of the old colleges breeds neither a particular respect for liberty nor a particular hatred of war', she wrote, 'it is clear that you must build your college differently' (Woolf, 1977, p. 39). Asking 'what should be taught in the new college, the poor college?', she replied thus:

> Not the arts of dominating other people; not the arts of ruling, of killing, of acquiring land and capital. . . The poor college must teach only the arts that can be taught cheaply and practised by poor people; such as medicine, mathematics, music, painting and literature. It should teach the arts of human intercourse; the art of understanding other people's lives and minds, and the little arts of talk, of dress, of cookery that are allied with them. The aim of the new college, the cheap college, should be not to segregate and specialise, but to combine. It should explore the ways in which mind and body can be made to co-operate; discover what new combinations make good wholes in human life. (Ibid, pp. 39–40)

Virginia Woolf's poor college is a fitting contrast to the million dollar science parks of steel and glass and 'megabuck' deals.

Virginia Woolf suggests a whole other agenda, another more meaningful curriculum for schools and colleges, but also for society. The significance of her argument is underlined by Dale Spender's enquiries into knowledge and control. Spender is interested in 'what we know in our society and how we come to know it'; 'We cannot trust what we know. It has been made and taught by individual human beings who have had (fallible) human reasons for making and teaching such knowledge, and we may or may not subscribe to those reasons. We need to ask ourselves *why* it is that we know what we know, and whose interests are being served' (Spender, 1982, pp. 1–2).

What are also important are the limitations placed on knowledge. Spender is concerned with what is not known or knowable in society; with repressed, suppressed and subjugated knowledges. What she addresses is the relation between knowledge and power, the relation with which we have been concerned throughout this book. What is taught in schools? Why is it taught? In whose interests is it taught in this way at this time? Above all, what is not taught? And why not? A formidable obstacle in the way of the reconstruction of human society is that schools can teach only what society knows. What is now of paramount importance, however, is what society has forgotten or denied. Spender's fundamental point is that schools cannot teach what society does not know. But that is precisely what will be needed.

Bibliography

Abbs, Peter (1987) 'Training Spells the Death of Education', *The Guardian*, 5 January.

Abercrombie, Nicholas, Hill, Stephen, and Turner, Bryan S. (1986) *Sovereign Individuals of Capitalism* (London: Allen and Unwin).

ACARD/ABRC (Advisory Council for Applied Research and Development/Advisory Board for the Research Councils) (1983) *Improving Research Links between Higher Education and Industry* (London: HMSO).

Adam Smith Institute (1985) 'Education Policy', in *The Omega File* (London: Adam Smith Institute).

Adam Smith Institute (1986) *Ex Libris* (London: Adam Smith Institute).

Adelstein, David (1969) 'Roots of the Present Crisis', in Andrew Cockburn and Robin Blackburn (eds) *Student Power* (Harmondsworth: Penguin).

Aglietta, Michel (1979) *A Theory of Capitalist Regulation* (London: New Left Books).

Aitken, Robert (1986) 'MSC, TVEI and Education in Perspective', *Political Quarterly*, 57(3) July–September, pp. 231–5.

Akin, William E. (1977) *Technocracy and the American Dream* (Berkeley: University of California Press).

Albig, William (1939) *Public Opinion* (New York: McGraw-Hill).

Albu, Austen (1963) 'Taboo on Expertise', *Encounter*, 21(1) July, pp. 45–50.

Allen, G. C. (1976) *The British Disease: A Short Essay on the Nature and Causes of the Nation's Lagging Wealth* (London: Institute of Economic Affairs, Hobart Papers 67).

Allison, Lincoln (1983) 'Is Britain's Decline a Myth?', *New Society*, 17 November, pp. 274–5.

American Library Association (1986) 'Less Access to Less Information about the US Government: 2'. Washington Office, December.

Anderson, Digby (ed.) (1984) *Trespassing? Businessmen's Views of the Education System* (London: Social Affairs Unit).

Anderson, Perry (1966) 'Origins of the Present Crisis', in Perry Anderson and Robin Blackburn (eds) *Towards Socialism* (Ithaca, New York: Cornell University Press).

Anderson, Perry (1987) 'Figures of Descent', *New Left Review*, 161, January–February, pp. 20–77.

Annual Review of Government Funded R&D (1985) (London: HMSO).

Apple, Michael W. (1982) 'Curriculum and the Labor Process: The Logic of Technical Control', *Social Text*, (5), Spring, pp. 108–25.

Archer, Jeffrey (1985) Interview on BBC Radio 4, 'The World This Weekend', 6 October, Reported in *The Times*, 7 October.

Arnold, Erik and Guy, Ken (1986) *Parallel Convergence: National Strategies in Information Technology* (London: Frances Pinter).

Ashby, Eric (1963) *Technology and the Academics: An Essay on Universities and the Scientific Revolution* (London: Macmillan).

Ashworth, John M. (1982) 'Reshaping Higher Education in Britain', *Journal of the Royal Society of the Arts*, 130, pp. 713–29.

Ashworth, John M. (1984) 'The University as a Business', *IEEE Proceedings*, 131, Part A (8) November, pp. 635–41.

Ashworth, John M. (1985) 'What Price an Ivory Tower? University-Industry Relationships', *Higher Education Review*, 17(2), pp. 31–43.

Athanasiou, Tom (1987) 'Artificial Intelligence as Military Technology', unpublished manuscript.

Atkinson, Dick (1972) 'The Politics of Academic Freedom' in Trevor Pateman (ed.), *Counter Course* (Harmondsworth: Penguin).

Atkinson, John (1985) 'Flexibility: Planning for an Uncertain Future', *Manpower Policy and Practice*, 1, pp. 26–9.

Atkinson, Paul, Dickinson, Hilary and Erben, Michael (1986) 'The Classification and Control of Vocational Training for Young People' in Stephen Walker and Len Barton (eds), *Youth, Unemployment and Schooling* (Milton Keynes: Open University Press).

Atkinson, Paul, Rees, Teresa L., Shone, David and Williamson, Howard (1982) 'Social and Life Skills: The Latest Case of Compensatory Education' in Teresa L. Rees and Paul Atkinson (eds), *Youth Unemployment and State Intervention* (London: Routledge and Kegan Paul).

AT&T (American Telegraph and Telephone) (1985) Advertisement in *New York Review of Books*, 9 May, p. 5.

Bagehot, Walter (1872) *The English Constitution* (London: Kegan Paul, Trench, Trubner and Co., 1929).

Bailey, Charles (1984) *Beyond the Present and the Particular: A Theory of Liberal Education* (London: Routledge and Kegan Paul).

Baker, Kenneth (1980) *Hansard*, 11 July, col. 938.

Baker, Kenneth (1982) 'Towards an Information Economy', Department of Trade and Industry, 7 September.

Baker, Kenneth (1983) *Information Technology – The Path to Greater Freedom or to 1984* (London: Department of Industry, 6 January).

Baker, Kenneth (1987) 'Market Gardening', *Times Higher Education Supplement*, 3 July, p. 23.

Baldry, Tony (1986) *Education: 'No Easy Answers'* (London: Tory Reform Group).

Ball, Alan and Gordon, Alan (1985) *Employer Liaison with Schools*, IMS Report no. 108 (Brighton: Institute of Manpower Studies).

Ball, Christopher (1986) Foreword to *Transferable Personal Skills in Employment: the Contribution of Higher Education* (London: National Advisory Board for Public Sector Higher Education, May).

Balogh, Janet (1982) *Profile Reports for School-Leavers* (York: Longmans for Schools Council).

Bamford, James (1983) *The Puzzle Palace: America's National Security Agency and its Special Relationship with Britain's GCHQ* (London: Sidgwick and Jackson).

Barker, Bernard (1983) 'The Myth of Technology: The Manpower Services Commission and the Comprehensive School', *Head Teachers Review*, Winter, pp. 4–5.

Barnaby, Frank (1982) 'Microelectronics in War' in G. Friedrichs and A. Schaff (eds), *Microelectronics and Society: For Better or for Worse* (Oxford: Pergamon Press).

Barnaby, Frank (ed.) (1984) *Future War: Armed Conflict in the Next Decade* (London: Michael Joseph).

Barnaby, Frank (1986) *The Automated Battlefield* (London: Sidgwick and Jackson).

Barnett, Corelli (1972) *The Collapse of British Power* (London: Eyre Methuen).

Barnett, Corelli (1975) 'Further Education and the Development of an Industrial Society', *Coombe Lodge Reports*, 8(14), pp. 899–915.

Barnett, Corelli (1979) 'Technology, Education and Industrial and Economic Strength', *Journal of the Royal Society of Arts*, 127(5271) February, pp. 117–30.

Barnett, Corelli (1986a) *The Audit of War: The Illusion and Reality of Britain as a Great Nation* (London: Macmillan).

Barnett, Corelli (1986b) 'The Truth of British Decline', *Management Today*, April, pp. 84–8, 139.

Barnouw, Eric (1978) *The Sponsor: Notes on an American Potentate* (New York: Oxford University Press).

Beach, General Sir Hugh (1983) *The Protection of Military Information: Report of the Study Group on Censorship*, Ministry of Defence (London: HMSO) December, Cmnd 9112.

Beechey, Veronica (1987) 'It's Off To Work We Go?', *Marxism Today*, May, pp. 28–32.

Beer, Samuel H. (1982) *Britain Against Itself: The Political Contradictions of Collectivism* (London: Faber and Faber).

Bell, Daniel (1973) *The Coming of Post-Industrial Society: A Venture in Social Forecasting* (Harmondsworth: Penguin, 1976).

Bell, Daniel (1980) 'The Social Framework of the Information Society' in Tom Forester (ed.) *The Microelectronics Revolution* (Oxford: Blackwell).

Benn, Caroline and Fairley, John (1986) *Challenging the MSC: On Jobs, Training and Education* (London: Pluto Press).

Berg, Ivar (1970) *Education and Jobs: The Great Training Robbery* (New York: Praeger).

Berliner, Wendy (1987) 'Spare a thought for the Micro', *The Guardian*, 19 May.

Bernal, J. D. (1935) 'Universities, Science and Society', *Time and Tide*, 22 June, pp. 949–52.

Bernays, Edward L. (1923) *Crystallizing Public Opinion* (New York: Boni and Liveright).

Bernays, Edward L. (1952) *Public Relations* (Norman: University of Oklahoma Press, 1980).

Bernstein, Basil (1975) *Class, Codes and Control, vol. 3 (Towards a Theory of Educational Transmissions)* (London: Routledge and Kegan Paul).

Better Schools (1985), Cmnd 9469, March (London: HMSO).

Beynon, Huw (1984) *Working for Ford* 2nd edn (Harmondsworth: Penguin).

Blackburn, R. M. and Mann, Michael (1979) *The Working Class in the Labour Market* (London: Macmillan).

Blythe, John, Brace, Diane, Henry, Tony (1979) *Teaching Social and Life Skills* (Cambridge: National Extension College/Association for Liberal Education).

Bok, Derek (1982) *Beyond the Ivory Tower* (Cambridge, MA: Harvard University Press).

Boorstin, Daniel J. (1978) *The Republic of Technology: Reflections on our Future Community* (New York: Harper and Row).

Borgmann, Albert (1984) *Technology and the Character of Contemporary Life* (Chicago: University of Chicago Press).

Bracken, Paul (1983) *The Command and Control of Nuclear Forces* (New Haven: Yale University Press).

Braverman, Harry (1974) *Labor and Monopoly Capital: The Degradation of Work in the Twentieth Century* (New York: Monthly Review Press).

Broadfoot, Patricia (1986) 'Records of Achievement: Achieving a Record?' in Patricia Broadfoot (ed.) *Profiles and Records of Achievement: A Review of Issues and Practice* (London: Holt, Rinehart and Winston).

Broughton, John M. (1981) 'Piaget's Structural Development Psychology: Function and the Problem of Knowledge', *Human Development*, 24, pp. 257–85.

Broughton, John M. (1985) 'The Surrender of Control: Computer Literacy as Political Socialization of the Child' in Douglas Sloan (ed.) *The Computer in Education: A Critical Perspective* (New York: Teachers College Press).

Brown, Michael *et al.* (1985) *No Turning Back: A New Agenda from a Group of Conservative MPs* (London: Conservative Political Centre).

Brown, Michael *et al.* (1986) *Save Our Schools* (London: Conservative Political Centre).

Brzoska, Michael (1983) 'Economic Problems of Arms Production in Western Europe – Diagnoses and Alternatives' in Helena Tuomi and Raimo Vayrynen (eds) *Militarization and Arms Production* (London: Croom Helm).

BSSRS Technology of Political Control Group (1985) *Technocop: New Police Technologies* (London: Free Association Books).

Burgess, Tyrell (ed.) (1986) *Education for Capability* (London: NFER-Nelson).

Burgess, Tyrell and Adams, Elizabeth (1986) 'Records for All at 16' in Patricia Broadfoot (ed.) *Profiles and Records of Achievement: A Review of Issues and Practice* (London: Holt, Rinehart and Winston).
Burnham, David (1983) *The Rise of the Computer State* (London: Weidenfeld and Nicolson).
Burrows, William E. (1986) *Deep Black: Space Espionage and National Security* (New York: Random House).
Business Roundtable (1985) 'International Information Flow: A Plan for Action', New York, January. Cited in Herbert I. Schiller (1986) 'The Erosion of National Sovereignty by the World Business System', in Michael Traber (ed.) *The Myth of the Information Revolution* (London: Sage).
Callaghan, James (1976) 'Towards a National Debate', *Education*, 22 October, pp. 332–3.
Callaghan, James (1978) 'Prime Minister Announces Major Programme of Support for Microelectronics' (Press Office: 10 Downing Street) 6 December.
Callahan, Raymond E. (1962) *Education and the Cult of Efficiency: A Study of the Social Forces that have Shaped the Administration of the Public Schools* (Chicago: University of Chicago Press).
Campbell, Christy (1982) *War Facts Now* (London: Fontana).
Campbell, Duncan (1980) 'Society Under Surveillance' in Peter Hain *et al.* (1980) *Policing the Police, vol. 2* (London: Calder).
Campbell, Duncan (1984) 'Civil Liberties in the Nuclear Age' in Peter Wallington (ed.) *Civil Liberties 1984* (London: Martin Robertson).
Campbell, Duncan (1987) 'The Parliamentary By-pass Operation', *New Statesman*, 23 January, pp. 8–12.
Campbell, Duncan and Connor, Steve (1986) *On the Record: Surveillance, Computers and Privacy* (London: Michael Joseph).
Canan, James (1982) *War in Space* (New York: Harper and Row).
Carey, James T. (1975) *Sociology and Public Affairs: The Chicago School* vol. 16, Sage Library of Social Research (Beverly Hills: Sage).
Carey, James T. (1983) 'High-Speed Communication in an Unstable World', *Chronicle of Higher Education*, 27 July, p. 48.
Carey, James T. (1987) 'High Technology and Higher Education', in Steven E. Goldberg and Charles R. Strain (eds) *Technological Change and the Transformation of America* (Carbondole: Southern Illinois University Press).
Carnoy, Martin and Castells, Manuel (1984) 'After the Crisis?', *World Policy Journal*, Spring, pp. 495–515.
Casson, Herbert N. (1911) *Ads and Sales: A Study of Advertising and Selling from the Standpoint of the New Principles of Scientific Management* (Chicago: A. C. McClurg & Co).
Castoriadis, Cornelius (1982) 'From Ecology to Autonomy', *Thesis Eleven*, (3), pp. 8–22.
Castoriadis, Cornelius (1984) *Crossroads in the Labyrinth* (Brighton, Sussex: Harvester).
Castoriadis, Cornelius (1984/5) 'Reflections on "Rationality" and "Development" ', *Thesis Eleven*, (10/11), pp. 18–36.

CBI (1985) *Managing Change: The Organisation of Work* (London: Confederation of British Industries).

Centre for Educational Research and Innovation (1986) *New Information Technologies: A Challenge for Education* (Paris: Organisation for Economic Co-operation and Development).

Chalmers, Malcolm (1983) *The Cost of Britain's Defence* (London: Housemans).

Chandler, Alfred D. Jr. (1977) *The Visible Hand: The Managerial Revolution in American Business* (Cambridge, MA: Harvard University Press).

Chandler, Daniel (1984) *Young Learners and the Microcomputer* (Milton Keynes: Open University Press).

Chandler, Daniel and Marcus, Stephen (1985) *Computers and Literacy* (Milton Keynes: Open University Press).

Chapman, Paul G. and Tooze, Michael J. (1987) *The Youth Training Scheme in the United Kingdom* (London: Gower).

Cherrington, Ruth (1987) 'The Changing Relationship between Industry and Education: the intermediary role of technology' (mimeo). British Sociological Association Annual Conference, University of Leeds, April.

Childs, Harwood L. (1965) *Public Opinion: Nature, Formation and Role* (Princeton: Van Nostrand).

Chitty, Clyde (1986) 'TVEI: The MSC's Trojan Horse', in Caroline Benn and John Fairley (eds) (q.v., above).

Choukas, Michael (1965) *Propaganda Comes of Age* (Washington DC: Public Affairs Press).

CIHE (1987) *Towards a Partnership: Higher Education-Government-Industry* (London: Council for Industry and Higher Education).

Cline, Ray S. (1978) 'The US Intelligence Machine' in *The US War Machine* (London: Salamander Press).

CNAA (1982) 'Policy Statement: Implications of the Development of Information Technology for CNAA Undergraduate Courses'. Publication 2a/27, 27 December (London: Council for National Academic Awards).

Coates, David and Hillard, John (eds) (1986) *The Economic Decline of Modern Britain: The Debate between Left and Right* (Brighton, Sussex: Harvester).

Cockburn, Andrew (1983) *The Threat: Inside the Soviet Military Machine* (London: Hutchinson).

Coffield, Frank, Borrill, Carol, and Marshall, Sarah (1986) *Growing Up at the Margins: Young Adults in the North East* (Milton Keynes: Open University Press).

Cohen, Philip (1984) 'Against the New Vocationalism' in Inge Bates *et al.*, *Schooling for the Dole? The New Vocationalism* (London: Macmillan).

Cohen, Stanley (1979) 'The Punitive City: Notes on the Dispersal of Social Control', *Contemporary Crises*, 3(4), pp. 339–63.

Cohen, Stanley (1985) *Visions of Social Control* (Cambridge: Polity Press).

Cohen, Stephen and Zysman, John (1987) *Manufacturing Matters: The Myth of a Post-Industrial Economy* (New York: Basic Books).

Coleman, D. C. (1973) 'Gentlemen and Players', *Economic History Review*, 26(1), pp. 92–116.

Collins, Nigel (1986) 'MSC and the Education of Young People', *Political Quarterly*, 57(3) July–September, pp. 236–45.

Collins, Randall (1979) *The Credential Society* (New York: Academic Press).

Committee of Vice-Chancellors and Principals (1985) *Report of the Steering Committee for Efficiency Studies in Universities* (London: Committee of Vice-Chancellors and Principals).

Connor, H. and Pearson, Richard (1986) *Information Technology Manpower into the 1990s* (Brighton: University of Sussex, Institute of Manpower Studies).

Conservative Party (1987) *The Next Moves Forward: The Conservative Party Manifesto 1987* (London: Conservative Party).

Cooke, Philip (1987) 'Britain's New Spatial Paradigm: Technology, Locality and Society in Transition', *Environment and Planning* A, 19(10) October, pp. 1289–301.

Cooley, Mike (1981) 'The Taylorisation of Intellectual Work' in Les Levidow and Bob Young (eds) *Science, Technology and the Labour Process, vol. 1* (London: CSE Books) pp. 46–65.

Coriat, Benjamin (1979) *L'Atelier et le Chronomètre: Essai sur le Taylorisme, le Fordisme et la Production de Masse* (Paris: Christian Bourgois).

Cotgrove, Stephen F. (1958) *Technical Education and Social Change* (London: Allen and Unwin).

Council for Science and Society (1986) *UK Military R&D: Report of a Working Party* (Oxford: Oxford University Press).

CRAC/CBI (1987) Careers Research and Advisory Centre/Confederation of British Industry, *The Job Book 1987* (Cambridge: CRAC/CBI).

Crompton, Rosemary and Jones, Gareth (1984) *White-Collar Proletariat: Deskilling and Gender in Clerical Work* (London: Macmillan).

Cronin, Blaise and Martyn, John (1984) 'Public/private sector interaction: a review of issues with particular reference to document delivery and electronic publishing', *Aslib Proceedings*, 36(10) October, pp. 373–91.

Crosland, Anthony (1956) *The Future of Socialism* (London: Jonathan Cape).

Crossman, R. H. S. (1963) 'The Party of Science', *The Guardian*, 4 October.

CSU (1987), Central Services Unit, *Statistical Quarterly*, (30), May.

Curtis, Liz (1984) *Ireland: The Propaganda War* (London: Pluto Press).

Dahrendorf, Ralf (1982) *On Britain* (London: BBC Publications).

Dale, Barrie G. and Lees, Jayne (1986) *Quality Circle Programme Development: Some Key Issues* (Sheffield: Manpower Services Commission).

Dale, Roger (1986) 'Examining the Gift-Horse's Teeth: A Tentative Analysis of TVEI' in Stephen Walker and Len Barton (eds) *Youth, Unemployment and Schooling* (Milton Keynes: Open University Press).

Daniel, W. W. (1986) 'The Myth of the British Disease', *New Society*, 5 December.

Davidoff, Leonore (1973) *The Best Circles: Society Etiquette and the Season* (London: Croom Helm).

Davies, Bernard (1979) *In Whose Interests? From Social Education to Life Skills Training* (Leicester: National Youth Bureau) Occasional Paper 19.

Davies, Bernard (1986) *Threatening Youth: Towards a National Youth Policy* (Milton Keynes: Open University Press).

Davies, Nick (1985) 'BBC chiefs briefed by MI5 on union subversives', *The Observer*, 25 August, p. 1.

Davies, Nick and Black, Ian (1984) 'Subversion and the State', *The Guardian*, 17 April, p. 19.

Davy, John (1984) 'Mindstorms in the Lamplight', *Teachers College Record*, 85(4) Summer, pp. 549–58.

Dede, Christopher (1985) 'Educational and Social Implications', in Tom Forester (ed.) *The Information Technology Revolution* (Oxford: Blackwell).

Department of Commerce (1983) *High Technology Industries: Profiles and Outlooks, The Telecommunications Industry* (International Trade Administration, Washington DC: Government Printing Office) April.

Department of Employment (1985) *Employment: The Challenge for the Nation* Cmnd 9474 (London: HMSO).

Department of Trade and Industry (1988) *DTI – The Department for Enterprise* Cmnd 278 (London: HMSO).

DES (Department of Education and Science) (1982) 'The Future Development of Libraries and Information Services', Library Information Series, no. 2 (London: DES) quoted in Golding and Murdock, 1983, p. 73 (q.v., below).

DES (1986a) *City Technical Colleges: A New Choice of School* (London: Department of Education and Science/Central Office of Information) October.

DES (1986b) 'Results of the Survey of Microcomputers etc., in Schools – Autumn 1985', *Statistical Bulletin*, 18/86, December.

DES (1986c) Department of Education and Science, Department of Trade and Industry, Welsh Office, *School/Industry Links: A Directory of Organisations* (London: DES) March.

DES (1987) *Government Response to the ITAP Report 'Learning to Live with IT'* (London: HMSO).

DES/Welsh Office (1984) *Records of Achievement: A Statement of Policy* (London: Department of Education and Science/Welsh Office).

DES/Welsh Office (1987) *The National Curriculum, 5–16* (London: Department of Education and Science/Welsh Office) July.

De Vroey, Michel (1984) 'A Regulation Approach Interpretation of the Contemporary Crisis', *Capital and Class*, (23), Summer, pp. 45–66.

Dewey, John (1963) *Experience and Education* (New York: Collier).

Dickson, David (1974) *Alternative Technology and the Politics of Technological Change* (London: Fontana).

Dickson, David (1984) *The New Politics of Science* (New York: Pantheon).

Donaldson, Michael *et al.* (1987) *Skills for the Future* (Sheffield: University of Sheffield).

Dordick, Herbert S. (1986) *Understanding Modern Telecommunications* (New York: McGraw-Hill).

Dore, Ronald (1976) *The Diploma Disease* (London: Allen and Unwin).

Downs, Sylvia (1982) 'Who Learns Whom?', *Training and Development*, June, pp. 8–9.

Downs, Sylvia and Perry, Patricia (1984) 'Developing Learning Skills', *Journal of European Industrial Training*, 8(1), pp. 21–6.

Downs, Sylvia and Perry, Patricia (1986) 'Can Trainers Learn to take a Back Seat?', *Personnel Management*, March, pp. 42–5.

Dreyfus, Hubert L. (1980) 'Holism and Hermeneutics', *Review of Metaphysics*, 34, September, pp. 3–23.

Dreyfus, Hubert L. and Dreyfus, Stuart E. (1986) *Mind over Machine: The Power of Human Intuition and Expertise in the Era of the Computer* (Oxford: Basil Blackwell).

Dumas, Lloyd J. (1984) 'The Economics of Warfare', in Frank Barnaby (ed.) (q.v., above).

Duncan, K. D. and Kelly, C. J. (1983) *Task Analysis, Learning and the Nature of Transfer* (Sheffield: Manpower Services Commission).

Durham, Kenneth (1984) 'Re-funding Higher Education to Increase Technological Application and Growth', in Digby Anderson (ed.) (q.v., above).

Dwyer, Thomas (1980) 'Heuristic Strategies for Using Computers to Enrich Education', in Robert Taylor (ed.) *The Computer in the School: Tutor, Tool, Tutee* (New York: Teachers College Press).

Eckelmann, R. (1983) 'A Study of the International Competitive Position of the US Telecommunications Equipment Industry', in Department of Commerce (q.v., above).

Economist Intelligence Unit (1982) *Coping with Unemployment: The Effects on the Unemployed Themselves* (London: Economist Intelligence Unit) December.

Education Group (1981) *Unpopular Education: Schooling and Social Democracy in England since 1944* (London: Hutchinson).

Education and Training for Young People (1985) Cmnd 9482 (London: HMSO).

Edwards, Paul N. (1987) 'The Closed World: Systems Discourse and Military Thinking in Post World War Two Historical Consciousness'. Paper for the Conference on 'Directions and Implications of Advanced Computing', Computer Professionals for Social Responsibility. Seattle, Washington, 12 July.

Edwards, Richard (1979) *Contested Terrain: The Transformation of the Workplace in the Twentieth Century* (London: Heinemann).

Edwards, Terry (1984) *The Youth Training Scheme: A New Curriculum* (Lewes: Falmer Press).

Eisenhower, Dwight D. (1970) 'Liberty is at Stake', in Herbert I. Schiller and Joseph D. Phillips (eds) (q.v., below).

Ellul, Jacques (1965) *Propaganda* (New York: Knopf).

Eraut, Michael and Burke, John (1986) *Improving the Quality of YTS* (Brighton: Education Area, University of Sussex).

Evans, Christopher (1979) *The Mighty Micro: The Impact of the Computer Revolution* (London: Gollancz).

Evans, Keith (1975) *The Development and Structure of the English Educational System* (London: University of London Press).

Ezard, John (1983) 'Letter of the Law for War Reporters', *The Guardian*, 27 October.

Feigenbaum, Edward A. and McCorduck, Pamela (1984) *The Fifth Generation: Artificial Intelligence and Japan's Computer Challenge to the World* (London: Pan).

Ferguson, James R. (1983) 'Scientific Freedom, National Security, and the First Amendment', *Science*, 221, 12 August, pp. 620–24.

FEU (1982a), *A Basis for Choice: Report of a Study Group on Post-16 Pre-Employment Courses* (London: Further Education Unit) 2nd edn (First published June 1979).

FEU (1982b) *Basic Skills* (London: Further Education Unit).

FEU (1985a) *Supporting YTS* (London: Further Education Unit) 3rd edn (First published May 1983).

FEU (1985b) *Supporting TVEI* (London: Further Education Unit).

Field, Anne R. and Harris, Catherine L. (1986) 'The Information Business', *Business Week*, August 25, pp. 48–53.

Finlay, Marike (1987) *Powermatics: A Discursive Critique of New Communications Technologies* (London: Routledge and Kegan Paul).

Finn, Dan (1987) *Training Without Jobs: New Deals and Broken Promises* (London: Macmillan).

Finniston, Sir Montague (1980) *Report of the Committee of Inquiry into the Engineering Profession: Engineering our Future* (London: HMSO) January.

Flude, Michael (1983) 'The Social Democratic Party, Its Political Programme and Educational Policies: Revisionism Revisited and Re-Formed', in John Ahier and Michael Flude (eds) *Contemporary Education Policy* (London: Croom Helm).

Ford, Daniel (1985) *The Button: The Nuclear Trigger – Does it Work?* (London: Allen and Unwin).

Foremski, Tom (1986) 'Military Projects Draw US Crowds', *Computing*, October 30, p. 12.

Forester, Tom (ed.) (1985) *The Information Technology Revolution* (Oxford: Blackwell).

Foucault, Michel (1979) *Discipline and Punish: The Birth of the Prison* (Harmondsworth: Penguin).

Fowler, Graham (1985) 'What is TVEI?' *Liberal Education*, (54), Autumn, pp. 14–17.

Fowler, Graham (1986) 'CPVE: A Discordant Note', *Liberal Education*, (56), Summer, pp. 26–7.

Fullick, Leisha (1986) 'The MSC and the Local Community', in Caroline Benn and John Fairley (eds) (q.v., above).

Gamble, Andrew (1979) 'The Free Economy and the Strong State', in Ralph Miliband and John Saville (eds) *Socialist Register 1979* (London: Merlin).

Gamble, Andrew (1981) *Britain in Decline: Economic Policy, Political Strategy and the British State* (London: Macmillan).

Gansler, J. S. (1980) *The Defense Industry* (Cambridge, MA: MIT Press).

Gehlen, Arnold (1980) *Man in the Age of Technology* (New York: Columbia University Press).

Gershuny, Jonathan I. (1978) *After Industrial Society? The Emerging Self-Service Economy* (London: Macmillan).

Gershuny, Jonathan I. (1983) *Social Innovation and the Division of Labour* (Oxford: Oxford University Press).

Gershuny, Jonathan I. and Miles, Ian (1983) *The New Service Economy: The Transformation of Employment in Industrial Societies* (London: Frances Pinter).

Gerth, Hans H. and Mills, C. Wright (1967) *From Max Weber: Essays in Sociology* (London: Routledge and Kegan Paul).

Gervassi, Tom (1981) *Arsenal of Democracy 11: American Military Power in the 1980s and the Origins of the New Cold War* (New York: Grove Press).

Gerver, Elizabeth (1984) *Computers and Adult Learning* (Milton Keynes: Open University Press).

Giddens, Anthony (1981) *The Class Structure of the Advanced Societies* (London: Heinemann) 2nd edn.

Giddens, Anthony (1985) *The Nation-State and Violence: Volume Two of a Contemporary Critique of Historical Materialism* (Cambridge: Polity Press).

Giddens, Anthony (1987) *Social Theory and Modern Sociology* (Cambridge: Polity Press).

Giddens, Anthony and Stanworth, Philip (1978) 'Elites and Privilege', in Philip Abrams (ed.) *Work, Urbanism and Inequality: UK Society Today* (London: Weidenfeld and Nicolson).

Gill, Kenneth (1983) 'Chairman's Review', in Saatchi and Saatchi Company PLC, *Annual Report 1983*.

Girouard, Mark (1978) *Life in the English Country House: A Social and Architectural History* (New Haven: Yale University Press).

Girourd, Mark (1981) *The Return to Camelot: Chivalry and the English Gentleman* (New Haven: Yale University Press).

Gleeson, Denis and Hopkins, Michael (1987) 'Further Education without Tiers: Countering Tripartism in Post-Sixteen Further Education and Training', *Critical Social Policy*, (19) Summer, pp. 77–89.

Glover, Ian A. (1985) 'How the West was Lost? Decline in Manufacturing in Britain and the United States', *Higher Education Review*, 17(3), pp. 3–34.

Goddard, J. B. and Gillespie, A. E. (1986) 'Advanced Telecommunications and Regional Economic Development', *The Geographical Journal*, 152(3) November, pp. 383–97.

Golden, Frederic (1985) 'Here Come the Microkids', in Tom Forester (ed.) (q.v., above).

Goldberg, Steven E. and Strain, Charles R. (eds) (1987) *Technological Change and the Transformation of America* (Carbondale: Southern Illinois University Press).

Golding, Peter and Middleton, Susan (1982) *Images of Welfare* (Oxford: Martin Robertson).

Golding, Peter and Murdock, Graham (1986) 'Unequal Information: access and exclusion in the new communications marketplace', in Marjorie Ferguson (ed.) *New Communication Technologies and the Public Interest: Comparative Perspectives on Policy and Research* (London: Sage).

Goldsmith, Walter (1984) 'The Business of Education', in Digby Anderson (ed.) (q.v., above).

Gombrich, Ernst (1985) 'The Embattled Humanities', *Universities Quarterly*, 39(3) Summer, pp. 193–205.

Goode, Kenneth (1926) cited in Stephen R. Shapiro (1969) *The Big Sell – Attitudes of Advertising Writers About Their Craft in the 1920s and 1930s*, University of Wisconsin, Ph.D. thesis.

Gooding, Kenneth (1984) 'Ford's "do it only once" approach', *Financial Times*, 16 November.

Goodwin, Glenn A. and Humphreys, Laud (1982) 'Freeze-Dried Stigma: Cybernetics and Social Control', *Humanity and Society*, 6, November, pp. 391–408.

Gordon, Alan and Pearson, Richard (1984) *Manpower for Information Technology* (Brighton: University of Sussex, Institute of Manpower Studies) Report no. 83.

Gorz, André (1982) *Farewell to the Working Class: an Essay on Post-Industrial Socialism* (London: Pluto Press).

Gorz, André (1983) 'The Reconquest of Time', *Telos*, (55), pp. 212–25.

Gorz, André (1985) *Paths to Paradise: On the Liberation from Work* (London: Pluto Press).

Gouldner, Alvin (1976) *The Dialectic of Ideology and Technology* (London: Macmillan).

Government Statistical Services (1981), Cmnd 8236 (Privy Council Office: HMSO) April.

Graves, Robert and Hodge, Alan (1940) *The Long Week-End: A Social History of Great Britain, 1918–1939* (London: Faber and Faber).

Green, Andy (1986) 'The MSC and the Three-Tier Structure of Further Education', in Caroline Benn and John Fairley (eds) (q.v., above).

Greenbaum, Joan (1979) *In the Name of Efficiency: Management Theory and Shopfloor Practice in Data-Processing* (Philadelphia: Temple University Press).

Gregor, Ian (1983) 'Liberal Education: an Outworn Ideal?', in Nicholas Phillipson (ed.) *Universities, Society, and the Future* (Edinburgh: Edinburgh University Press).

Grubb, W. Norton (1984) 'The Bandwagon Once More: Vocational Preparation for High-Tech Occupations', *Harvard Educational Review*, 54(4) November, pp. 429–51.

Grubb, W. Norton (1987) 'Blinding Faith in the New Orthodoxy', *Times Higher Educational Supplement*, 26 June, p. 14.

Gummett, Philip (1986) 'What Price Military Research?', *New Scientist*, 19 June, pp. 60–63.

Haber, Samuel (1964) *Efficiency and Uplift: Scientific Management in the Progressive Era, 1890–1920* (Chicago: University of Chicago Press).

Habermas, Jürgen (1962) *Strukturwandel der Öffentlichkeit* (Darmstadt: Luchterhand).

Hakim, Catherine (1987) 'Trends in the flexible workforce', *Employment Gazette*, November, pp. 549–60.

Hall, Jackson (1985) 'The Centralist Tendency', *Forum*, 28(1) Autumn, pp. 4–6.

Hall, Stuart (1983) 'Education in Crisis', in Anne-Marie Wolpe and James Donald (eds) *Is There Anyone Here From Education?* (London: Pluto).

Hallin, Daniel (1986) *The 'Uncensored War': The Media and Vietnam* (New York: Oxford University Press).

Halsey, A. H. (1961) 'British Universities and Intellectual Life', in A. H. Halsey, J. Floud and C. A. Anderson (eds) *Education, Economy and Society: A Reader in the Sociology of Education* (New York: Free Press).

Halsey, A. H. (1986) *Change in British Society* (Oxford: Oxford University Press) 3rd edn.

Hanson, Dirk (1982) *The New Alchemists: Silicon Valley and the Microelectronics Revolution* (Boston: Little, Brown and Company).

Harding, Sandra (1986) *The Science Question in Feminism* (Milton Keynes: Open University Press).

Hargreaves, Andy (1977) 'Progressivism and Pupil Autonomy', *Sociological Review*, 25(3), pp. 585–621.

Hargreaves, Andy (1986) 'Record Breakers?', in Patricia Broadfoot (ed.) (q.v., above).

Harris, Robert (1983) *Gotcha! The Media, the Government and the Falklands Crisis* (London: Faber).

Harrison, J. F. C. (1957) 'The Victorian Gospel of Success', *Victorian Studies*, 1(2) December, pp. 155–64.

Hartung, William D. *et al.* (1985) *The Strategic Defense Initiative: Costs, Contractors and Consequences* (New York: Council on Economic Priorities).

Hattersley, Roy (1985) 'New Technology Policy'. Speech at the First London Business Computer Week, Earls Court Exhibition Centre, 5 June.

Hawkridge, David (1983) *New Information Technology in Education* (London: Croom Helm).

Hayes, Christopher *et al.* (1981) *Occupational Training Families* (Brighton: Institute of Manpower Studies).

Hayes, Christopher *et al.* (1982) *Foundation Training Issues* (Brighton: Institute of Manpower Studies).

Hayes, Christopher *et al.* (1983) *Training for Skill Ownership: Learning to Take It With You* (Brighton: Institute of Manpower Studies).

Hayes, Christopher and Fonda, Nickie (1982) 'The Privatisation of Skills', *Personnel Management*, October.

Heald, Gordon and Wybrow, Robert J. (1986) *The Gallup Survey of Britain, 1985* (Beckenham, Kent: Croom Helm).

Heddon, Russell (1981) quoted in *Business Week*, 3 August, p. 63.

Hersch, Seymour (1986) *'The Target is Destroyed': What Really Happened to Flight 007* (London: Faber).

Higher Education: Meeting the Challenge (1987), Cmnd. 114 (London: HMSO) April.

'Higher Education Output in Engineering: International Comparisons', *Employment Gazette*, December, pp. 603–10.

Hill, Christopher (1967) *The Pelican Economic History of Britain*, VOL. 2, *1530–1780: Reformation to Industrial Revolution* (Harmondsworth: Penguin, 1978).

Hillgate Group (1986) *Whose Schools? A Radical Manifesto* (London: Hillgate Group).

Hoag, Paul W. (1985) 'High-Tech Armaments, Space Militarization, and the Third World', in Colin Creighton and Martin Shaw (eds) *The Sociology of War and Peace* (London: Macmillan, 1987).

Hobsbawm, Eric J. (1968) *Industry and Empire: An Economic History of Britain since 1750* (London: History Book Club).

Hodges, Lucy (1985) 'School leavers get new computer test', *The Times*, 12 February.

Holland, Geoffrey (1987) quoted in *Youth Training News*, (36) February, p. 13.

Holloway, David (1983) *The Soviet Union and the Arms Race* (Yale: Yale University Press).

Holloway, John (1987) 'The Red Rose of Nissan', *Capital and Class*, (32) Summer, pp. 142–64.

Holt, Maurice (1983) 'Vocationalism: The New Threat to Universal Education', *Forum*, 25(3) Summer, pp. 84–6.

Hopkins, Adam (1978) *The School Debate* (Harmondsworth: Penguin).

Hopson, Barrie and Scally, Mike (1981) *Lifeskills Teaching* (London: McGraw-Hill).

Horowitz, David (ed.) (1969) *Corporations and the Cold War* (New York: Monthly Review Press).

House of Commons Defence Committee (1982a), First Report, session 1982–83. *The Handling of Press and Public Information During the Falklands Crisis*, VOL. 1, (London: HMSO) December.

House of Commons Defence Committee (1982b), Second Report from the Defence Committee, Session 1981–1982. *Ministry of Defence Organization and Procurement, vol. 1. Report and Minutes of Proceedings* (London: HMSO) 11 June.

House of Lords (1983), Select Committee on Science and Technology,

1982–83, *Engineering Research and Development* (London: HMSO).

House of Lords (1985), Select Committee on Science and Technology, Session 1984–85, 2nd Report, *Education and Training for New Technologies, VOL. 1, Report (48–1)* (London: HMSO) December.

Hunter, Laurence C. (1981) 'Employers' Perceptions of Demand', in Robert Lindley (ed.) (q.v., below).

Hurwitz, Donald L. (1983) *Broadcast 'Ratings': The Rise and Development of Commercial Audience Research and Measurement in American Broadcasting*, University of Illinois at Urbana-Champaign, Ph.D. thesis. (Available from University Microfilms International, Ann Arbor, MI 48106.)

Information Technology Skills Shortages Committee (1984) *The Human Factor – the Supply Side Problem. First Report* (London: Department of Trade and Industry).

Inman, Adm. Bobby R. (1982) 'A Government Proposal', *Aviation Week and Space Technology*, 8 February.

ITAP (Information Technology Advisory Panel) (1983) *Making a Business of Information: A Survey of New Opportunities* (London: HMSO) September.

ITAP (Information Technology Advisory Panel) (1986) *Learning to Live with IT* (London: HMSO).

Jahoda, Marie (1982) *Employment and Unemployment: A Social-Psychological Analysis* (Cambridge University Press).

Jaikumar, Ramchandram (1986) 'Postindustrial Manufacturing', *Harvard Business Review*, 86(6) November–December, pp. 69–76.

Jamieson, Ian (1980) *Capitalism and Culture: A Comparative Analysis of British and American Manufacturing Organisations* (Farnborough: Gower).

Jamieson, Ian (1985a) 'Corporate Hegemony or Pedagogic Liberation? The Schools-Industry Movement in England and Wales', in Roger Dale (ed.) *Education, Training and Employment: Towards a New Vocationalism?* (Oxford: Pergamon Press).

Jamieson, Ian (1985b) *Industry in Education: Developments and Case Studies* (London: Longman).

Jamieson, Ian (1986) 'The Case for Linking Schools and Industry', *Secondary Education*, 16(1) January, pp. 5–7.

Jamieson, Ian and Lighfoot, Martin (1982) *Schools and Industry* (London: Methuen).

Janowitz, Morris (1975) 'Sociological Theory and Social Control', *American Journal of Sociology*, 81(1) July, pp. 82–108.

Janus, Noreen (1984) 'Advertising and the Creation of Global Markets: The Role of the New Communication Technologies', in Vincent Mosco and Janet Wasko (eds) *The Critical Communications Review*, vol. 2 (Norwood, New Jersey: Ablex).

Januszczak, Waldemar (1985) 'The art world can't tell Jacob Duck from Donald', *The Guardian*, 28 December.

Januszczak, Waldemar (1986) 'No way to treat a thoroughbred', *The Guardian*, 15 February, p. 11.

Jasani, Bhupendra (ed.) (1982) *Outer Space – A New Dimension of the Arms Race* (London: Taylor and Francis).

Jasani, Bhupendra and Lee, Christopher (1984) *Countdown to Space War* (London: Taylor and Francis).

Jenkins, Clive and Sherman, Barry (1979) *The Collapse of Work* (London: Eyre Methuen).

Jenkins, Clive and Sherman, Barry (1981) *The Leisure Shock* (London: Eyre Methuen).

Jessop, Bob, Bonnett, Kevin, Bromley, Simon, Ling, Tom (1987), 'Popular Capitalism, Flexible Accumulation and Left Strategy', *New Left Review*, (165) September–October, pp. 104–22.

Johnson, R. W. (1986) *Shootdown: The Verdict on KAL 007* (London: Chatto).

Jonas, Hans (1984) *The Imperative of Responsibility: In Search of an Ethics for the Technological Age* (Chicago: Univeristy of Chicago Press).

Jonathan, Ruth (1983) 'The Manpower Services Model of Education', *Cambridge Journal of Education*, 13(2), pp. 3–10.

Jonathan, Ruth (1986) 'Education and the "Needs of Society"', in Anthony Hartnett and Michael Naish (eds) *Education and Society Today* (Lewes: Falmer Press).

Jones, Barry (1982) *Sleepers Wake! Technology and the Future of Work* (Brighton, Sussex: Wheatsheaf).

Jones, Ken (1983) *Beyond Progressive Education* (London: Macmillan).

Joseph, Sir Keith (1975) *Reversing the Trend* (Chichester: Rose).

Jungk, Robert (1979) *The Nuclear State* (London: Calder).

Kahn, Herman (1983) *The Coming Boom: Economic, Political, and Social* (New York: Simon and Schuster).

Kaldor, Mary (1981) *The Baroque Arsenal* (New York: Hill and Wang).

Kaldor, Mary (1983) 'Military R&D: Cause or Consequence of the Arms Race?', *International Social Science Journal*, 35(1), pp. 25–45.

Kaldor, Mary, Sharp, Margaret, and Walker, William (1986) 'Industrial Competitiveness and Britain's Defence', *Lloyds Bank Review*, (162) October, pp. 31–49.

Karas, Thomas (1983) *The New High Ground: Strategies and Weapons of Space-Age War* (New York: Simon and Schuster).

Kennaway, Alexander (1981) 'Never the Dominant Manufacturer', *The Guardian*, January 21, p. 17.

Kennedy, Gavin (1983) *Defence Economics* (London: Duckworth).

Kinnock, Neil (1986) *Making Our Way: Investing in Britain's Future* (Oxford: Blackwell).

Kistiakowsky, Vera (1986) 'Should University Researchers Accept SDI Funding?' *Technology Review*, January, pp. 10–12.

Klein, Rudolph (1987) 'Inside the Ivory Tower', *New Society*, 17 April.

Knight, Richard (1983) *Key Issues for Industry and Education*, Society of Education Officers, Occasional Paper 3 (London: Society of Education Officers).

Knightley, Phillip (1986) *The Second Oldest Profession: The Spy as Bureaucrat, Patriot, Fantasist and Whore* (London: André Deutsch).

Kogan, Maurice and Kogan, David (1983) *The Attack on Higher Education* (London: Kogan Page).

Kovel, Joel (1982/83) 'Theses on Technocracy', *Telos*, (54), Winter, pp. 155–61.

Kovel, Joel (1983) *Against the State of Nuclear Terror* (London: Pan).

Kraft, Philip (1977) *Programmers and Managers: The Routinization of Computer Programming in the United States* (New York: Springer-Verlag).

Kuhn, Deanna (1986) 'Education for Thinking', *Teachers College Record*, 87(4) Summer, pp. 495–512.

Kumar, Krishan (1978) *Prophecy and Progress: The Sociology of Industrial and Post-Industrial Society* (Harmondsworth: Penguin).

Labour Party (1961) *Science and the Future of Britain* (London: Labour Party).

Labour Party (1985) *Labour and Information Technology* (London: Labour Party).

Labour Party (1986) *Education Throughout Life* (London: Labour Party).

Labour Research, 'Lords on the Board', 74(2), December 1985, pp. 297–9.

Lamb, Chris (1987) 'From Liberal Corporatism to Techno-Corporatism? A Study of the Manpower Services Commission', *Local Government Studies*, 13(5) September–October, pp. 63–73.

Landes, David S. (1969) *The Unbound Prometheus: Technological Change and Industrial Development in Western Europe from 1750 to the Present* (Cambridge: Cambridge University Press).

Landon, Robert (1983) 'EIA Sees $490 billion Defense Budget by 1993', *Defense Electronics*, 15(11) November, pp. 164–172.

Large, Peter (1987) 'Parties Only a Grid Apart', *The Guardian*, 10 September.

Larson, Magali Sarfatti (1972) 'Notes on Technocracy: Some Problems of Theory, Ideology and Power', *Berkeley Journal of Sociology*, 17, pp. 1–34.

Lasch, Christopher (1980) 'Life in the Therapeutic State', *New York Review of Books*, 27(10) June 12, pp. 24–32.

Lasch, Christopher (1984) 'Chip of Fools', *New Republic*, 13 and 20 August, pp. 25–8.

Lasch, Christopher (1985) *The Minimal Self: Psychic Survival in Troubled Times* (London: Pan).

Lasch, Christopher (1987) 'Technology and its Critics: The Degradation of the Practical Arts', in Steven E. Goldberg and Charles R. Strain (eds) (q.v., above).

Lash, Scott and Urry, John (1987) *The End of Organised Capitalism* (Cambridge: Polity Press).

Lasswell, Harold D. (1941) *Democracy Through Public Opinion*. (Wisconsin: George Banta Publishing Company) (The Eleusis of Chi Omega, vol. 43, no. 1, Part 2).

Lasswell, Harold D. (1977) 'The Vocation of Propagandists' (1934), in *On Political Sociology* (Chicago: University of Chicago Press).

Laudon, Kenneth C. (1986) *Dossier Society: Value Choice in the Design of National Information Systems* (New York: Columbia University Press).

Lawson, Nigel (1983) 'Changing Employment Patterns: Where Will the New Jobs Be?' Chancellor of the Exchequer's paper to NEDC (83)58: 28 November.

Lawson, Nigel (1984) 'Speech at the Annual Meeting of the International Monetary Fund', Washington. Reported and quoted in *The Guardian*, 26 September.

Lawton, Denis (1984) *The Tightening Grip: Growth of Central Control of the School Curriculum* (London: University of London, Institute of Education) Bedford Way Papers 21.

Leadbeater, Charlie (1987) 'In the Land of the Dispossessed', *Marxism Today*, April, pp. 18–25.

Leigh, David (1980) *The Frontiers of Secrecy: Closed Government in Britain* (London: Junction Books).

Leigh, David and Lashmar, Paul (1985) 'Revealed: How MI5 Vets BBC Staff; The Blacklist in Room 105', *The Observer*, 18 August, p. 1, 9.

Levin, Henry and Rumberger, Russell (1983) 'The Low-Skill Future of High-Tech', *Technology Review*, August–September, pp. 18–21.

Levitt, T. (1976) 'The Industrialization of Service', *Harvard Business Review*, 54(5) September–October, pp. 63–74.

Lewis, D. A. and Martyn, J. (1986) 'An Appraisal of National Information Policy in the United Kingdom', *Aslib Proceedings*, 38(1), pp. 35–42.

Leyland, David G. (1986) 'Commercialism and Corporate Strategy in British Higher Education', *Higher Education Review*, 19(1) Autumn, pp. 23–33.

Lin, Herbert (1985) 'The Development of Software for Ballistic-Missile Defense', *Scientific American*, 253(6) December, pp. 32–9.

Lindley, Robert M. (ed.) (1981) *Higher Education and the Labour Market* (Guildford, University of Surrey: Society for Research into Higher Education).

Link, Henry C. (1932) *The New Psychology of Selling and Advertising* (New York: Macmillan).

Lipietz, Alain (1982) 'La Double Complexité de la Crise', in Jean-Claude Delaunay (ed.) *Actualité du Marxisme*, vol. 1 (Paris: Anthropos).

Lipietz, Alain (1986) 'New Tendencies in the International Division of Labour: Regimes of Accumulation and Modes of Regulation', in Allen J. Scott and Michael Storper (eds) *Production, Work, Territory: The Geographical Anatomy of Industrial Capitalism* (Boston: Allen and Unwin).

Lipietz, Alain (1987) *Mirages and Miracles: The Crises of Global Fordism* (London: Verso).

Lippmann, Walter (1922) *Public Opinion* (London: Allen and Unwin).

Lippmann, Walter (1925) *The Phantom Public* (New York: Harcourt, Brace and Co).

Lipsky, Abram (1925) *Man the Puppet: The Art of Controlling Minds* (New York: Frank-Maurice, Inc).

Littler, Craig R. (1982) *The Development of the Labour Process in Capitalist Societies* (London: Heinemann).

Lorenz, Christopher (1982) 'Roots of the British Malaise', *Financial Times*, September 15.

Lovering, John (1987) 'The Atlantic Arms Economy: Towards a Military Regime of Accumulation?' *Capital and Class*, (33), Winter, pp. 129–55.

Lowe, Julian (1985) 'Science Parks in the U.K.', *Lloyds Bank Review*, April, pp. 31–42.

Lumek, Roberta (1984) 'Information Technology and Libraries', *Library Management*, 5(3), pp. 1–60.

Lynd, Robert S. (1933), with the assistance of Alice C. Hanson, 'The People as Consumers', in President's Research Committee on Social Trends, *Recent Social Trends in the United States* (London: McGraw Hill).

Lyotard, Jean-François (1979) *La Condition Postmoderne: Rapport sur le Savoir* (Paris: Minuit).

McCrone, John (1985) 'Keeping MAD Intact', *Computing*, May 2, pp. 14–15.

McCulloch, Gary, Jenkins, Edgar, Layton, David (1985) *Technological Revolution? The Politics of School Science and Technology in England and Wales Since 1945* (Lewes: Falmer Press).

MacMurray, John (1935) *Reason and Emotion* (London: Faber and Faber).

Maddock, Sir Ieuan (1983) *Civil Exploitation of Defence Technology. Report to the Electronics EDC and Observations by the Ministry of Defence* (London: NEDO) February.

Mann, P. Q. (1984) 'Reassessing the Sakhalin Incident', *Defence Attaché*, (3), pp. 41–56.

Marchand, Roland (1985) *Advertising the American Dream: Making Way for Modernity, 1920–1940* (Berkeley: University of California Press).

Marsh, Jan (1982) *Back to the Land: The Pastoral Impulse in Victorian England from 1880 to 1914* (London: Quartet).

Marsh, Peter (1982) 'Britain Faces up to Information Technology', *New Scientist*, 96(1335) 9 October, pp. 634–8.

Marshall, M. (n.d.) 'Women's Education in the North of Scotland', unpublished manuscript.

Martin, James (1978) *The Wired Society* (Englewood Cliffs: Prentice-Hall).

Martin, Ron (1987) 'The New Economics and Politics of Regional Restructuring: The British Experience'. Paper presented at the International Conference on 'Regional Policy at the Crossroads', University of Leuven, Belgium, 22–24 April.

Marx, Gary T. (1985) 'I'll Be Watching You: Reflections on the New Surveillance', *Dissent*, Winter, pp. 26–34.

Marx, Gary T. and Reichman, Nancy (1984) 'Routinizing the Discovery of Secrets', *American Behavioral Scientist*, 27(4) March, pp. 423–52.

Marx, Leo (1987) 'Does Improved Technology Mean Progress?', *Technology Review*, 90(1) January, pp. 33–41, 71.

Massiter, Cathy (1985) 'The Spymasters Who Broke Their Own Rules', *The Guardian*, 1 March, p. 13.

Meighan, Roland and Reid, William (1982) 'How Will the "New Technology" Change the Curriculum?', *Journal of Curriculum Studies*, 14(4), pp. 353–8.

Melman, Seymour (1970) *Pentagon Capitalism* (New York: McGraw-Hill).

Miller, Robert L. (1986) 'The Road to a Job', *Times Higher Education Supplement*, 7 February, p. 14.

Mills, C. Wright (1953) *White-Collar: The American Middle Classes* (New York: Oxford University Press).

Mills, C. Wright (1963) *Power, Politics and People* (New York: Oxford University Press).

Ministry of Defence (1983) *The Protection of Military Information. Report of the Study Group on Censorship*, Cmnd. 9112 (London: HMSO) December.

Minsky, Marvin (1977) 'Applying Artificial Intelligence to Education', in Robert J. Seidel and Martin L. Rubin (eds) *Computers and Communications: Implications for Education* (New York: Academic Press).

Mohr, Charles (1985) 'Soviets May Choose Countermeasures and More Missiles', *International Herald Tribune*, 11 March, p. 8.

Moon, Jeremy and Richardson, J.J. (1984) 'Policy-Making with a Difference? The Technical and Vocational Education Initiative', *Public Administration*, 62, Spring, pp. 23–33.

Moore, Jr., Barrington (1966) *The Social Origins of Dictatorship and Democracy: Lord and Peasant in the Making of the Modern World* (Harmondsworth: Penguin, 1969).

Moore, Robert (1984) 'Schooling and the World of Work', in Inge Bates *et al.* (eds) *Schooling for the Dole? The New Vocationalism* (London: Macmillan).

Morrison, Ian (1983) 'Profiling – A GCE for Personality?', *Liberal Education*, (49), Summer, pp. 11–14.

MSC (n.d.) *Instructional Guide to Social and Life Skills* (London: Manpower Services Commission).

MSC (1981) *A New Training Initiative: An Agenda for Action* (Sheffield: Manpower Services Commission).

MSC (1984) *Core Skills in YTS, Part 1* (Sheffield: Manpower Services Commission).

Mumford, Lewis (1964) 'Authoritarian and Democratic Technics', *Technology and Culture*, 5, pp. 1–8.

Mumford, Lewis (1967) *The Myth of the Machine* (London: Secker and Warburg).

Mungham, Geoff (1982) 'Workless Youth as a "Moral Panic"', in Teresa L. Rees and Paul Atkinson (eds) *Youth Unemployment and State Intervention* (London: Routledge and Kegan Paul).

Murray, Robin (1985) 'Benetton Britain: The New Economic Order', *Marxism Today*, November, pp. 28–32.

NAB (1986a) *Partnership in Progress: The Links between Polytechnics and Colleges and Industry in Engineering, Computing and Technology* (London: National Advisory Body for Public Sector Higher Education).

NAB (1986b) *Transferable Personal Skills in Employment: The Contribution of Higher Education* (London: National Advisory Body for Public Sector Higher Education).

Naisbitt, John (1984) *Megatrends: Ten New Directions Transforming Our Lives* (London: Macdonald & Co).

Natanson, Charles E. (1969) 'The Militarization of the American Economy', in David Horowitz (ed.) (q.v., above).

NEDC (National Economic Development Council) (1980) *Computer Manpower in the '80s: The Supply and Demand for Computer Related Manpower to 1985*, Electronic Computers Sector Working Party (London: NEDO).

NEDC (National Economic Development Council) (1983) *Education and Industry* (London: NEDO).

NEDC (National Economic Development Council) (1984) *Crisis Facing UK Information Technology* (London: NEDO) September.

NEDC/MSC (1984) *Competence and Competition: Training and Education in the Federal Republic of Germany, the United States and Japan* (London: NEDO/Manpower Services Commission).

Nelkin, Dorothy (1972) *The University and Military Research: Moral Politics at MIT* (Ithaca: Cornell University Press).

Nelkin, Dorothy (1984) *Science as Intellectual Property* (New York: Macmillan).

Neil, Andrew (1983) 'The Information Revolution: the new freedom will mean the end of old-fashioned capitalism and socialism', *The Listener*, 23 June, pp. 2–4, 22.

Neisser, Ulric (1966) 'Computers as Tools and as Metaphors', in Charles Dechert (ed.) *The Social Impact of Cybernetics* (Notre Dame: University of Notre Dame Press).

Newby, Howard (1977) *The Deferential Worker: A Study of Farm Workers in East Anglia* (Harmondsworth: Penguin, 1979).

Newby, Howard (1979) *Green and Pleasant Land? Social Change in Rural England* (Harmondsworth: Penguin, 1980).

Noble, David F. (1977) *America by Design: Science, Technology and the Rise of Corporate Capitalism* (New York: Knopf).

Noble, David F. (1984) *Forces of Production: A Social History of Industrial Automation* (New York: Knopf).

Noble, Douglas (1985) 'Microcomputers in Schools', Paper Presented to the Symposium on New Technologies, Work and Education, Montreal, 28–30 March.

Noble, Douglas (1986) 'Education and Technology: Some Unexplained Questions', unpublished manuscript.

Norman, Colin (1981) *The God That Limps: Science and Technology in the Eighties* (New York: Norton and Company).

OECD (1984) *Industry and University: New Forms of Co-operation and Collaboration* (Paris: Organisation for Economic Co-operation and Development).

Office of Technology Assessment (1986) *Strategic Defenses: Ballistic Defense Technologies; Anti-Satellite Weapons, Countermeasures, and Arms Control* (New Jersey: Princeton University Press).

Olson, James (1987) Reported in *International Communications Week*, 10 April.

O'Neill, John (1986) 'The Disciplinary Society: From Weber to Foucault', *British Journal of Sociology*, 37(1) March, pp. 42–60.

Orwell, George (1937) *The Road to Wigan Pier* (Harmondsworth: Penguin, 1967).

O'Shea, Tim and Self, John (1983) *Learning and Teaching with Computers: Artificial Intelligence in Education* (Brighton: Harvester).

Paisley, William (1985) 'Children, New Media, and Microcomputers: Continuities of Research', in Milton Chen and William Paisley (eds) *Children and Microcomputers: Research on the Newest Medium* (Beverly Hills: Sage).

Papert, Seymour (1979) 'Computers and Learning', in Michael L. Dertouzos and Joel Moses (eds) *The Computer Age: A Twenty-Year View* (Cambridge, MA: MIT Press).

Papert, Seymour (1980) *Mindstorms: Children, Computers, and Powerful Ideas* (Brighton: Harvester).

Parkes, D. L. (1985) 'Competition . . . and Competence? Education, Training and the Roles of the DES and MSC', in Ian McNay and Jenny Ozga (eds) *Policy-Making in Education: The Breakdown of Consensus* (Oxford: Pergamon).

Parnas, David Lorge (1985) 'Software Aspects of Strategic Defense Systems', *American Scientist*, 73, September–October, pp. 432–40.

Partington, Geoffrey (1987) 'The Disorientation of Western Education', *Encounter*, 68(1) January, pp. 5–15.

Peacock, Alan (1984) 'Introduction', in Digby Anderson (ed.) (q.v., above).

Peacock (1986) *Report of the Committee on Financing the BBC*, Chairman: Professor Alan Peacock. Cmnd. 9824 (London: HMSO).

Pearson, Richard (1983) *Industry and Higher Education: Future Collaboration*, IMS Report no. 79 (Brighton: Institute of Manpower Studies).

Pearton, Maurice (1982) *The Knowledgeable State: Diplomacy, War and Technology since 1830* (London: Burnett Books).

Perkin, Harold (1969) *The Origins of Modern English Society, 1780–1880* (London: Routledge and Kegan Paul).

Pepper, David (1984) *The Roots of Modern Environmentalism* (London: Croom Helm).

Peston, Maurice (1985) 'Higher Education: Financial and Economic Aspects', *Royal Bank of Scotland Review*, (148), December, pp. 3–17.

Piore, Michael and Sabel, Charles (1984) *The Second Industrial Divide: Possibilities for Prosperity* (New York: Basic Books).

Pollard, Sidney (1982) *The Wasting of the British Economy: British Economic Policy 1945 to the Present* (London: Croom Helm).

Pope, Daniel (1983) *The Making of Modern Advertising* (New York: Basic Books).

Porter, Leslie (1984) 'Coming Lately to the Economic Facts of Life', in Digby Anderson (ed.) (q.v., above).

Poster, Mark (1984) *Foucault, Marxism and History* (Cambridge: Polity Press).

Postman, Neil (1986) *Amusing Ourselves to Death: Public Discourse in the Age of Show Business* (London: Heinemann).

Potter, David M. (1954) *People of Plenty: Economic Abundance and the American Character* (Chicago: University of Chicago Press).

Powell, Enoch (1986) 'A Policy that Sells Universities Short', *The Guardian*, 3 November.

Pratley, Beryl (1985) *Signposts '85: A Review of 16–19 Education* (London: Further Education Unit).

Price, Geoffrey (1984/85) 'Universities Today: Between the Corporate State and the Market', *Universities Quarterly*, 39(1) Winter, pp. 43–58.

Proxmire, William (1970) 'Retired High-Ranking Military Officers Employed by Large Contractors', in Herbert I. Schiller and Joseph Phillips (eds) (q.v., below).

Pyle, C. H. (1982) 'The Invasion of Privacy', in G. Benjamin (ed.) *The Communications Revolution in Politics* (New York: Academy of Political Science).

Pym, Sir Francis (1983) 'The Revolution Laissez-Faire and Socialism Cannot Handle', *The Guardian*, 10 October.

Pym, Sir Francis (1985) *The Politics of Consent* (London: Sphere).

Radice, Giles (1986) *Equality and Quality: A Socialist Plan for Education* (London: Fabian Society).

Ranson, Stewart (1984) 'Towards a Tertiary Tripartism: New Codes of Social Control and the 17+', in Patricia Broadfoot (ed.) *Selection, Certification and Control: Social Issues in Educational Assessment* (Lewes: Falmer Press).

Ranson, Stewart (1985a) 'Changing Relations between Centre and Locality in Education', in Ian McNay and Jenny Ozga (eds) *Policy-Making in Education: The Breakdown of Consensus* (Oxford: Pergamon).

Ranson, Stewart (1985b) 'Contradictions in the Government of Educational Change', *Political Studies*, 33, pp. 56–72.

Raven, John (1982) 'Education and the Competencies Required in Modern Society', *Higher Education Review*, 15(1) Autumn, pp. 47–57.

Raven, John (1984) *Competence in Modern Society: Its Identification, Development and Release* (London: H. K. Lewis).

Reagan, Ronald (1983) 'Text of Reagan Address on Defense Policy', *Congressional Quarterly*, March 26, pp. 631–3.

Reeder, David (1981) 'A Recurring Debate: Education and Industry', in Roger Dale *et al.* (eds) *Education and the State, Volume 1: Schooling and the National Interest* (Lewes: Falmer Press).

Report by the Minister for the Arts on Library and Information matters during 1983 (1983), Cmnd 9109 (London: HMSO).

Reppy, Judith (1983) 'The United States', in Milton Leitenberg and

Nicole Ball (eds) *The Structure of the Defense Industry* (London: Croom Helm).

Richelson, Jeffrey T. and Ball, Desmond (1986) *The Ties That Bind: Intelligence Co-operation Between the UK/USA Countries* (London: Allen and Unwin).

Roberts, Albert (1987) 'Swings and Roundabouts in the Park', *Times Higher Education Supplement*, 13 March, p. 16.

Robertson, James (1985) *Future Work: Jobs, Self-Employment and Leisure after the Industrial Age* (Aldershot: Gower/Maurice Temple Smith).

Robertson, J. A. S., Briggs, J. M. and Goodchild, A. (1982) *Structure and Employment Prospects of the Service Industries*, Research Paper no. 30 (London: Department of Employment).

Robins, Kevin and Webster, Frank (1985) ' "The Revolution of the Fixed Wheel": Information, Technology and Social Taylorism', in Philip Drummond and Richard Paterson (eds) *Television in Transition* (London: British Film Institute).

Robins, Kevin and Webster, Frank (1986) 'The Media, the Military and Censorship', *Screen*, 27(2) March–April, pp. 57–63.

Robins, Kevin and Webster, Frank (1987) 'Information as Capital: A Critique of Daniel Bell', in Jennifer Daryl Slack and Fred Fejes (eds) *The Ideology of the Information Age* (Norwood, New Jersey: Ablex).

Robins, Kevin and Webster, Frank (1988) 'Athens without Slaves . . . or Slaves without Athens? The Neurosis of Technology', *Science as Culture*, (3), 7–53.

Roderick, Gordon and Stephens, Michael (1978) *Education and Industry in the Nineteenth Century: The English Disease?* (London: Longman).

Roderick, Gordon and Stephens, Michael (eds) (1981) *Where Did We Go Wrong? Industrial Performance, Education and the Economy in Victorian England* (Lewes: Falmer Press).

Roderick, Gordon and Stephens, Michael (eds) (1982) *The British Malaise: Industrial Performance, Education and Training in Britain Today* (Lewes: Falmer Press).

Roizen, Judith and Jepson, Mark (1985) *Degrees for Jobs: Employer Expectations of Higher Education* (Guildford: SRHE & NFER-Nelson).

Roobeek, Annemieke J. M. (1987) 'The Crisis in Fordism and the Rise of a New Technological Paradigm', *Futures*, 19(2) April, pp. 129–54.

Rose, Michael (1985) *Re-Working the Work Ethic: Economic Values and Socio-Cultural Politics* (London: Batsford).

Roszak, Theodore (1986) *The Cult of Information: The Folklore of Computers and the True Art of Thinking* (Cambridge: Lutterworth Press).

Rourke, Francis E. (1961) *Secrecy and Publicity: Dilemmas of Democracy* (Baltimore: Johns Hopkins Press).

RPPITB (1982) *The Way Forward: A Practical Proposal for Introducing Changes in the School Curricula*. Fourth Report of the Study Group on the Education/Training of Young People (Brentford: Rubber and Plastics Processing Industry Training Board).

Rustin, Michael (1986) 'The Idea of the Popular University: A Historical Perspective', in Janet Finch and Michael Rustin (eds) *A Degree of Choice? Higher Education and the Right to Learn* (Harmondsworth: Penguin).

Ruthven, Kenneth (1984) 'Computer Literacy and the Curriculum', *British Journal of Educational Studies*, 32(2) June, pp. 134–47.

Ryan, Paul (1984) 'The New Training Initiative After Two Years', *Lloyds Bank Review*, (152), April, pp. 31–45.

SDP (1983) *Education and Training* (London: Social Democratic Party).

St John-Brooks, Caroline (1985) *Who Controls Training? The Rise of the Manpower Services Commission*, Fabian Tract 506 (London: Fabian Society).

Saatchi & Saatchi Company plc (1985) *Review of Advertising Operations 1984* (London: Saatchi & Saatchi).

Sagan, Scott D. (1985) 'Nuclear Alerts and Crisis Management', *International Security*, 9(4) Spring, pp. 99–139.

Sampson, Anthony (1978) *The Arms Bazaar: From Lebanon to Lockheed* (New York: Viking).

Samuel, Raphael (1977) 'Workshop of the World: Steam Power and Hand Technology in mid-Victorian Britain', *History Workshop Journal*, 3, pp. 6–72.

Sanderson, Michael (1972) *The Universities and British Industry, 1850–1970* (London: Routledge and Kegan Paul).

Sanderson, Michael (1983) *Education, Economic Change and Society in England, 1780–1870* (London: Macmillan).

Sardello, Robert J. (1984) 'The Technological Threat to Education', *Teachers College Record*, 85(4) Summer, pp. 631–9.

Schiller, Dan (1982) *Telematics and Government* (Norwood, New Jersey: Ablex).

Schiller, Herbert I. (1981) *Who Knows: Information in the Age of the Fortune 500* (Norwood, New Jersey: Ablex).

Schiller, Herbert I. (1984) *Information and the Crisis Economy* (Norwood, New Jersey: Ablex).

Schiller, Herbert I. (1987) 'Old Foundations for a New (Information) Age', in Jorge R. Schement and Leah Lievroux (eds) *Competing Visions, Complex Realities: Aspects of the Information Society* (Norwood, New Jersey: Ablex).

Schiller, Herbert I. and Phillips, Joseph (eds) (1970) *Super-State: Readings in the Military-Industrial Complex* (Urbana: University of Illinois Press).

Schiller, Anita R. and Schiller, Herbert I. (1988) 'Libraries, Public Access to Information and Commerce', in Vincent Mosco and Janet Wasko (eds) *The Political Economy of Information* (Madison: University of Wisconsin).

Schudson, Michael (1984) *Advertising: The Uneasy Persuasion* (New York: Basic Books).

Schultze, Quentin J. (1978) *Advertising, Science, and Professionalism,*

1885–1917, University of Illinois at Urbana-Champaigne, Ph.D. thesis.

Schwarz, Bill (1987) 'The Thatcher Years', in Ralph Miliband and John Saville (eds) *Socialist Register 1987* (London: Merlin).

Scott, John (1982) *The Upper Classes: Property and Privilege in Britain* (London: Macmillan).

Scott, Peter (1986) 'The British Disease and its Cures', *Times Higher Education Supplement*, 15 August.

Scruton, Roger, Ellis-Jones, Angela and O'Keefe, Dennis (1985) *Education and Indoctrination* (London: Sherwood Press).

Seale, Clive (1984) 'FEU and MSC: Two Curricular Philosophies and their Implications for the Youth Training Scheme', *The Vocational Aspect of Education*, 36(93) May, pp. 3–10.

Searle, John (1984) 'Beer Cans and Meat Machines', *The Listener*, 15 November, pp. 14–16.

Segal, H. P. (1985) *Technological Utopianism in American Culture* (Chicago: University of Chicago Press).

Selbourne, David (1986) 'The Comprehensive Failure of the Left', *The Guardian*, 12 May.

Seldon, Arthur (1986) *The Riddle of the Voucher* (London: Institute of Economic Affairs).

Shaiken, Harley (1984) *Work Transformed: Automation and Labor in the Computer Age* (New York: Holt, Rinehart and Winston).

Shamoon, Stella (1984) 'Why Global Advertising "Is It" ', *The Observer*, 23 September.

Sharp, Rachel and Green, Anthony (1975) *Education and Social Control* (London: Routledge and Kegan Paul).

Shattuck, John (1986) 'Federal Restrictions on the Free Flow of Academic Information and Ideas', *Government Information Quarterly*, 3(1), pp. 5–29.

Sheerman, Barry (1986) *Education and Training: Options for Labour* (London: House of Commons).

Shils, Edward (1967) 'Privacy and Power', in Edward Shils (1975) *Center and Periphery: Essays in Macrosociology* (Chicago: University of Chicago Press).

Silver, Harold (1980) *Education and the Social Condition* (London: Methuen).

Simon, Brian (1965) *The Two Nations and the Educational Structure, 1780–1870* (London: Lawrence and Wishart).

Simon, Herbert A. (1977) 'What Computers Mean for Man and Society', *Science*, 195, 18 March, pp. 1186–91.

Slee, Peter (1986) 'Concern for Skills', *Universities Quarterly: Culture, Education and Society*, 40(1) Winter, pp. 163–70.

Sloan, Alfred P. (1965) *My Years with General Motors* (London: Sidgwick and Jackson).

Sloan, Douglas (1984) 'On Raising Critical Questions about the Computer in Education', *Teachers College Record*, 85(4) Summer, pp. 539–47.

Smith, Dan and Smith, Ron (1983) *The Economics of Militarism* (London: Pluto Press).

Smith, Diane (1985) 'The Commercialization and Privatization of Government Information', *Government Publications Review*, 12, pp. 45–63.
Smith, Duncan and Wootton, Richard (1986) *Exploring Enterprise: School and Business Perspectives* (New York: Longman).
Smith, John and Park, George (1987) *A Strategy for IT: Labour and Information Technology* (London: Labour Party).
Smith, Leslie (1984) *Ability Learning* (London: Further Education Unit).
Smith, Evelyn (1985) 'Young Enterprise – Practical Experience for Tomorrow's High Flyers?', *Employment Gazette*, November, pp. 429–33.
Smiths Industries (1986) Recruitment Advertisement in *The Guardian*, 14 November.
Snoddy, Raymond (1986) 'An Information Revolution', *Financial Times*, 24 March, p. 13.
Southwood, Peter (1985) *The UK Defence Industry: Characteristics of the Main UK Defence Equipment Manufacturers which are also Relevant to a Credible Arms Conversion Strategy*, University of Bradford: Peace Research Reports no. 8, September.
Speier, Hans (1950) 'Historical Development of Public Opinion', *American Journal of Sociology*, 55, January, pp. 376–88.
Spender, Dale (1982) *Invisible Women: The Schooling Scandal* (London: Writers and Readers).
Stares, Paul (1985) *Space Weapons and US Strategy: Origins and Development* (London: Croom Helm).
Starsmore, Sandra C. (1987) *A Comparative Study of the Attitudes and Perceptions of Computer Education in Respect of Children with Differing Social Backgrounds in the 9–11 Age Range* (Oxford Polytechnic: Modular Course Dissertation, Applied Education/Sociology).
Statement of the Defence Estimates 1985, presented to Parliament by the Secretary of State for Defence, 1985 (London: HMSO).
Statistical Abstract of the United States 1986 (1985), US Department of Commerce, December.
Stead, R. H. (1985) *Taking It With You: An Experiment in Computer Assisted Profiling for Basic Skills in a Youth Custody Centre* (London: Further Education Unit).
Stevenson, John (1984) *British Society 1914–1945* (Harmondsworth: Penguin).
Stevenson, John and Cook, Chris (1977) *The Slump: Society and Politics During the Depression* (London: Cape).
Stockholm International Peace Research Institute (SIPRI) (1985) *World Armaments and Disarmament: SIPRI Yearbook 1985* (London: Taylor and Francis).
Stronach, Ian (1984) 'Work Experience: The Sacred Anvil', in Carol Varlaam (ed.) *Rethinking Transition: Educational Innovation and the Transition to Adult Life* (Lewes: Falmer Press).
Stone, Lawrence (1965) *The Crisis of the Aristocracy, 1558–1641* (Oxford: Clarendon Press).
Stone, Lawrence and Stone, Jeanne C. Fawtier (1984) *An Open Elite? England 1540–1880* (Oxford: Clarendon Press).

Stonier, Tom (1981) 'A Little Learning is a Lucrative Thing', *Times Higher Education Supplement*, 1 May.

Stonier, Tom (1983) *The Wealth of Information: A Profile of the Post-Industrial Economy* (London: Thames Methuen).

Stonier, Tom and Conlin, Cathy (1985) *The Three Cs: Children, Computers and Communication* (Chichester: Wiley and Sons).

Swinnerton-Dyer, Peter (1985) 'Higher Education into the 1990s', *Higher Education Review*, 17(2) Spring, pp. 9–18.

Tedlow, Richard S. (1979) *Keeping the Corporate Image: Public Relations and Business, 1900–1950* (Greenwich, Connecticut: Jai Press).

Thatcher, Margaret (1982) 'Speech at the Opening Ceremony of I.T. '82 Conference'. Press Office, 10 Downing Street, 8 December.

Thatcher, Margaret (1983), Interviewed by G. Bull, *The Director*, 37(2) September, pp. 22–7.

Thompson, Edward P. (1963) *The Making of the English Working Class* (London: Gollancz).

Thompson, Edward P. (1970a) 'The Business University', *New Society*, 19 February, pp. 301–7.

Thompson, Edward P. (1970b) *Warwick University Ltd* (Harmondsworth: Penguin).

Thompson, Edward P. (1974) 'Patrician Society, Plebian Culture', *Journal of Social History*, 7, pp. 382–405.

Thompson, Edward P. (1978) 'Eighteenth-Century English Society: class struggle without class?', *Social History*, 3(2), pp. 133–65.

Thompson, Edward P. (1980) 'Notes on Exterminism, the Last Stage of Civilization', *New Left Review*, (121), May–June, pp. 3–31.

Thompson, F. M. L. (1963) *English Landed Society in the Nineteenth Century* (London: Routledge and Kegan Paul).

Thompson, John B. (1982) 'Ideology and the Social Imaginary', *Theory and Society*, 11(5) September, pp. 659–81.

Thompson, Kenneth (1984) '"Education for Capability": A Critique', *British Journal of Education Studies*, 32(3) October, pp. 203–12.

Thompson, Paul (1983) *The Nature of Work* (London: Macmillan).

Thorn-EMI (1980) *Annual Report*.

Toffler, Alvin (1970) *Future Shock* (London: Bodley Head).

Toffler, Alvin (1980) *The Third Wave* (New York: Bantam, 1981).

Townsend, Christina (1982) *Skills Needed on Young People's Jobs*, VOL. 1 (Brighton: Institute of Manpower Studies).

Townsend, Peter (1981) 'By restricting the flow of information, the Government is restricting the right to free and open discussion of the industrial, economic and social conditions of Britain', *The Guardian*, 15 July, p. 15.

Trachtenberg, Alan (1982) *The Incorporation of America: Culture and Society in the Gilded Age* (New York: Hill and Wang).

Training for Jobs (1984), Cmnd. 9135 (London: HMSO).

Trevelyan, G. M. (1944) *English Social History: A Survey of Six Centuries, Chaucer to Queen Victoria* (London: Longman, Green and Co., 1948).

Tucker, Anthony (1985) 'Who Really Needs Eureka?' *The Guardian*, 1 August.
Tuomi, Helena and Vayrynen, Raimo (1982) *Transnational Corporations, Armaments and Development* (Aldershot: Gower).
Turkle, Sherry (1984) *The Second Self: Computers and the Human Spirit* (London: Granada).
Turner, John (1987) 'Employer's Eye View', *View*, (32), Summer, pp. 15–17.
Turney, Jon (1987) 'Science Parks Fail to bring Home Industrial Bacon', *Times Higher Education Supplement*, 24 April, p. 10.
Useem, Michael (1984) *The Inner Circle: Large Corporations and the Rise of Business Political Activity in the US and UK* (New York: Oxford University Press).
Vincent, Brieda and Vincent, Tom (1985) *Information Technology and Further Education* (London: Kogan Page).
Waddilove, Ken (1985) 'Let the Micros Rot!' *The Guardian*, 19 February.
Waddington, John (1987) 'Developing Effective Industry/Education Links', *TVEI Insight*, (9), June, p. 17.
Wainwright, Hilary and Elliott, Dave (1982) *The Lucas Plan: A New Trade Unionism in the Making?* (London: Allison and Busby).
Walkerdine, Valerie (1984) 'Developmental Psychology and the Child-Centred Pedagogy: the Insertion of Piaget into Early Education', in Julian Henriques *et al.*, *Changing the Subject: Psychology, Social Regulation and Subjectivity* (London: Methuen).
Warnock, Mary (1988) 'Universities: The New Civil Service?', *New Society*, 12 February, p. 24.
Watson, John, Foreword to Henry C. Link, 1932 (q.v., above).
Watts, Anthony G. (1983) *Work Experience and Schools* (London: Heinemann).
Webster, Frank and Robins, Kevin (1986) *Information Technology: A Luddite Analysis* (Norwood, New Jersey: Ablex).
Weizenbaum, Joseph (1983) 'The Computer in Your Future', *New York Review of Books*, 27 October, pp. 58–62.
Wellington, J. J. (1985) *Children, Computers and the Classroom* (London: Harper and Row).
Westinghouse Corporation (1982a) *Annual Report 1982*.
Westinghouse Corporation (1982b) *Second Quarter Report*.
Whyte, George (1986) 'Enterprise Training in YTS', *Youth Training News*, (30) June, p. 9.
Wicklein, J. (1981) *Electronic Nightmare: The New Communications and Freedom* (New York: Viking).
Wiener, Martin J. (1981) *English Culture and the Decline of the Industrial Spirit, 1850–1980* (Cambridge: Cambridge University Press).
Wilkinson, Barry (1983) *The Shopfloor Politics of New Technology* (London: Heinemann).
Williams, Frederick (1982) *The Communications Revolution* (New York: Mentor, 1983).

Williams, Martha (1985) 'Electronic Databases', *Science*, 228(4698) 26 April, pp. 445–6.

Williams, Raymond (1973) *The Country and the City* (St Albans: Paladin, 1975).

Williams, Shirley (1985) *A Job to Live: the Impact of Tomorrow's Technology on Work and Society* (Harmondsworth: Penguin).

Wilson, Andrew (1968) *The Bomb and the Computer* (London: Barrie and Rockliff).

Wilson, Harold (1963) 'Labour and the Scientific Revolution', in Report of the 62nd Annual Conference. Scarborough, September 30–October 4 (London: Labour Party).

Winner, Langdon (1986) *The Whale and the Reactor: A Search For Limits in an Age of High Technology* (Chicago: University of Chicago Press).

Wolin, Richard (1984/85) 'Modernism vs Postmodernism', *Telos*, (62), Winter, pp. 9–29.

Woolf, Virginia (1977) [1938] *Three Guineas* (Harmondsworth: Penguin).

Woolhouse, John (1984) 'Technical and Vocational Education Initiative', *Perspectives*, (14), March, pp. 73–80.

Working Together – Education and Training (1986) Cmnd. 9823 (London: HMSO).

Young, David (1984) 'Coping With Change: The New Training Initiative', *Journal of the Royal Society of Arts*, 132, June, pp. 449–59.

Young, Rt Hon. Lord (1985a) 'A Nation Learning to Change', *The Times*, 26 March.

Young, Rt Hon. Lord (1985b) 'Fewer Rules, More at Work', *The Times*, 17 May.

Young, Rt Hon. Lord (1985c) *Enterprise Regained* (London: Conservative Political Centre).

Young, Rt Hon. Lord (1987) quoted in *Youth Training News* (36), February, p. 13.

YTS (1987) 'Enterprise in YTS', *Youth Training News* (36), February pp. 13–20.

Zegveld, Walter and Enzing, Christien (1987) *SDI and Industrial Technology Policy: Threat or Opportunity?* (London: Frances Pinter)

Zuckerman, Lord (1987a) 'Reagan's Highest Folly', *New York Review of Books*, 34(6) April 9, pp. 35–41.

Zuckerman, Lord (1987b) 'What Price Star Wars?', *New York Review of Books*, 34(7) April 23, pp. 8–13.

Index